Intersecting Journeys

Intersecting Journeys

THE ANTHROPOLOGY OF
PILGRIMAGE AND TOURISM

EDITED BY
Ellen Badone and
Sharon R. Roseman

UNIVERSITY OF ILLINOIS PRESS
URBANA AND CHICAGO

© 2004 by the Board of Trustees
of the University of Illinois
All rights reserved
Manufactured in the United States of America
C 5 4 3 2 1

∞ This book is printed on acid-free paper.

Library of Congress Cataloging-in-Publication Data
Intersecting journeys : the anthropology of pilgrimage
and tourism / edited by Ellen Badone and Sharon R. Roseman.
p.   cm.
Includes bibliographical references and index.
ISBN 0-252-02940-2 (cloth : alk. paper)
1. Pilgrims and pilgrimages. 2. Culture and tourism.
I. Badone, Ellen. II. Roseman, Sharon R., 1963–
BL619.P5I67   2004
306.6—dc22   2004002538

For my parents, Gloria and Frank—S. R.

For Steve, Amy, and Robin—E. B.

CONTENTS

ACKNOWLEDGMENTS

We are grateful to the Social Sciences and Humanities Research Council of Canada, McMaster University, and Memorial University of Newfoundland for their financial support of our research and this book project. We would also like to thank our many students, colleagues, and friends who provided research assistance and advice, in particular: Stephen R. G. Jones, Wayne Fife, Patricia Lane, Faydra Shapiro, Amanda White, Vicki Hill, Christine Aylward, and Libby Toews. We are very grateful to Larry Taylor and a second anonymous reviewer for reading the manuscript so carefully and for providing many helpful suggestions. Throughout the publication process, Liz Dulany and her staff at the University of Illinois Press have provided excellent editorial advice.

Intersecting Journeys

1   Approaches to the Anthropology of Pilgrimage and Tourism

ELLEN BADONE AND SHARON R. ROSEMAN

In this English translation, Dutch novelist Cees Nooteboom power-fully described how he readied himself for his final approach to the famous Catholic pilgrimage site of Santiago de Compostela:

> There is no one to be seen on that high mound, nothing at all, a somewhat bare field, a closed chapel, a few boulders. I climb onto one of them and stare into the distance, and then, slowly, as if a veil is lifting, I discover the cathedral, almost hidden behind a ripple of green hills and a transparent screen of trees, three fragile towers drawn in infinitesimal detail, a vision in a dream, and *whether I like it or not, an indefinable chemistry floods my heart with their joy,* and I sit there until the dusk creeps up the slope and the cars down in the misty valley turn on their lights and beam towards the city in sinuous ribbons of light. Here I am at last, now I can arrive in Santiago. (1997, 333; emphasis added)

It was the third time that Nooteboom had visited Santiago, and his reasons for doing so, although tied up with his overall passion for the country of Spain, are self-avowedly not "religious" in the sense imparted by most formal defi-nitions of the term: "It will not in my case be a pilgrimage to the apostle, rather to an earlier, shadowy self, the recapture of a past passage" (5).

In accounts such as Nooteboom's that reflect on experiences of journey-ing to a variety of destinations for innumerable and often multiple reasons, var-ious shadings of meaning underlie concepts such as "pilgrimage" and "tour-ism." Anthropologists and others interested in the cultural and social significance of human travel have to make sense of these nuances that are con-tained in both written documents and oral testimonies. Drawing on diverse theoretical approaches to the study of pilgrimage and tourism, contributors to this volume explore a variety of case studies ranging from modern-day walking pilgrimages to Santiago, to North American *Star Trek* fan conventions.

As the chapters in this book indicate, rigid dichotomies between pilgrimage and tourism, or pilgrims and tourists, no longer seem tenable in the shifting world of postmodern travel. A key basis for distinguishing between pilgrimage and tourism involves assumptions about the beliefs and motivations of travelers who undertake journeys to religious shrines. One of the perennial problems in ethnography has been precisely the difficulty of attaining clear insight into the motivations and inner experiences of Others, perhaps in part because motivations and experience are often contradictory or poorly understood by ethnographic actors themselves. However, the observation that pilgrims may have mixed motivations is neither rare nor particularly recent: among the large number of medieval Europeans who traveled to Santiago de Compostela and Canterbury, it is not likely that all were propelled by uniquely pious motives (see Smith 1992, 7–8). Likewise, can we guarantee that present-day tourists who come to locations such as Rome or Jerusalem in search of culture and heritage will leave those sites unmoved by religious inspiration?

In any case, interpretations of travel as religious in character hinge upon the meanings attached to the term "religious." The contributors to this volume hold with Durkheim that notions of divinity and the sacred arise from and symbolize the social collectivity. From this perspective, it is not surprising that collective experiences like sporting events, *Star Trek* conventions, or mobilization for war generate "religious" emotions. Likewise, we follow Clifford Geertz (1973) in conceptualizing religion as a quest for meaning, interpretability, and the "really real." Hence, touristic travel in search of authenticity or self-renewal falls under the rubric of the sacred, collapsing the distinction between secular voyaging and pilgrimage. Such an approach can illuminate the motivations and experiences of those business and recreational travelers who make time in their hectic schedules to visit places such as the location of the fatal car crash where Princess Diana perished in Paris, views of the embattled homes of West Bank Palestinians, or the scarred site in Lower Manhattan where the World Trade Center used to stand.

Starting from the premise that dichotomous distinctions between the sacred and the secular obscure more than they illuminate, we seek to highlight the similarities between two categories of travel, pilgrimage and tourism, that have frequently been regarded as conceptual opposites. The popular depiction of the tourist as a superficial hedonist seems far removed from the image of the pious pilgrim motivated by faith to undertake arduous and ascetic journeys to centers of religious devotion. Yet, as Victor and Edith Turner (1978, 20) have observed, "A tourist is half a pilgrim, if a pilgrim is half a tourist." Moreover, as Nelson Graburn points out in this volume, the terms "pilgrims" and "tourists" can be potent in native discourses that seek to appropriate resources or advance particular interests. Perhaps it is always necessary to pose the questions, Pilgrims or tourists for whom, from whose perspective, in what contexts, and why?

In the remainder of this introductory chapter, we set the context for this set of essays within the framework of existing anthropological literature on pilgrimage and tourism, ending with a discussion of the parallels between pilgrimage and touristic journeys.

From Communitas to Contestation

Although predated by earlier studies of particular pilgrimage sites (e.g., Wolf 1958), the work of Victor and Edith Turner represents the first broad-ranging theoretical model for the anthropological interpretation of pilgrimage (Turner 1974; Turner and Turner 1978). Taking as his point of departure the work of French folklorist Arnold van Gennep on rites of passage, Victor Turner developed the notions of liminality and communitas. Deriving from the Latin *limen,* meaning threshold, the term "liminal" aptly describes the condition of ritual participants who have symbolically exited one social "space" or state but have not entered a new one: they are figuratively poised over the threshold, or "betwixt and between," two social worlds (Turner 1969, 107).

The most significant aspect of liminality is its capacity to generate communitas, "a relational quality of full unmediated communication, even communion" with other individuals, "which combines the qualities of lowliness, sacredness, homogeneity, and comradeship" (Turner and Turner 1978, 250). In contrast to the communitas of the liminal state, Turner opposes the concept of structure, an ordered and rule-governed arrangement of relationships between groups and institutions and between statuses and roles that persists through time despite changes in the identity of the individuals who occupy particular positions (1969, 126). For Turner, communitas develops in the interstices of social structure: among the poor, outcasts, and those like artists and religious virtuosos who consciously remove themselves from some of the constraints of society.

Moving from rites of passage in preindustrial societies, Turner and Turner seek to locate the liminal in the religious systems of societies characterized by the "'historical' or 'salvation' religions" (1978, 3). In these contexts, they suggest, pilgrimage replaces the rite of passage as the primary locus of liminality and communitas (Turner 1974, 182; Turner and Turner 1978, 3–7). Through the journey to a distant holy place, the pilgrim is separated from the rule-governed structures of mundane social life, becoming both geographically and socially marginal. Turner (1974) argues that pilgrimage centers are frequently found in peripheral locations distinct from centers of political and economic influence. Thus, the pilgrimage shrine is spatially liminal, but for the pilgrim it also "represents a threshold, a place and moment 'in and out of time'" where "direct experience of the sacred, invisible or supernatural order" can be expected (197).

As Turner and Turner suggest, the popular, individualistic, and charismatic character of pilgrimage renders it problematic from the point of view of orthodox religious authorities in many traditions (1978, 31). Significantly, it is the "touristic" aspects of pilgrimage journeys that sacred authorities frequently condemn, such as sightseeing or participation in markets or fairs. From the Turners' point of view, however, these activities represent an important aspect of the total pilgrimage process and should not be ignored in anthropological analyses. The nonliturgical features of pilgrimage also give rise to communitas, even if such activities are not declared legitimately "religious" (37).

It is somewhat difficult to evaluate the extent to which Victor Turner's seminal ideas about liminality and communitas in the pilgrimage process are supported empirically. Several of the studies in this volume suggest that these modes of sociality are often a component of the experience of individual pilgrims (see especially the chapters by Paula Holmes-Rodman, Nancy Frey, and Jennifer Porter). However, many other ethnographic accounts from diverse cultural settings pose a serious challenge to the Turnerian approach by demonstrating that the quality of antistructure and the experience of communitas are largely absent from specific pilgrimage contexts. While communitas may be one element of the pilgrimage experience, this social and emotional quality cannot be assumed to exist in all pilgrimages; nor can the concept be used as a master key to unlock the meaning and significance of pilgrimage for all participants in every cross-cultural setting. Moreover, Turner's work has been the subject of several theoretical critiques. Notably, E. Alan Morinis has argued that the attempt to apply the same structural framework developed for rites of passage to pilgrimage seriously distorts our understanding of the latter, more complex, and diverse ritual phenomenon (1984, 257–60; 1992, 8). Likewise, British anthropologists John Eade and Michael Sallnow (1991) argue against a global, essentialist approach that focuses on the universal characteristics and social functions of pilgrimage. Rather, they advocate analyzing each specific pilgrimage in terms of its particular social context and its "historically and culturally specific behaviours and meanings" (3, 5).

For Eade and Sallnow, pilgrimages must be viewed as arenas for the conjunction of competing discourses. Each category of pilgrims brings its own construction or understanding of the significance and meaning of the pilgrimage journey and shrine. Likewise, resident religious specialists at pilgrimage centers offer yet another discourse about the pilgrimage process (Eade and Sallnow 1991, 5). While pilgrimage may involve consensus and communitas, it also involves divisiveness and discord (2–3). The power of a pilgrimage shrine derives from its capacity to function as a "religious void, a ritual space capable of accommodating diverse meanings and practices," and its ability to "offer a variety of clients what each of them desires" (15).[1]

In analyzing the competing discourses associated with pilgrimage sites, Eade and Sallnow direct attention toward three coordinates: person, place, and text (1991, 9). In the eyes of pilgrims, the power of a shrine can result from its association with a particularly holy person, from its location at a place where the divine realm made itself manifest in the human world, or from its character as illustration of a sacred text (6–9). Following the work of Eade and Sallnow, anthropologist Simon Coleman and art historian John Elsner maintain that elements of person, place, and text work together to determine the particular character of pilgrimage sites (1995, 202). However, in their broadly comparative study, *Pilgrimage Past and Present in the World Religions,* Coleman and Elsner also focus on the importance of a fourth element—movement—which they see as central to the pilgrimage process: "It is the experience of travel and the constant possibility of encountering the new which makes pilgrimage distinct from other forms of ritual in the religions we have examined" (206).

For Coleman and Elsner, pilgrimage holds the potential for both communitas and contestation. A similar, flexible approach is exemplified in Jill Dubisch's postmodern and experiential study of the Greek Orthodox shrine of the Church of the Annunciation on the Aegean island of Tinos (1995). Like communitas, liminality from Dubisch's perspective "is not an inherent feature of pilgrimage to Tinos, but is variable, situational and fluctuating" (97). Dubisch's approach is valuable in pointing the way to a nondeterministic use of Turner's categories that would allow the anthropologist to invoke the ideas of liminality and communitas when they illuminate particular ethnographic situations, without the necessity of attempting to fit all pilgrimage-related phenomena into a rigidly preconceived theoretical framework.[2]

Tourism as Individual Quest

Extending the notion of the transformative experience of religious pilgrimage, Nelson Graburn (1977, 1983, 1989) and Dean MacCannell (1976) have produced the most astute and wide-ranging theoretical analyses of how modernist touristic travel may fulfill individuals' need for periodic spiritual renewal. The work of Graburn and MacCannell responds to a history of negative evaluations of mass tourism that depict it as a trivial subject for academic investigation and "a frivolous inauthentic activity characteristic of the pseudo-events of modern capitalist society" (Graburn 1983, 15).[3]

Graburn (1977, 22–23) argues that modern tourism fulfills similar purposes to those of earlier categories of travel, such as premodern European and Asian pilgrimages, by providing "structurally-necessary ritualized breaks in routine that define and relieve the ordinary." Following Edmund Leach (1961), Graburn outlines how touristic journeys—like religious ceremonial occasions, such as Easter or Yom Kippur—mark the passage of time both cyclically and in a linear fashion. Individuals' annual cycles are divided into "profane" (ordinary, working) and "sacred" (nonordinary, holy, or holiday) periods that are repeated from year to year. Graburn notes that modern Western conceptions of the purpose of these travel experiences include the notion that the nonordinariness, excitement, and relaxation from the normal duties of life allow people on holiday to symbolically "re-create" and thus "renew" themselves for the return to their working lives (1977, 22; see also Löfgren 1999; and Nash 1977, 1989).

MacCannell's classic study *The Tourist* is fundamentally an in-depth exploration of the structure of "modern mass leisure" and the motivations that underlie it (1976, 3). Like Graburn (1977, 1989), MacCannell argues that modern individuals respond to their routinized work lives by regularly seeking out the inverse in leisure activities. In MacCannell's formulation, however, these individuals embark on journeys that are primarily quests for an "authenticity" that is missing in their everyday lives. MacCannell's emphasis on the search for meaning through experiences of the "authentic" away from home supports the parallel drawn by Graburn between secular touristic journeys and religious pilgrimages. Unlike focal pilgrimage destinations, however, tourists' itineraries lead them through a myriad of different "sights" that may even include the workplaces of Others, resulting in what MacCannell terms "staged authenticity" (1976, 57–76, 91–107). As opposed to Daniel Boorstin (1964), however, MacCannell does not equate either the tourist's quest for authenticity or the host's staging of authentic spaces as "pseudo"-experiences.[4]

Following Graburn and MacCannell, British sociologists Ian Reader and Tony Walter and the contributors to their multidisciplinary volume *Pilgrimage in Popular Culture* (1993) underscore the parallels between pilgrimage and tourism, arguing that the category "pilgrimage" need not be confined to explicitly religious settings, such as temples, mosques, or cathedrals. These researchers highlight the implicitly religious character of travel to ostensibly secular sites, such as Graceland (King 1993) or the Little Bighorn battlefield in Montana (Sellars and Walter 1993). Like Turner (1992), they also draw attention to the theme of death and its transcendence as well as the role of the dead—saints and cultural heroes—in providing a focus for both pilgrimage and touristic travel (Reader and Walter 1993, 17–21).

An important additional series of examples of travel that can be seen to blur distinctions between tourism as "personal quest" and pilgrimage deals with individuals who are engaged in what some term "roots tourism," in reference to Alex Haley's novel *Roots* (1971). For example, in his study of the touristic development of Elmina Castle and Cape Coast Castle in Ghana, staging points for the transatlantic slave trade between 1700 and 1850, Edward Bruner (1996) observes that for many African American visitors, these castles "are sacred ground not to be desecrated." As he points out, "many African Americans come to Ghana in a quest for their roots, to experience one of the very sites from which their ancestors may have begun the torturous journey to the New World" (291). Likewise, Paulla Ebron (1999) provides a detailed analysis of the structural and experiential aspects of an African American "homeland tour" or "heritage tour" to Senegal and Gambia that was sponsored by the multinational corporation McDonald's. Although she refers to the participants as "tourists" and "travelers," in her analysis she underscores that this journey is an example of a "pilgrimage tour" that is fundamentally about "confirming or creating an identity that is reunited with the African past" (923). The tours described by Bruner and Ebron share similarities with other journeys undertaken by individuals back to the areas where their ancestors came from, whether the travelers themselves are at one or many generations' remove from these "homelands." Other examples of this type of roots-oriented travel can be found in many contexts, including Europe (see Danforth 1989, 183–87; Delaney 1990; Lehmann 1993; and Neville 1979) and Israel (see Habib, 2004; Mittelberg 1999; Storper-Perez and Goldberg 1994; Shapiro 2000; and Zerubavel 1995, 119–37).[5]

Commenting on the issue of tourism as personal quest, Bruner (1991, 247) disparages the "elitism" articulated by Boorstin (1964) and others in their dismissal of tourists. At the same time, however, Bruner argues forcefully against Western travel companies' reliance on a social discourse that opposes two images: that of the unchanging Third World "native object," and that of the Western tourist who is promised that on vacation trips she or he will experience not only the renewal that results from relaxation but also a "total transformation of self" (1991, 239). For Bruner, the inverse of this dominant discourse normally prevails: not only do many Western tourists return from holiday largely unchanged but also it is frequently the "natives" who are forced dramatically to transform themselves in order to accommodate tourists.

Indeed, the same sort of critical analysis could be applied to anthropological travelers, some of whom—like pilgrims and tourists—also seek meaningful experiences and significant personal transformations by undertaking field-work journeys far from home (Bruner 1989; see also Badone 1991, and in this volume; Danforth 1989; and Holmes-Rodman, in this volume). Since such quests often take anthropologists among people who at one time were wide-ly characterized as having maintained more "authentic" cultural identities than those prevalent in Western societies, anthropological fieldwork has con-tributed to a discourse that constructs a wide existential gap between the "self" and the "Other" (Fabian 1983; see also Crick 1985; Dubois 1995; Gewertz and Errington 1989; and Herzfeld 1987). As Bruner (1991, 240–41) emphasizes, however, discourses relying on such modernist notions as the existence of easily discernible, unitary "truths" and clear distinctions between the "au-thentic" and the "inauthentic" have largely been surpassed in anthropologi-cal writing (see, e.g., Harrison 2003, 208; and MacDonald 1997).

Tourism, as an expression of the desire to discover and order the ecumene, the known world, and to construct links between the self—perceived to be located on the margins—and an Other—perceived to be situated at an authen-tic and sacred center—may well constitute a key trope in the worldview of the privileged members of contemporary wealthy nations located in Western Europe, North America, and East Asia (compare Harrison 2003). Clearly, as Crick (1995, 211) has argued, anthropologists share much common ground with tourists, including the material infrastructure required for travel, roman-tic motivations for exploring the world, and the tendency to exoticize the Other. Crick paints the similarities between anthropologists and tourists in a fundamentally negative light, situating both anthropological and touristic travel in a direct line of descendance from colonialism and suggesting that both anthropologists and tourists "travel to collect and expropriate what they value from the other and then tell of their journeys" (210–11). The contribu-tors to this volume agree with Crick's view that "structurally, anthropologists and tourists have overlapping identities" (211). Where we part company with Crick, however, concerns the assumption that such structural parallels nec-essarily involve only exploitation and cultural appropriation.

A World in Motion: The Impact of Postcolonial Critiques

The ascendance of theoretical frameworks in anthropology that emphasize mobility and border crossings over previous approaches that analyzed the world as though it were divided into static and bounded social units has had major implications for research on tourism, pilgrimage, and other forms of travel. A cluster of related themes—including travel and travelers, displacement, new cosmopolitans, postmodern "nomads," borders, transculturalism, and migrations—have come to dominate much of the literature in anthropology and related fields since the 1990s. These new metaphors reflect a world in which there is an unprecedented number of people traveling across wide distances as immigrants, refugees, labor migrants, or temporary sojourners as well as tourists and pilgrims. These voyages have been accompanied by the emergence of postcolonial, feminist, and diasporic challenges to the androcentric and "white" West as a unique center of theoretical advances and global politics (e.g., Mohanty 1988; and Spivak 1987). As James Clifford (1989, 185), for example, has emphasized, "Theory is always written from some 'where,' and that 'where' is less a place than *itineraries*."

The idea of "travel," rather than that of "place," has thus had a major impact on postmodern theories of society. One now reads analyses that emphasize that, like individuals and objects, theories (Said 1983) as well as cultures can best be imagined as "traveling" or "touring" (Clifford 1992; Rojek and Urry 1997). These new metaphors are especially relevant to studies of tourism since earlier characterizations described tourists, much like explorers, military officers, missionaries, and anthropologists, as uniquely mobile "travelers" who displaced themselves to locations where they were hosted by homebound insiders. Now, some conceive that "every center or home is someone else's periphery or diaspora" (Clifford 1989, 179; see also Appadurai 1991; and Marcus 1995, on the emergence of "multi-sited ethnography"). Moreover, like many of anthropologists' "key informants" and interpreters (Clifford 1992, 97), touristic or pilgrimage "hosts" are frequently individuals who have had as many or more experiences of travel than their "guests" (Macdonald 1997, 155; Ong 1999; Tsing 1993).

Intersecting Journeys: The Anthropology of Pilgrimage and Tourism

With the ascendance of travel and other forms of mobility as key metaphors for contemporary cultural theory, there has been a related inquiry into the symbolic constructions underpinning the images that have been created of various travel figures, ranging from the nineteenth-century male *flâneur* (stroller) to the late twentieth century's self-consciously antitourist, "nomadic" travel writer (Clifford 1989, 183). One has to ask the question of where, within this kaleidoscope of juxtaposed images, now lies the distinction between "religious" pilgrims and "secular" tourists. For each of these concepts, too, can be the source of theoretical play:

"Pilgrimage" seems to me a more interesting comparative term to work with. It includes a broad range of Western and non-Western experiences and is less class and gender-biased than "travel." Moreover, it has a nice way of subverting the constitutive modern opposition: traveler/tourist. But its "sacred" meanings tend to predominate—even though people go on pilgrimages for secular as well as religious reasons. And in the end, for whatever reasons of cultural bias, I find it harder to make "pilgrimage" stretch to include "travel" than the reverse. (Clifford 1992, 110)

This problematizing of the boundaries between pilgrims and tourists is supported by etymological inquiries. As Valene Smith (1992) points out, although the most widespread current use of the term "pilgrim" refers to someone on a "religious journey," the Latin *peregrinus* from which "pilgrim" is derived "suggests broader interpretations, including foreigner, wanderer, exile, and traveler, as well as newcomer and stranger." Similarly, she explains, the English word "tourist" derives from the Latin root *tornus*, which refers to someone "who makes a circuitous journey—usually for pleasure—and returns to the starting point" (1).

Smith goes on to argue, however, that although pilgrims often use the same infrastructure as tourists and, like them, can undertake journeys only if they have the necessary "discretionary income, leisure time, and social sanctions permissive of travel" (1992, 1), it is necessary to develop more refined definitions and typologies rather than to collapse the two concepts in the broader one of "traveler." One general approach positions tourism and pilgrimage as lying at either end of a conceptual continuum (3). Along these lines, John Eade (1992), Mary Lee Nolan and Sidney Nolan (1989, 1992), and Boris Vukonić (1992) have demonstrated that pilgrimage shrines are also frequently attractions for vacationers engaged partly in "religious tourism" rather than in pilgrimage journeys.

Furthermore, in different historical periods people have fulfilled their spiritual needs through travel to locations with no apparent public or religious shrine, as Smith suggests, referring to ecotourism (1992, 14), and as both Graburn (1977, 1989) and Turner and Turner (1978) have highlighted: "Even when people bury themselves in anonymous crowds on beaches, they are seeking an almost sacred, often symbolic, mode of communitas, generally unavailable to them in the structured life of the office, the shop floor or the mine" (20). Similarly, following the work of both Turner (1974) and Mircea Eliade (1969, 27–56), Erik Cohen (1992a, 50–55; 1992b) claims that in premodern times pilgrims moved toward sacred "centers" while people journeying for noninstrumental purposes moved toward the "Other," located on the peripheries. Over the last few centuries, however, these structural differences have been transformed, as tourists attempting to retreat from geographic centers of industry and finance frequently created new centers in formerly peripheral locations and thereby emerged as the new variety of "pilgrim-tourists," discussed by MacCannell (1976) and others.

Finally, although pilgrims have been characterized as quintessentially premodern travelers and structural precursors to tourists, such labels should not distract our attention from the existence today of mass pilgrimages that possess deep cultural significance in the postmodern era. How, then, can the theoretical insights of postmodern theory be applied to the study of religious pilgrims in the contemporary period? The religious significance, deep histories, and routinized itineraries of most pilgrimages have meant that, to a greater degree than tourists, pilgrims have been self-conscious about the purpose of their journeys to pilgrimage shrines, often being guided by printed guidebooks, oral narratives, and a plethora of cultural signs displayed by previous pilgrims. One might assume, moreover, that religious pilgrims would be less likely to think about their journeys in the self-ironic terms ascribed to those travelers whom Maxine Feifer (1985), John Urry (1990), and others have called "post-tourists."[6] Is the same true, however, of pilgrims' ideas about the significance of the journeys of fellow pilgrims—some of whom may be accused of having nonreligious (e.g., commercial) as opposed to spiritual motivations for traveling on pilgrimage routes, and others who might be characterized as choosing less "authentic" modes of travel and thus lessening the spiritual validity of their personal sacrifice (see, e.g., Starkie 1957, 324)? As the essays in this volume demonstrate, it is in such contestations over meaning that centers, like journeys, are continuously emergent and perpetually in motion.

Discussion of Contributions

It seems appropriate to begin this collection with Paula Holmes-Rodman's literary and humanistic evocation of the experience of being a pilgrim and the experience of the ethnographer studying pilgrimage (chapter 2). This reflexive chapter re-creates for the reader the full sensory impact of the sustained physical movement involved in the annual pilgrimage made on foot by Native American and Hispanic Catholics to the healing shrine of El Santuario de Chimayo in northern New Mexico. Holmes-Rodman explores the ambiguous position of the ethnographer on pilgrimage: an observer who becomes over the course of the journey a participant, a friend, an honorary niece and daughter of fellow pilgrims, and a suffering body in need of healing but ultimately remains an unbeliever. Holmes-Rodman's experience on the route to Chimayo is surprisingly close to the Turnerian representation of pilgrimage. Like initiates, the pilgrims are segregated by gender into separate men's and women's groups for the journey. They are stripped of their identities, wearing identical blue pilgrimage T-shirts and taking off all jewelry, including wedding rings. The liminality of the 135-mile walk is heightened by the fact that only the leaders are allowed to wear watches. For the ordinary pilgrims, this is truly time out of time. Likewise, the order of day and night is inverted, as pilgrims are awakened at 2 A.M. to do their walking in the cool hours of early morning. For Holmes-Rodman, this liminality generated communitas, as the women in her group of pilgrims tended each other's blisters, sang together on the road, and comforted one another in their exhaustion.

The third chapter, by Simon Coleman, portrays the complexity and variety of the discourses that cluster around a pilgrimage center, in this case Walsingham, England's Nazareth, where an exact replica of Christ's childhood home is said to have been constructed in pre-Norman times. Walsingham was a popular pilgrimage destination in the Middle Ages but was largely forgotten after the sixteenth century, until its revival in the late nineteenth century. Since Walsingham is claimed as a sacred center by both the Roman Catholic and the Anglican Churches, the twentieth-century history of this site provides numerous examples of the competition and contestation that Eade and Sallnow (1991) claim is characteristic of the pilgrimage process.

As Coleman points out, there are many different types of visitors to Walsingham. For some, the "parish pilgrims," travel to Walsingham helps reinforce a well-defined Roman Catholic or Anglican identity and provides a link to a wider historical and religious context beyond the level of the local parish. At Walsingham, these pilgrims experience the Turnerian sense of communitas that comes from the consciousness of belonging to a deeply rooted religious tradition. However, Walsingham also attracts "heritage pilgrims" who are interested in experimenting with new liturgical practices, blurring the distinctions between Anglicanism and Roman Catholicism, and for them a visit to the beach, a walk in the countryside, or fellowship in one of Walsingham's pubs becomes part of an individualized pilgrimage itinerary. Often, such visitors know little about the official church narratives concerning Walsingham. As Coleman shows, Walsingham has now developed into a site of generalized religious heritage as well as spiritual and secular tourism, and for some visitors, he writes, "the boundaries between tourism and pilgrimage have become attenuated if not impossible to detect."

Walsingham, like Santiago de Compostela, provides an interesting case of what might be termed an inversion of pilgrimage. Both Santiago and Walsingham are believed to constitute direct links to the Holy Land. In the case of Walsingham, this link is constructed through mimesis: the site's sacredness derives from the fact that it is the location of a replica of the Holy House in Nazareth. The relics of St. James, who is said to have preached Christianity in the Iberian Peninsula, form the link between Santiago and the Holy Land. At both sites, the distances that are bridged are temporal as well as geographical: the relics and the replica of the Holy House connect visitors to the time of Christ as well as to the place where he lived. In these two cases, the shrines derive part of their sacredness from their tangible evocation of other, yet more sacred, centers in the Holy Land. The pilgrim to Walsingham or Santiago does not have to travel the whole distance to Nazareth or Jerusalem, for the Holy Land has moved closer to the pilgrim's home through mimesis, replication, and the movement of relics. In a process similar to that which underlies the construction of Lourdes grottoes in Ireland (Taylor 1995, 198), at Walsingham and Santiago it is the center that has traveled to the pilgrim on the periphery, inverting the usual order of pilgrimage (see Coleman and Elsner 1995, 104–6).

Coleman also emphasizes the role of Walsingham as a national shrine, an embodiment of a supposedly unchanging rural English past. Similarly, Santiago de Compostela has historically been linked to the identity of the Galician nation within the Spanish state. With the designation of Santiago as a European City of Culture for the year 2000, however, the city is developing into a symbol of an emergent, supranational, European identity. As Sharon Roseman shows in chapter 4, through her analysis of a bid formulated by municipal officials in Santiago promoting their city as a candidate to become a European City of Culture, the pilgrimage route to Santiago serves as a potent symbol of European unity. The bid suggests that through the centuries thousands of culturally diverse Europeans traveled the same route to Santiago and that an ethos of tolerance and unity developed among them over the course of the pilgrimage. Santiago is described in the bid as a cosmopolitan center shaped by the cultural exchanges among pilgrims from many different backgrounds. Owing to its historical status as a Christian pilgrimage destination, therefore, Santiago is portrayed as being ideally suited to serve as a focal point for the pluralistic culture of the European Union.[7] Travel to Santiago in the year 2000 is presented in the bid as an extension of pilgrimage, no longer an overtly Christian journey but nonetheless serious travel with the goal of promoting tolerance, solidarity, and creative expression among the peoples of Europe. Once again, the Turnerian ideal of communitas echoes in the language of the Santiago bid.

Nancy Frey, in chapter 5, takes a different approach to the Santiago pilgrimage, providing an ethnography of the experiences of travelers on the Camiño,[8] or Pilgrimage Way, and after their return home. Relative to much of the literature on both pilgrimage and tourism, Frey's work is innovative in its focus on the aftermath of travel: the lasting impact of a journey on the traveler's subsequent quotidian life.

As Frey shows, present-day travel along the Camiño de Santiago on foot or bicycle crosscuts the categories of pilgrimage and tourism. Although many of the travelers Frey interviewed consider themselves pilgrims, they were rarely motivated by explicitly Roman Catholic or other religious concerns to undertake the pilgrimage. Many of these pilgrims hoped that the physical act of traveling to Santiago would help them achieve a parallel inner journey of self-discovery and self-transformation. Like the "heritage pilgrims" who see Walsingham as "the launching point for liturgical and interpretative creativity" (Coleman, in this volume), a large number of the travelers on the Camiño are urban, middle-class, and well educated. For these pilgrims, the Camiño provides the opportunity to develop meaningful contacts with nature and with other people, as well as relief from the alienation of routinized daily life at home. This alienation is symbolized for pilgrims by the technology and speed of modern means of transportation. In contrast, travel on foot or bicycle is valorized by pilgrims because it symbolizes authenticity and genuine empathy with others, the "I-Thou" relationship defined by theologian Martin Buber and referred to by Turner in his description of communitas. Indeed, Frey's ethnographic material provides unexpected support for the Turnerian model of pilgrimage. For the travelers with whom Frey spoke, the pilgrimage was an extraordinary experience, "a series of meaningful contacts—human, physical, geographic, emotional—involving all of the senses." The journey to Santiago is liminal in the sense of being divorced from the normal rules and obligations of everyday structured life. Upon their return home, many of these pilgrims experienced dissonance and sought to find ways to prolong the communitas of the Camiño and the insights gained from journeying. Significantly, as in the Walsingham pilgrimage, travelers on the Camiño seek authenticity and communitas through re-creation of the medieval past.

Like Roseman's chapter, those by Mark Tate (chapter 6) and Nelson Graburn (chapter 7) deal with the intersection between religion, tourism, identity (national and local), and the political promotion of a city. Tate analyzes the processions of Holy Week in the northern Spanish city of León. He focuses on an application made by one of the city's confraternities, or religious brotherhoods, to have its Holy Friday procession designated as of "National Touristic Interest" by the Spanish secretary of state for tourism. As in the examples of Walsingham and Santiago, the Holy Week processions are valorized as authentic because of their connection to a traditional past that is assumed to be unchanging. Tourists are expected to be attracted to the processions because these rituals offer the opportunity to "experience an urban-based 'tradition' that is religiously oriented." Thus, the León application implicitly assumes that touristic travel to the city for Holy Week will not be motivated by religion. In contrast, the citizens of León are presented in the application as participants in the processions or as spectators who are distinguished from tourists by virtue of a greater religious interest in the processions. Tate suggests that this distinction between religious insiders and secular tourist outsiders is a false one. He maintains that many Leonese citizens—like tourists from other parts of Spain—relate to the processions as secular spectators. Other Leonese residents leave the city to engage in touristic activities during Holy Week, using the holiday as an opportunity to rest, travel, and pursue entertainment.[9]

As the Japanese Buddhist priests discussed in Graburn's chapter point out, even ostensibly secular visitors to a religious attraction may undergo a religious or spiritual experience. Furthermore, Graburn argues that it is difficult if not impossible to distinguish between tourists who visit a temple for its architectural value and religious devotees who travel to the same site regardless of its age and heritage value.[10] These two observations apply equally to spectators at the Leonese Holy Week processions. Moreover, following Graburn's (1977) framework, those Leonese residents who travel as tourists to other destinations during Holy Week can be interpreted as participating in a religious quest for meaning and self-renewal.

Graburn's chapter analyzes the conflict that developed during the mid-1980s between civil and religious authorities in Kyoto concerning a plan to collect a tax on visitors to thirty-seven of the city's temples in order to raise money for historic preservation. As in the Leonese case, visitors to Kyoto, whether classified as tourists or pilgrims, are important to the city's economy. The Kyoto tax strike provides a salient case study of the contestation that can develop in the context of a pilgrimage center. At issue was the key question, are temples religious institutions or tourist attractions? Graburn points out that during the tax strike certain actors emphasized the binary opposition between tourism and pilgrimage, while other actors chose to ignore this duality. It seems clear from Graburn's chapter, however, that the distinctions between pilgrimage and tourism are more likely to be blurred in Japan than in the Western contexts described in the other chapters in this collection. This overlapping of categories may in part stem from the fact that most Japanese do not think of religion as a separate, compartmentalized domain, set apart from other aspects of life. As Graburn notes, the ancient Buddhist pattern of pilgrimage has provided the prototype for contemporary Japanese tourism. Religious practices are rarely absent from nonpilgrimage travel in Japan. Even secular attractions frequently have small shrines or altars near the entrance so that visitors may pray or call upon the Buddha for blessing. In a parallel fashion, modern pilgrimages in Japan also include elements of recreation and promote secular values, such as national pride or family solidarity. On the basis of the Japanese evidence, Graburn rightly cautions that researchers should avoid a Western or Christian bias, evident in both the Turnerian and the Eade and Sallnow models, when developing theoretical perspectives for pilgrimage.

Wayne Fife's essay (chapter 8) seeks to extend the concept of pilgrimage by applying it metaphorically to British missions in Papua New Guinea between 1871 and 1914. Like Morinis (1984, 1992), Fife argues that pilgrimage can involve inner as well as outer journeying and that interaction between self and Other lies at the center of the pilgrimage experience. Viewed from this perspective, British missionaries in New Guinea can be understood as embarking on a voyage of self-transformation, during which they sought to become ever more perfect Christians, while at the same time transforming the "heathen" Others they encountered. In some respects, these turn-of-the-century missionaries were similar to Frey's present-day Santiago pilgrims, who also seek inner transformation through physical movement, although the Santiago pilgrims rarely speak in the Christian idiom used by Fife's Protestant missionaries.

Fife suggests that our definition of pilgrimage should be expanded to encompass the concept of journeying to a place that is not yet sacred but that can be rendered sacred through the activities of pilgrims. Missionaries to New Guinea saw themselves as working to create a sacred space that would only be fully realized in the future, with the complete conversion of the native population. In the meantime, missionaries set up compounds or stations, separate Christian settlements for missionaries and converts near indigenous villages. These "civilized" compounds were viewed by missionaries as sacred space, set apart from the darkness that they believed characterized most of New Guinea.

While the time span involved in the missionary pilgrimages that Fife describes is longer than the duration of most conventional pilgrimage journeys, lasting up to twenty years, it is clear that for the missionaries the time spent in New Guinea was a liminal period outside the boundaries of their structured lives in Britain. In this respect, the experience of New Guinea missionaries corresponds to the Turnerian model of pilgrimage.

Like Fife, Jennifer Porter sets out to broaden the boundaries of the concept of pilgrimage in her essay (chapter 9) on *Star Trek* conventions. Following Morinis (1984, 1992), Porter suggests that pilgrimage represents a quest for a "place or state in which intensified ideals not attainable at home are embodied." Starting from this assumption, she shows that for many *Star Trek* fans convention attendance involves the pursuit of sacred ideals that are actualized in the convention itself. Significantly, these ideals coincide with those defined as sacred in the "cult of man" that Durkheim predicted would become the religion of complex, industrialized societies: individualism, liberalism, freedom, justice, equality, and tolerance for diversity. In the context of *Star Trek,* these values are expressed as the doctrine of IDIC—Infinite Diversity in Infinite Combination.

Porter maintains that, in contrast to more traditional pilgrimages, the particular location of *Star Trek* conventions is unimportant to most fans. Even the process of journeying to the convention assumes secondary significance. The "center" that attracts these pilgrims is a dialogic one, not localized geographically, but rather a fluid and shifting community of fans that meets, interacts, shares opinions, and negotiates understandings.

Finally, in the concluding chapter to this volume, Ellen Badone takes up once again the theme of the parallels that underlie the journeys made by pilgrims, tourists, and ethnographers. Examining the emotional, intellectual, spiritual, and physical dimensions of these forms of travel, she argues that both pilgrimage and tourism, like ethnography, situate social actors in liminal border zones that generate creative and complex reinterpretations of experience and renegotiations of identity.

One point is clear: at the dawn of the twenty-first century, the appeal of movement and the attraction of centers remain undiminished, as unprecedented numbers of visitors travel to Lourdes, Rome, Jerusalem, Santiago de Compostela, Ground Zero, and *Star Trek* conventions (Fainberg 2003; Lichfield 1999). Ethnographic analysis of the conflicts over resources and meanings associated with such sites, as well as the communitas they inspire, provides compelling evidence reemphasizing the links between pilgrimage and tourism. As the essays in this collection demonstrate, studies of these forms of journeying are at the forefront of postmodern debates about movement and centers, global flows, social identities, and the negotiation of meanings.

Notes

1. In his introduction to the second edition of *Contesting the Sacred,* Eade (2000, xiv) acknowledges that the theoretical argument of the first edition may have "overstated" the deconstruction of pilgrimage "as both a category and a structure." Nonetheless, he (correctly, in our view) identifies the main contribution of *Contesting the Sacred* as a "critique of the grand narrative tradition" regarding pilgrimage (xxi). He also provides an excellent detailed overview of anthropological research on pilgrimage that appeared in the decade following the first edition, much of which was inspired by that seminal volume. Like ourselves, Eade draws attention to the convergence during the 1990s of

anthropological work on various forms of journeying in the postmodern, globalized world system, including pilgrimage, tourism, and the travels of migrants and refugees (xviii–xix).

2. Like Dubisch, Taylor (1995) also notes that communitas and the sense of liminal separation from everyday life are a potential, but not inevitable, feature of pilgrimage. Writing of the Irish Catholic pilgrimage to Lough Derg, Taylor is attentive to the ways in which gender and social class influence the experience of participants. He suggests that in this particular context Turner's model most closely approximates the experience of middle-class pilgrims (196–97).

3. For examples of this point of view, see Boorstin 1964 and Fussell 1980. For a good summary of this trend, see Crick 1989, 307–10.

4. In a later collection of essays, MacCannell (1992) extends his argument that many tourists and especially "natives" (whom he now calls "ex-primitives") are aware of the paradox that their lives are "staged" in order to satisfy tourists' quest for meaning that they do not find at home: "The encounter between tourist and 'other' is the scene of a shared Utopian vision of profit without exploitation, logically the final goal of cannibal economics shared by ex-primitives and postmoderns alike" (28). See Fine and Speer (1985) for an ethnographic case study that seeks to illustrate the five processes that MacCannell identifies as leading to touristic "sight sacralization."

5. Following her Scottish study (1979), Neville (1987) documents a form of roots-based travel in the southern United States that she characterizes as pilgrimage. This involves members of extended kin groups living in widely separated locations who return to their ancestral homes annually for family reunions and church or cemetery homecomings that combine festive elements with Protestant religious services.

6. A number of authors have used the terms "post-tourist," "post-tourism," and "postmodern tourist" in efforts to characterize and analyze the consumption practices of middle-class and elite tourists in the context of global capitalism and postmodern theoretical frameworks. Feifer (1985, 259–71) alludes to the way in which the expansion of mass media has made it possible for audiences to passively consume vivid representations of faraway and "different" places while sitting in their homes. Smith (1992, 10) notes a similar process among millions of "born again" Christians in the United States who regularly make "TV pilgrimages" in response to the draw of television evangelists. Unlike the cynical "antitourist" or the devout American Christian watching a church service from home, however, the "outward-bound" post-tourist does travel, possesses a postmodern sense of irony, and comfortably parodies the romantic tourist of an earlier time period by self-consciously buying kitsch and eating meals in evidently "tourist" restaurants. Later authors, such as John Urry (1990), more fully elaborate the theoretical implications of the postmodern consumption of tourist sights. The post-tourist concept highlights the fact that although many individuals' rhetorical technique when distinguishing themselves from mass tourists is to use labels such as "traveler" and "trekker" (Cohen 1992b, 54; Errington and Gewertz 1989), post-tourists have different tactics. They are intellectually playful when on holiday, fully recognizing "that they are a tourist and that tourism is a game, or rather a whole series of games with multiple texts and no single, authentic tourist experience" (Urry 1990, 100). Bauman (1996) explores the categories "pilgrim" and "tourist," among others, in his discussion of the shift from modern to postmodern identity.

7. As historian Jonathan Sumption demonstrates, however, medieval pilgrimages seldom promoted cultural exchanges among pilgrims of diverse origins, in part because of the language barriers separating people from different regions of Europe: "It would be pleasant to learn that pilgrims returned from their travels with minds broadened by the experience of strange people and unfamiliar customs. But it would be the reverse of the truth. . . . All too often, those who lived on the pilgrimage roads regarded pilgrims as fair game to be plundered at will. The pilgrims in turn had little incentive to understand their hosts, and viewed them with that uncomprehending contempt which uneducated people commonly accord to foreigners" (1975, 192).

8. Here, we use the Galician term *camiño,* although the Castilian *camino,* used by Frey in chapter 5, may be more familiar to some readers.

9. See Crain (1996, 1997) and Murphy (1994) on the emergence of the Andalusian El Rocío *romería* (pilgrimage to a local shrine) tradition as a religious event that draws large numbers of spectators and provides a focus for the contestation of meanings among insiders and between insiders and outsiders.

10. Indeed, as Coleman's chapter indicates, even for the religious devotee, age and architectural quality may enhance the sacredness and authenticity of a shrine.

References Cited

Appadurai, Arjun. 1991. "Global Ethnoscapes: Notes and Queries for a Transnational Anthropology." In *Recapturing Anthropology: Working in the Present.* Ed. Richard G. Fox. 191–210. Santa Fe: School of American Research Press.

Badone, Ellen. 1991. "Ethnography, Fiction, and the Meanings of the Past in Brittany." *American Ethnologist* 18:518–45.

Bauman, Zygmunt. 1996. "From Pilgrim to Tourist—or a Short History of Identity." In *Questions of Cultural Identity.* Ed. Stuart Hall and Paul Du Gay. 18–36. London: Sage.

Boorstin, Daniel J. 1964. *The Image: A Guide to Pseudo-Events in America.* New York: Harper and Row.

Bruner, Edward M. 1989. "Of Cannibals, Tourists, and Ethnographers." *Cultural Anthropology* 4 (4): 439–49.

———. 1991. "Transformation of Self in Tourism." *Annals of Tourism Research* 18:238–50.

———. 1996. "Tourism in Ghana: The Representation of Slavery and the Return of the Black Diaspora." *American Anthropologist* 98:290–304.

Clifford, James. 1989. "Notes on Travel and Theory." *Inscriptions* 5:177–88.

———. 1992. "Traveling Cultures." In *Cultural Studies.* Ed. Lawrence Grossberg, Cary Nelson, and Paula A. Treichler. 96–112. London: Routledge.

Cohen, Erik. 1992a. "Pilgrimage and Tourism: Convergence and Divergence." In *Sacred Journeys: The Anthropology of Pilgrimage.* Ed. E. Alan Morinis. 47–61. New York: Greenwood Press.

———. 1992b. "Pilgrimage Centers: Concentric and Excentric." *Annals of Tourism Research* 19:33–50.

Coleman, Simon, and John Elsner. 1995. *Pilgrimage Past and Present in the World Religions.* Cambridge, Mass.: Harvard University Press.

Crain, Mary M. 1996. "Contested Territories: The Politics of Touristic Development at the Shrine of El Rocío in Southwestern Andalusia." In *Coping with Tourists: Euro-*

pean Reactions to Mass Tourism. Ed. Jeremy Boissevain. 27–55. Oxford: Berghahn Books.

———. 1997. "The Remaking of an Andalusian Pilgrimage Tradition: Debates regarding Visual (Re)presentation and the Meanings of 'Locality' in a Global Era." In *Culture, Power, Place: Explorations in Critical Anthropology.* Ed. Akhil Gupta and James Ferguson. 291–311. Durham, N.C.: Duke University Press.

Crick, Malcolm. 1985. "'Tracing' the Anthropological Self: Quizzical Reflections on Fieldwork, Tourism and the Ludic." *Social Analysis* 17:71–92.

———. 1989. "Representations of International Tourism in the Social Sciences: Sun, Sex, Savings, and Servility." *Annual Review of Anthropology* 18:307–44.

———. 1995. "The Anthropologist as Tourist: An Identity in Question." In *International Tourism, Identity and Change.* Ed. Marie-Françoise Lanfant, John B. Allcock, and Edward M. Bruner. 205–23. London: Sage.

Danforth, Loring. 1989. *Firewalking and Religious Healing: The Anastenaria of Greece and the American Firewalking Movement.* Princeton, N.J.: Princeton University Press.

Delaney, Carol. 1990. "The *Hajj:* Sacred and Secular." *American Ethnologist* 17:513–30.

Dubisch, Jill. 1995. *In a Different Place: Pilgrimage, Gender, and Politics at a Greek Island Shrine.* Princeton, N.J.: Princeton University Press.

Dubois, Laurent. 1995. "'Man's Darkest Hours': Maleness, Travel, and Anthropology." In *Women Writing Culture.* Ed. Ruth Behar and Deborah A. Gordon. 306–21. Berkeley: University of California Press.

Eade, John. 1992. "Pilgrimage and Tourism at Lourdes, France." *Annals of Tourism Research* 19:18–32.

———. 2000. Introduction to *Contesting the Sacred: The Anthropology of Pilgrimage.* Ed. John Eade and Michael Sallnow. ix–xxvii. Urbana: University of Illinois Press.

Eade, John, and Michael J. Sallnow. 1991. Introduction to *Contesting the Sacred: The Anthropology of Christian Pilgrimage.* Ed. John Eade and Michael Sallnow. 1–29. London: Routledge.

Ebron, Paulla. 1999. "Tourists as Pilgrims: Commercial Fashioning of Transatlantic Politics." *American Ethnologist* 26:910–32.

Eliade, Mircea. 1969. *Images and Symbols.* New York: Sheed and Ward.

Errington, Frederick, and Deborah Gewertz. 1989. "Tourism and Anthropology in a Post-Modern World." *Oceania* 60:37–54.

Fabian, Johannes. 1983. *Time and the Other.* New York: Columbia University Press.

Fainberg, Denise. 2003. "A Pilgrim, but a Tourist, Too." *New York Times,* Travel Section, June 29, 11–12.

Feifer, Maxine. 1985. *Going Places: The Ways of the Tourist from Imperial Rome to the Present Day.* London: Macmillan.

Fine, Elizabeth C., and Jean Haskell Speer. 1985. "Tour Guide Performances as Sight Sacralization." *Annals of Tourism Research* 12:73–95.

Fussell, Paul. 1980. *Abroad: British Literary Travelling between the Wars.* New York: Oxford University Press.

Geertz, Clifford. 1973. "Religion as a Cultural System." In *The Interpretation of Cultures.* 87–125. New York: Basic Books.

Gewertz, Deborah, and Frederick Errington. 1989. "Tourism and Anthropology in a Post-Modern World." *Oceania* 60:37–54.

Graburn, Nelson H. H. 1977. "Tourism: The Sacred Journey." In *Hosts and Guests: The Anthropology of Tourism.* Ed. Valene L. Smith. 17–31. Philadelphia: University of Pennsylvania Press.

———. 1983. "The Anthropology of Tourism." In "The Anthropology of Tourism," ed. Nelson H. H. Graburn. Special issue, *Annals of Tourism Research* 10:9–33.

———. 1989. "Tourism: The Sacred Journey." In *Hosts and Guests: The Anthropology of Tourism.* Ed. Valene L. Smith. 2nd ed. 21–36. Philadelphia: University of Pennsylvania Press.

Habib, Jasmin. 2004. *Israel, Diaspora, and the Routes of National Belonging.* Toronto: University of Toronto Press.

Haley, Alex. 1971. *Roots.* Garden City, N.J.: Doubleday.

Harrison, Julia. 2003. *Being a Tourist: Finding Meaning in Pleasure Travel.* Vancouver: University of British Columbia Press.

Herzfeld, Michael. 1987. *Anthropology through the Looking Glass: Critical Ethnography in the Margins of Europe.* Cambridge: Cambridge University Press.

King, Christine. 1993. "His Truth Goes Marching On: Elvis Presley and the Pilgrimage to Graceland." In Reader and Walter 1993, 92–112.

Leach, Edmund R. 1961. "Time and False Noses." In *Rethinking Anthropology.* 132–36. London: Athlone Press.

Lehmann, Albrecht. 1993. "German Refugees of 1945 and Their Integration into West Germany." *Ethnologia Europea* 23:125–33.

Lichfield, John. 1999. "Miracles and Masses." *The Independent,* Sunday Review Section, December 12.

Löfgren, Orvar. 1999. *On Holiday: A History of Vacationing.* Berkeley: University of California Press.

MacCannell, Dean. 1976. *The Tourist: A New Theory of the Leisure Class.* New York: Schoken Books.

———. 1992. *Empty Meeting Grounds: The Tourist Papers.* London: Routledge.

MacDonald, Sharon. 1997. "A People's Story: Heritage, Identity and Authenticity." In Rojek and Urry 1997, 155–75.

Marcus, George E. 1995. "Ethnography in/of the World System: The Emergence of Multi-Sited Ethnography." *Annual Review of Anthropology* 24:95–117.

Mittelberg, David. 1999. *The Israel Connection and American Jews.* Westport, Conn.: Praeger.

Mohanty, Chandra. 1988. "Under Western Eyes: Feminist Scholarship and Colonial Discourses." *Feminist Review* 30 (Autumn): 60–88.

Morinis, E. Alan. 1984. *Pilgrimage in the Hindu Tradition: A Case Study of West Bengal.* New York: Oxford University Press.

———. 1992. "Introduction: The Territory of the Anthropology of Pilgrimage." In *Sacred Journeys: The Anthropology of Pilgrimage.* Ed. E. Alan Morinis. 1–27. Westport, Conn.: Greenwood.

Murphy, Michael Dean. 1994. "Class, Community and Costume in an Andalusian Pilgrimage." *Anthropological Quarterly* 67 (2): 49–61.

Nash, Dennison. 1977. "Tourism as a Form of Imperialism." In *Hosts and Guests: The Anthropology of Tourism.* Ed. Valene L. Smith. 33–47. Philadelphia: University of Pennsylvania Press.

———. 1989. "Tourism as a Form of Imperialism." In *Hosts and Guests: The Anthropology of Tourism*. Ed. Valene L. Smith. 2nd ed. 37–52. Philadelphia: University of Pennsylvania Press.

Neville, Gwen Kennedy. 1979. "Community Form and Ceremonial Life in Three Regions of Scotland." *American Ethnologist* 6:93–109.

———. 1987. *Kinship and Pilgrimage: Rituals of Reunion in American Protestant Culture*. New York: Oxford University Press.

Nolan, Mary Lee, and Sidney Nolan. 1989. *Christian Pilgrimage in Modern Western Europe*. Chapel Hill: University of North Carolina Press.

———. 1992. "Religious Sites as Tourism Attractions in Europe." *Annals of Tourism Research* 19:68–78.

Nooteboom, Cees. 1997. *Roads to Santiago*. Trans. Ina Rilke. New York: Harcourt Brace. (First published in Dutch in 1992.)

Ong, Aihwa. 1999. *Flexible Citizenship: The Cultural Logics of Transnationality*. Durham, N.C.: Duke University Press.

Reader, Ian, and Tony Walter, eds. 1993. *Pilgrimage in Popular Culture*. London: Macmillan.

Rojek, Chris, and John Urry, eds. 1997. *Touring Cultures: Transformations of Travel and Theory*. London: Routledge.

Said, Edward. 1983. *The World, the Text and the Critic*. Cambridge, Mass.: Harvard University Press.

Sellars, Richard West, and Tony Walter. 1993. "From Custer to Kent State: Heroes, Martyrs and the Evolution of Popular Shrines in the U.S.A." In Reader and Walter 1993, 179–200.

Shapiro, Faydra L. 2000. "Building and Being Built: Constructing Jewish Identities on an Israel Experience Program." Ph.D. diss., McMaster University.

Smith, Valene L. 1992. "Introduction: The Quest in Guest." In "Pilgrimage and Tourism: The Quest in Guest," ed. Valene L. Smith. Special issue, *Annals of Tourism Research* 19:1–17.

Spivak, Gayatri C. 1987. *In Other Worlds: Essays in Cultural Politics*. London: Methuen.

Starkie, Walter. 1957. *The Road to Santiago: Pilgrims of St. James*. New York: E. P. Dutton.

Storper-Perez, Danielle, and Harvey E. Goldberg. 1994. "The Kotel: Toward an Ethnographic Portrait." *Religion* 24:309–32.

Sumption, Jonathan. 1975. *Pilgrimage: An Image of Medieval Religion*. London: Faber and Faber.

Taylor, Lawrence J. 1995. *Occasions of Faith: An Anthropology of Irish Catholics*. Philadelphia: University of Pennsylvania Press.

Tsing, Anna Lowenhaupt. 1993. *In the Realm of the Diamond Queen: Marginality in an Out-of-the-Way Place*. Princeton, N.J.: Princeton University Press.

Turner, Victor. 1969. *The Ritual Process: Structure and Anti-Structure*. Ithaca, N.Y.: Cornell University Press.

———. 1974. "Pilgrimages as Social Processes." In *Dramas, Fields and Metaphors: Symbolic Action in Human Society*. 166–230. Ithaca, N.Y.: Cornell University Press.

———. 1992. "Death and the Dead in the Pilgrimage Process." In *Blazing the Trail*. Ed. Edith Turner. 29–47. Tucson: University of Arizona Press.

Turner, Victor, and Edith L. B. Turner. 1978. *Image and Pilgrimage in Christian Culture: Anthropological Perspectives.* New York: Columbia University Press.

Urry, John. 1990. *The Tourist Gaze: Leisure and Travel in Contemporary Societies.* London: Sage.

Vukonić, Boris. 1992. "Medjugorje's Religion and Tourism Connection." *Annals of Tourism Research* 19:79–91.

Wolf, Eric R. 1958. "The Virgin of Guadalupe: A Mexican National Symbol." *Journal of American Folklore,* no. 71:34–39.

Zerubavel, Yael. 1995. *Recovered Roots: The Making of Israeli National Tradition.* Chicago: University of Chicago Press.

2 "They Told What Happened on the Road": Narrative and the Construction of Experiential Knowledge on the Pilgrimage to Chimayo, New Mexico

PAULA ELIZABETH HOLMES-RODMAN

Over the past thirty years, Native American and Hispanic Catholics have made an annual pilgrimage to the shrine of El Santuario de Chimayo, located in a small village in northern New Mexico. Groups of pilgrims converge on the shrine of Chimayo in the month of June, after having walked over one hundred miles from five different directions. Chimayo is host to pilgrims and tourists year-round. Each year, especially during Holy Week, millions journey thirty miles north of Santa Fe to El Santuario de Chimayo, an adobe church built by the Spaniards in the 1800s near a sacred Tewa Indian site. Pilgrims, who often arrive on crutches or in wheelchairs and carry large wooden crosses on their shoulders, post small votive images of ailing body parts in the room called *El Pocito* (the little hole), which houses medicinal sand. More than two thousand pilgrims gather on Good Friday alone at this sacred spot. Local traditions hold that if you touch, eat, or step on the earth from the *santuario* you can be healed (Kraker 1997, 77).

In 1997, on the silver anniversary of the Pilgrimage for Vocations in the Archdiocese of Santa Fe, I joined an all-women group of devotees who left for the pilgrimage from the city of Albuquerque, New Mexico. While there is little official history written about the Pilgrimage for Vocations, participants all come to the journey with some level of knowledge of the pilgrimage's history—largely a combination of memory, rumor, and individual and collective past experiences. The night before our group was to arrive in Chimayo just a dozen miles away, Rosita, a fellow pilgrim from Albuquerque, distributed pamphlets commemorating the twenty-fifth anniversary of the Pilgrimage for Vocations, for which she had collected and arranged photographs. On the cover was a collage of pictures of previous years' pilgrimages overlaid with the crest of the Archdiocese of Santa Fe; inside was a brief history of journeying to Chimayo past and present. This is what the women and I read that last night on the road:

> In a small valley twenty five years ago, the Spirit of God touched a small group of men who began a spiritual journey that continues today. The following is a brief history of the Pilgrimage for Vocations.
>
> Father Michael O'Brien, pastor in the village of Estancia in 1972, had promised a fishing trip to young men who had helped him paint the church. When he asked them where they would want to go, Rosendo Barela Jr. responded "to Chimayo." Fr. Mike asked how they were going to get there. The response was "walking!" The young men responded with enthusiasm, even though it was over 100 miles. That was the simple beginning of the journey. . . .
>
> In 1980, . . . Fr. Mike became the Spiritual Director and Donald Martinez Sr. accepted the responsibility of being the first *"Rector."*[1] Joe Vigil was the first *peregrino* [pilgrim] to be ordained a priest. He walked in 1976. Fr. Arturo Tafoya was the first *peregrino* to become a Bishop. This year, 350 *peregrinos* made the pilgrimage. Theme: "Come Walk With Me" . . .
>
> 1982—In addition to the Northern and Southern routes, this year's pilgrimage from the East and West were added. Women did not walk this year. *Peregrinos* now looked forward to completing their cross by walking all four directions. Theme: *"Que Vivo Cristo Rey!"* ["Christ the King Lives!"] . . .
>
> Father Ed Savilla is responsible for allowing the women return to walk [*sic*] for the June Pilgrimage. They had walked one year in 1981. In 1990, women came from the northern route and since then, continue to do the pilgrimage in June. This year, the women walked from the north, and the men from the south. After this year, one route was added every year until the four routes were back in place. The fifth route was added for the twenty fifth anniversary.
>
> Pilgrimage throughout the years has been a renewed experience for all those who walk. It is a journey for the spirit as well as the body, and a tradition in the Roman Catholic Church since the Middle Ages. . . .
>
> It is beautiful to know and share experiences that take place during such a prayerful journey. There are several reasons pilgrims give for going on pilgrimage. It may be for a family member, an illness, for forgiveness of personal debt, for personal favors, in thanksgiving for a blessing or miracle in their life, or just to pray for all vocations in life, especially for the increase of religious vocations. All of the pilgrims are committed to the sacrifice they will make for their own spiritual growth. (1997 pamphlet, Archdiocese of Santa Fe)

This pamphlet was the only "official" guide to the pilgrimage I ever received. I found out later that copies were distributed to all the men and women pilgrims that night before their arrival, and while Rosita had made a key contribution with her photographs, the idea, format, and editing of the pamphlet resided with those priests and organizers from the Archdiocese of Santa Fe. The pamphlet relates a narrative of how a divinely inspired yet spontaneous "lay" idea of walking to Chimayo became the archdiocese's annual Pilgrimage for Vocations—organized and routinized in terms of its historic link to tradition in the Catholic Church; its movement of men and women separately on the land; and its purpose of renewal and growth of body and spirit through sacrifice. The pilgrimage is ascribed official biblical themes and purpose—the increase of religious vocations—and asserts shared personal meanings such as forgiveness and thanksgiving.

The women appeared pleased to receive the pamphlet and praised Rosita for her work on the cover, yet its contents did not seem to change or challenge their own understandings of what pilgrimage was all about. This "official" reminder of the motivations for walking was quickly folded away; it had little effect on the meaning of their six days of walking or on their anticipation of the next day's arrival at Chimayo. The women I was with that evening seemed to find resonance in this framing of their experiences; the official interpretive prompts in the pamphlet were "true" but not complete or definitive. The paper was soon put aside, distant and out of sight, and the more immediate business of blisters, prayers, sharing, and sleep quickly attended to.

Go back one year. In the late summer of 1996, I had traveled from Toronto, Ontario, to Albuquerque, New Mexico, by train to carry out some preliminary doctoral research on contemporary Native American devotion to Kateri Tekakwitha, a seventeenth-century Mohawk saint. Devotees meet annually at the Tekakwitha Conference, and that year the gathering of over two thousand Native Americans was held at the University of New Mexico in Albuquerque. On the second day of the meetings, I found myself in the campus cafeteria, holding a lunch tray and looking for a place to sit. I could feel many eyes on me, blond and alone in a long skirt. I imagined that I looked lost but would later find out that many of the Native American devotees assumed that I was a nun. I was finally invited to sit and eat with two Acoma Pueblo women, Ann and her aunt Grace. Relieved by their hospitality and interest in me, I began to talk excitedly about how much I loved what I had seen so far of New Mexico and that I hoped to return to do research on Kateri there. Ann leaned back in her chair, smiled at our budding friendship, and then said, "Well, Paula, if you *really* want to know about our land and our people, *you should walk the land with us.* Every year, we walk one hundred miles to Chimayo, all the women together from one direction. It's in June. You should come back and walk with us. *Then you'll see.*" Grace agreed with her niece. I was thrilled and flattered by the invitation, and I enthusiastically answered, "yes!" that I would indeed try to return the following summer and join them. I imagined that the walk might be a grand adventure—a kind of supertourism guided by locals—and hoped that my participation might aid my acceptance as an anthropologist among the people I intended to research. Little did I know that not only the pilgrimage itself but the many journeys I took before and since would prove so revelatory of both self and Other.

When I walked in 1997, the official theme of the pilgrimage was this New Testament passage: "Were not our hearts burning within us as He was talking to us on the road? . . . Then they told what had happened on the road and how He had been made known to them in the breaking of the bread" (Luke 24:32, 35). This message—embossed on our commemorative blue T-shirts, printed at the top of every official letter and page of instructions I received—came to touch me deeply. In Luke's "original" narrative, two disciples of Jesus are walking along the road to Emmaus, deep in conversation about the recent crucifixion of their leader and his absence from his tomb. Jesus, unrecognized, joins the travelers who tell him about their recent experiences. Evening draws near, and Jesus, still perceived to be a stranger, is invited by the disciples to share a meal. Jesus gives a blessing, breaks the bread, and shares it with the travelers, who have a sudden and dramatic understanding of their companion's real identity. Their "eyes were opened," an "AH-HA" moment, one might say; then Jesus vanishes. The disciples marvel about what just happened: "Were not our hearts burning within us while He was talking to us on the road?" Soon they *share their story* with others: "Then they told what had happened on the road and how He had been made known to them in the breaking of the bread." For me, this briefest of stories, clipped from a gospel and recast as the official direction and meaning of a week's walking, became a vision of my own journey as a dialectic of movement and stillness, voice and silence, listening and storytelling.

In this chapter, I hope to demonstrate through my own account of the pilgrimage how experiential knowledge is gained through both physical movement as well as the informal narratives that are braided into collective journeys. I seek to evoke for the reader the experience of being simultaneously a reluctant pilgrim, an awkward anthropologist, and a curious tourist as well as some of the contradictions and transformations that such multiple identities imply and demand. In addition, I explore the issue of the anthropologist's voice, both its presence and absence, its noise and its silence, en route and later in the telling of anthropological tales. In so doing, I hope to elicit discussion about the larger issues of being both an insider and an outsider in the field, and the role that the intense experience of participation in a pilgrimage plays in the anthropologist's meaning-making of the event. Finally, I hope to evoke the broader anthropological conversation about the kinds of selves that people find and lose away from home (Ellis and Flaherty 1992, 6, 178).

I begin with excerpts from letters sent to me by Ann during the nine months prior to my participation in the pilgrimage. Ann was to be the spiritual director of our group; she and our *rectora,* Maria, would form the leadership team for that week. I received personal letters from Ann as well as mailings meant to spiritually prepare all the women in our group. Looking back, I realize that these letters shaped my expectations and understanding of what was to happen on the road to Chimayo. They served as a kind of lay guidebook and as local interpretive prompts, providing not only practical advice regarding clothing and supplies, as any tour book might do, but also personal encouragement and promises of an ineffable "AH-HA" experience.

The main section of this chapter is my own narrative of my 1997 pilgrimage experience—jotted down en route, written in full in the few days following my return, and edited and enhanced in the writing of this chapter. My aim in this section is to take readers with me on the pilgrimage, let them experience the pilgrimage with the senses and the emotions, and through the telling of this one journey perhaps lead them to reflect on the nature of pilgrimage itself.

This movement from the "ethnography of the particular" (Abu-Lughod 1991, 149) to generalization is perhaps especially relevant in the study of pilgrimage. In my attempts to understand the women's beliefs and motivations, perhaps beyond those so uniformly stated in the pamphlet, I also found myself stepping betwixt and between my own multiple identities, motivations, and meanings, all of which remained (and remain) in motion. In problematizing the very categories of pilgrims and pilgrimages, and in tracing their constructions, conflicts, communions, and contestations, we are led, perhaps, back to an individual journey (Dubisch 1995, 34, 46). What follows is the story of one such experience.

• • •

Dear Paula,
September 26, 1996
I know you will love the pilgrimage, everything you have seen and experienced will all come together; and you will reach that "AH-HA" stage (so this is what it's all about stage). . . . When you get blisters, you will really be at that "AH-HA" stage—ha! ha! ha! . . . Not only will you see our beautiful country by foot, but you will see and experience so much more—the people, they are pilgrim people with so much love and care to share with us pilgrims. . . . Especially during the time when we reach "that place" where night and day meet—fantastic! You will experience this for one whole week from Sunday to Saturday!!!!! God is so good to us. You will meet beautiful, spiritual women, young girls from 13 to 79 years of age, who will be on pilgrimage with us—come to us as Sisters-in-Christ. . . . It is so beautiful to ex-

perience, you will love it!! . . . I hope I don't scare you off, but this is the best advice I try to give new pilgrims who ask what they need to do to prepare. We . . . are praying that you will be able to come join us on this pilgrimage, but you must also pray.

November 19, 1996

Fill in the June application; I'll "walk" you through it. Mark "*guadalupana*,"[2] this is for women pilgrims, men are known as *peregrinos*. . . . Just beautiful—I am getting all excited for you, makes me remember my first time! . . . Anyway, love hearing from you. Will continue to pray for you, so you can join us during our June Pilgrimage.

January 30, 1997

We have received your application. I am happy to welcome you into this holy adventure.

February 28, 1997

Sending the information we spoke about. This should give you some ideas as to what to expect. The more you walk will toughen your feet, and if you are going to get blisters at least you will be less likely since your feet should be in condition to the long walks. Again, like I mentioned, the longer walks you take, the better. . . . Since you cannot be here with us during our [fund-raising] breakfasts, [practice] walks, and retreat, [our leader] asks that you pray for all of us, including yourself. After all, you are one of us pilgrims. . . . On the list, there are several mandatory items—now these are a must. Like the hat, large brimmed hat, to shade you from the sun. The hats are always worn. . . . Cotton shirts work best—they are cooler. However, it is best if the socks are not 100% cotton—this way you will not get blisters. We have found that when we wear 100% cotton socks, we have experienced more blisters! . . . We all send our love and prayers. Keep walking, praying. God loves you.

May 22, 1997 [letter to all the women pilgrims in Ann's group]

Welcome Sisters-In-Christ! We are all in for a great week! . . . My sisters who are on their very first pilgrimage, we welcome you! . . . We ask and encourage our experienced pilgrims to help your new sisters. Teach and encourage them when they come to you for any type of assistance or advice. Share with love the knowledge and wisdom you have learned from your pilgrimage. If a sister is having a hard day, show her the "tricks," how to make the "donuts" [round bandages with holes in the middle for blisters], or anything else you feel she needs to know. Maybe this is the year you will share your knowledge and wisdom our Lord has given you. For our Lord has instructed us to "love one another constantly!" Our Lord asks us to give our gifts away—this will lighten our load and make our pilgrimage easier. . . . So, as we journey this beautiful route, let's enjoy the sacredness of one another as Sisters-in-Christ, and especially as women. . . . Rest—and until we see one another on June 1, may our Lord bless you and your family.

Ann signed all her letters to me and the other women: "Until then I remain, A Sister-in-Christ."

The night before we began to walk, I received a card from Ann's aunt Grace. Grace was the eldest in our group, and at "somewhere in her seventies," she was a veteran of the pilgrimage and one of the first women who walked in 1981. Once again, she was making the trek to Chimayo, this time helping as a "trucker." That night, she silently slipped a small envelope in my hand and then waited while I opened it. She had written inside, "I'll be praying for you, as you walk with Jesus, He is with you all the time night and day." I was deeply moved by her gift to me of her own strength, endurance, and faith before I took my first step on the road to Chimayo.

Talking on the Road: The Ethnographer's Field Notes

Monday, May 26, Albuquerque

Ann picked me up from the airport, more excited and far less wary than I am about what lies ahead. She continues my training to be a pilgrim, which includes a lot of talk about "donuts" and socks as well as descriptions of how the "pilgrim people" will meet and feed us along the way. We will depend entirely on their food offerings to us as we walk through their communities. I can't quite picture how this works.

Tuesday, May 27, Albuquerque

Grace took me to visit the graves of her family today and to see her home in the old part of Acoma Pueblo, high on a mesa. There, in the shadow of the towering adobe church, Grace knelt, stroking the peeling whitewashed cross that marked the sandy mound where her husband lay. "This is Paula, my friend from Canada," she told him, "pray for her; it's her first pilgrimage." I went for a fifteen-mile "practice walk" with Ann tonight. We walked west on Route 66 as the day dimmed. The setting sun warmed our backs as we watched its reflection on the Sandia Mountains; the lights of the city started to glow, the tired bars came to life, and teens blared by in expensive cars. I could feel my first two pilgrimage blisters forming as Ann and I chatted about our families, the pilgrimage, and the land of New Mexico. No notes, no tape recorder, just walking. Ann says that the pilgrimage route is really 135 miles (not 100). But with no watches and covered road signs, nobody talks about distance once we start. In fact, the leaders (the only ones who are allowed to wear watches—to make sure that we get up on time and meet our *encuentros* [rendezvous] and Masses when planned) will lie to you if you ask, "How much further?" and answer, "Just over that hill." "But it never is," says Ann with a laugh.

Wednesday, May 28, Albuquerque

Just got back from stocking up my "blister kit." It turns out I need rubbing alcohol, needles and thread, and much more moleskin than I brought. "Bring lots to share," Ann said.

Thursday, May 29, Albuquerque

I am waiting for Ann in the shabby motel room I rented for a week. She is very keen on us/me doing as many "practice walks" as possible before the pilgrimage. Seems counterintuitive to me. All this doesn't feel quite like fieldwork yet. (Later) We walked eight miles tonight—down by the Rio Grande with lots of dogs, bikes, and mosquitoes. Toward the end of our walk, Ann asked me a question I had been dreading: "So what church does your family go to back home?" Ann already knows I am not Catholic, and for her this does not pose a problem for my participation in the pilgrimage. But I think she assumes I am a baptized and practicing Christian of some sort. I gave a vague but truthful answer. "My grandparents went to the United Church, and my mom did too."[3] "Uh-huh," Ann nodded and then told me what to do during the evening Masses. "You will just go up to receive communion with the other women, but when you get to the front of the line, put your hand over your mouth and shake your head. Tell Father 'no' and ask for his blessing instead. As guadalupanas, *we do everything together*—pray, sleep, talk—so it is important that we all receive communion and blessings together." Time for bed; feeling kind of "Other" myself tonight.

Sunday, June 1, Albuquerque

Pilgrimage begins today, and I'm not off to a very good start. Last night, I tripped over the motel bed leg and tore off most of my big toenail. It's all bloody and hurts like crazy. I awkwardly bandage it, slip on my sandals, and begin the mile or so walk to church. Ann and Grace have invited me to the 9:30 A.M. Mass and "blessing of the pilgrims" at their church in town. Once again, I was out of step. The "blessing" consisted of calling the pilgrims up to the front of the church for special prayers after the Mass had ended. Ann, Grace, and the half-dozen or so men and women who would be participating in the pilgrimage were all wearing their official blue T-shirts. Ann's invitation had neglected this detail, and I was wearing a long dress. Shoulder to shoulder we stood—they, a wash of brown skin, black hair, and bright blue T-shirts, and me—taller, paler, blonder, and dressed in pink. The congregation reached out their arms to us from their pews and prayed for safety and spiritual growth for us all.

It's sometime in the evening. I have no watch. We had to remove them along with all jewelry (including wedding rings). Dressed in pajamas and sitting alone on my sleeping bag on the hard floor, I feel naked and stripped. I mumble to myself that this must be the "precommunitas disassociation" part.[4] There's just a few minutes before night prayers and lights out. We'll be up at 2:00 A.M. tomorrow, starting early to avoid walking during the hottest part of the day. But until then, we are settled in the gym of an Albuquerque church—sleeping bags, cots, and duffel bags litter the floor. We have been divided into four groups of six or seven; each of the groups occupies one corner of the gym. I have six in my group. These are the women I am to sleep, eat, pray, walk, shower, talk, cry, and journey with for the next week. They look like friendly strangers now. I am loaded down with rosaries, chaplets,[5] and blessings. Formations, silence, commands, whistles. *Siempre!* (Always!) says Maria, our *rectora. Listas!* (Ready!) we reply loudly and in unison. We are always ready, we assure our leader. I can see the emergence of a new, strict order. This journal will have to go in the baggage truck. It is too big to carry in my waist pouch if I take the extra socks and moleskin I'm told I will need. I plan to write in the afternoons when we stop.

Just before bed, Maria came around to each of us and blessed us by making a cross on each of our foreheads with her finger dipped in holy oil. "Tomorrow we will begin our journey," she whispered in my ear as I nestled into my sleeping bag. "We will love each other and travel together." I drifted off bathed in the red light of the exit sign with the trace of her fingers still on my forehead.

Monday June 2, Bernalillo

It's sometime in the afternoon—two or three maybe—after showers and before Mass, which starts at five. We were up at 2:00 A.M. and stopped walking at 12:30 P.M. I feel totally disoriented—no time, no place, just these strangers who are instant companions. As I write, I am sitting on my sleeping bag and soaking my feet in a plastic basin of water, Clorox bleach, and *osha* root, a local plant known for its healing properties. We are spending the night in the parish hall of a church in Bernalillo whose congregants are our hosts for this first day. The women around me are chatting, stretching, snoozing, and treating their blisters, which involves running a needle and thread through a blister and leaving the knotted thread in to allow it to drain and heal.

We walked twenty-three miles today, I am told. I feel unexpectedly well—just a sunburn, despite a hat and sun block, and a few big blisters on my feet. Since I am one of only four or five "new girls" (out of thirty or so total), Carol, a fellow pilgrim and nurse by trade, offers to teach me the right way to take care of my blisters. In return, she says that I can *show the new girls next year.* Our leaders, Maria and Ann, tell us repeatedly that *we all are here as pilgrims,* not nurses or anything else. We are all supposed to learn to take care of our own feet and help others, especially those on pilgrimage for the first time. Many of the women have participated annually in this pilgrimage for a half-dozen times or more, and like Grace and Ann, intend to continue to do so until they are unable to walk at all. The "new girls"—including me—are enthusiastically welcomed, coddled a bit, taught in both subtle and overt ways, *and* expected to return the following year.

I can't tape-record during the walk, as I had planned. My recorder is too heavy to carry in my waist pouch and is becoming a burden both physically and metaphorically. We walk single file and have enforced periods of silence—the first hour of each morning and when we resume walking after a break. There are songs to sing and prayers to recite, all of which are printed in the palm-size prayer and song book created by the archdiocese for the pilgrimage. There are also times for conversation, walking side by side in twos and threes, time for hands to be held, arms to be grasped, jokes to be made.

We have a few hours of free time now, but I'm too tired to think and write more than sun-stroked letters on this journal page. The early morning hours are so beautiful—cool and blue with long shadows, barking dogs, and fading stars—a sly prelude to the intense heat and brightness the sun will bring. In the light of day, people honk, swear, wave, stare, and bless us as they pass us on the road.

In the first silenced hour this morning, lulled almost into sleep by the rhythmic footsteps of running shoes on pavement and the swing of light of the *rectora's* lantern, I suddenly looked up into the trees that lined the highway. There, against the hunter green of the nighttime woods was a row of shadows—bundled figures shuffling with bent heads against the darkness, led by an elongated cross. It took a brief moment to realize that I was seeing a reflection of ourselves. Later, in my group's good-night discussion, I mentioned what I had seen and said that I thought it was beautiful. "A vision!" several proclaimed. Oh, how lucky I was to have been given a vision so early on, one woman said. And another—there are so many stories of visions that women receive on pilgrimage. Maria—over there in the corner—ask her what she saw two years ago. Wonder, admiration, initiation, perhaps a bit of envy, a knowledge that recounting what I had seen made it communal, claimed as a gift by the whole group.

Mass, dinner: canned peaches, salad, grape punch, bread, pasta. We are getting up at 1:00 A.M. tomorrow. My days and hours are all mixed up, and I barely sleep—so tired that I feel tuned out of reality (or maybe tuned in). It all seems like such a rush—get in line, formation, prayers from the booklet—the same prayers in the morning, before and after each meal, the *Angelus*[6] at 6:00 A.M., noon, and 6:00 P.M., night prayers, rosaries, and then "time off," which is not off at all. I'm not sure what (or all) of this is pilgrimage. It seems a bit like a quick trip with a strict tour guide—no natural motion or exploration, as I had imagined. My companions seem to "get" why we do all the prayers and songs and lines over and over. I don't.

I feel the most "foreign" of the pilgrims. Affectionately, I am called "Blondie" by my "sister *guadalupanas*." But tonight, my sense of difference is embodied in many ways. I can hear another group "sharing" stories about their day on the other side of the room. Evening prayers start soon. I don't feel like myself. I don't feel like a pilgrim. And I sure don't feel like an anthropologist. Perhaps I am a misguided tourist who missed the bus headed to "that place," where the promised "AH-HA" moment would happen. Now my guides and companions speak a language I can neither hear nor understand. For them, these metered steps forward increase faith, imprint authenticity, and promise a destination where great spiritual renewal will transpire. Meanwhile, I am foolishly seeking some kind of transformation/information/acceptance en route to an unknown place in an utterly foreign landscape. . . . Exhaustion ends this trail of thoughts. Sleep—and a brief prayer for silence.

Tuesday June 3, Jemez Valley

Sometime in the late afternoon . . . I only have a few minutes before Mass, so I write quickly. My feet are a bleeding and blistered mess. I wore sport sandals with socks rather than the advised running shoes for the first days and have thus hobbled myself further. More sunburn, deep cough, bladder infection— my body is less inspired than my spirit by the walking. We started at 2:15 this morning. Beyond another beautiful dawn, our walking seemed to last forever—25 miles, church visits, and nuns to receive and feed us along the way. We weave into small communities, share food, weave out to the road, travel, and in again. I am starting to *see* the land and its people—in motion.

Now—stop—it's time for a meal, more Mass, and sleep. I am feeling twitches of anger at the incessant urgency and forced difference of the Mass. Walking feels purposeful, methodical. Even the songs and rosaries we sing as we walk draw and wind me into the center of this communitas. Mass feels like I am being suddenly spun out. No one has said anything to me about my unusual practice of refusal of communion. Still, I imagine their questions and assumptions about my spiritual state as I dumbly cover my mouth, shake and bow my head to the priest, and quietly return to my pew—empty of Body and Blood, incommunicado.

Wednesday June 4, Jemez Valley

2:00 P.M. (I find myself sneaking peeks at clocks in churches and parish halls—a grasp at grounding since my body and the sun lie.) We are back, showered, resting, soaking our feet, and making more "donuts." We—we?—did seventeen miles today—all uphill! We walked up into the Jemez Mountains—up Ponderosa Hill on a gravel and sand logging trail. With all the jokes about the "workout" factor of our walking, good-hearted complaints about cellulite and our aching muscles, I suppose we could be mistaken for clients at a spa—except that we eat too much. Peanuts, hard candies, homemade cookies from family members back in Albuquerque, orange sections, and cut-up bananas emerge from the water truck every few miles—washed down by green Dixie cups of cold water or cranberry juice. And then there are the meals—or rather, the hosts—the old women who rise even before we do to make breakfast; the tribal governor who sponsors our lunch at the pueblo recreation center and gives a speech about how we are welcome and he is honored; and the young people who buzz around us at long tables in the parish halls, offering us more bread, more punch, more chili. No, the meals are not about food, nor the walking about exercise, but both are about sacrifice, a backing and forthing of giving and gift.

I am feeling the rhythm. Morning broke on a land all misty green with brilliant sunshine and noisy birds. Women walked hand in hand or arm in arm, especially up the steep parts. The growing sense of communal love and common cause I feel overwhelms me—and clearly the others too at times. I found myself singing the Canadian folk song "Four Strong Winds"[7]—a song from my own land about traveling and moving on. I sang it to an older woman who had fallen behind on a hill, taking her hand while we walked up the steepest part. I sang it again to a young woman—only seventeen—it's her first time too. She had grown quiet and withdrawn as the miles passed, and I could see in her eyes that her heart was somewhere else. This kind of physical expression of support seems so normal but somehow unreal—like it wouldn't happen outside of pilgrimage time and place. But then, in "real time," I could not walk the way I have. I hardly recognize my body—the way it feels and what it can do.

I woke up weepy and shaky this morning as the gym lights were suddenly turned on to signal the start of our day. Even though we have only a brief wisp of time to get dressed and packed before prayers and breakfast, I sat on the edge of my bed totally immobilized by exhaustion. Sarah, who had slept next to me, must have seen the tears welling up in my eyes. She stopped rolling up her mat and knelt beside me, and taking my hand, she promised me that today would be a good day. "Thanks," I whispered, choking, then hurried to get dressed. I had no choice but to continue. In the next few moments, the community of women came alive, blurry-eyed "good mornings" emerged from limping and stiff bodies—their motion carried me forward.

The Jemez Mountains rose like the deep exhalations of the land. At 6:00 A.M. we stopped to say the *Angelus,* check our feet, and rest awhile. I sat on a ridge at what seemed like the top of the world, took off my dusty running shoes and my sweaty and bloody socks, let a cool breeze heal my torn feet, and looked out on a verdant world I had never seen before.

Two priests joined us for today's walk—men, but not men, and they did not disturb the community of women, but rather infused fresh energy and singing voices into us. My emotions are so mixed: annoyance—at the faith of these women, which I don't share, at the whole Catholic Church for its endlessness and monotony—to feeling compassion for the women I walk with and awe at the generosity of our hosts along the way and at the act of pilgrimage itself. I hear a lot of talk about "applying what you learn on pilgrimage to daily life," virtues like perseverance, patience, discipline, compassion. For me, these virtues have become radically embodied in walking. I feel as though I too have learned these lessons, although perhaps within a different framework than my fellow Catholic pilgrims.

Night prayers are like this: sitting on sleeping bags in a soft circle, reading poems, reciting "Footprints in the Sand,"[8] telling stories and wishes; the scent of artificial rose from the bright pink candle in the Our Lady of Guadalupe[9] tin in the middle of our circle; murmurs of prayers and Spanish conversation from other groups in the long, dirty gym; the smell of Clorox as we soak our feet and prepare bandages for the next day. Drifting off, I feel that perhaps I am on the right path.

Saturday June 7, Albuquerque, Looking Back

The last few days were characterized by bursts and drains of experience, all gone so fast. I feel like I've eaten a big meal too quickly and just now have time to digest. Twenty-four hours of togetherness with thirty women takes its toll on an anthropologist's methods. I found myself hiding in toilet stalls of parish halls to jot a few words down in private before quickly returning to the group so I would neither be missed nor provoke worry about my health with a long absence in the bathroom. These dashes between center and periphery and then back again with the purpose of cultivating memory for future storytelling strike me as quite odd. Even my dramatically scaled back "field methods" (no tape recorder, no camera, so little time to write) seem intrusive on the steps, words, and emotions of the pilgrimage experience.

I am back in Albuquerque, body at rest. I sit here dazed by the fragile knowledge that through my motions of the last week, I now have a kin of kinds—mothers, aunties, and sisters all over New Mexico. This morning, we walked into the Santuario de Chimayo after twelve miles in the freezing and pouring rain. As I passed through the old wooden doors of the church, I could not help the tears spilling onto my cheeks, and when I embraced the women around me and felt their strong arms, tired bodies, and warm, wet faces against mine, a choking river burst forth from me. For what seemed like an eternity, we held and blessed each other, and then, as the other four groups from the other directions arrived, we sang and clapped their drenched and spent bodies into the church to take their places on the pews beside us. The last mile, all the pilgrims sing this song over and over, rounds of which I still hear in my head.

> Vienen con alegría, Señor.
> Cantando. Vienen con alegría, Señor.
> Los que caminan por la vida, Señor.
> Sembrando tu paz y amor.

> [We come with joy, Lord.
> Singing. We come with joy, Lord.
> Those who are walking for life, Lord.
> Spreading your peace and love.]

Grace—Aunt Grace, as she wants me to call her—hugged me close, crying, "You are my child." It feels like a dream—all of us huddled on the worn wooden pews, craving candle warmth, singing, cheering. After, later, exhaustion becomes peace and awe for the beauty of the New Mexico landscape and the communion with my fellow *guadalupanas*. The women and the land *walked me*, and I was not unmoved. I remain changed by a journey I can't quite retrace.

But let me try to follow the trail back. On Thursday, we walked through the Jemez Valley—forest, vapors of green and blue, sharp smell of *piñon*, icy creek, sparse farms, horses and cows who line up and stare as we stagger by, singing Spanish songs of praise and joy, murmuring Hail Marys and Our Fathers. Then there's the infectious laughter. Barbara, a tall, quiet military woman, gained a voice late in the week. I noticed her because of her collection of T-shirts, which were each embossed with a different Catholic phrase, bit of doctrine, or prayer. Thursday, in the exhausted hours of the early afternoon, she suddenly stepped out of our line formation and led us in making up military chants. With a great sense of fun, mocking a general leading her troops, she taught us to sing and march (left, left, left-right-left) to the following:

I don't know but I've been told [she sings]
I don't know but I've been told [we echo back]
Chimayo is mighty close,
Chimayo is mighty close,
Sound off
Jeee-zus
Sound off
Is Lord
Jesus is Lord, Jeee-zus is Lord!

Beyond and behind all this—the sound of feet on the ground, echoes of "how are you doing, *mi hija* [my daughter]?" "you're hurting, aren't you?" and arms grabbed and hands held.

My feet kept me grounded—blisters on blisters, open wounds, and an infected big toenail. On the insistence of the *rectora,* I was sent to the Los Alamos Medical Center along with two other women whose feet were deemed to be seriously hurt. A little toe surgery, bulky bandages, and a big dose of antibiotics left me in more pain and wondering if I could walk the next day. The thought that I might not be able to broke my heart. Exhaustion and anger washed over me. After all the health problems I had struggled with all year, one stupid toe was going to keep me from finishing the pilgrimage?! My side trip to the hospital caused me to miss Mass, for which I was actually sorry. After dinner, I sat alone on my sleeping bag, not wanting to "share" anymore. Grace came to me just before lights out, crying, so sorry that I was hurting, telling me to take her strength to carry on. She held me and talked about how Jesus suffered on the cross and that I was helping him carry the cross with my own wounds. And then Lisa came by a few minutes later with a story of how one year she had prepared so diligently for the pilgrimage and then, because of an illness in the family, was unable to go. She told me how disappointed, angry, sad, and frustrated she too had been, but how she had learned that there are many kinds of pilgrimage and sacrifice and that it was God's desire that she be with her family that year. A lesson: "There are different kinds of journeys, Paula. You don't have to walk to be with us."

Friday morning the *rectora* again decided my next step. Because of an increased risk of further infection and injury, I was not to walk the first seven miles through a steep canyon. I was instructed to wait at the hall with the driver of the medical van, help clean up breakfast dishes, and then meet them when the road became paved. I knew Maria was right, but I didn't want to be separated from my group; I resented the inevitable difference my injuries imposed.

I would not be alone for long. No sooner had I waved my companions good-bye, tidied up after breakfast, and stretched out to rest than the women from my group streamed back into the parish hall. Some were running, others were limping, tears, fear etched on their blanched faces. What happened? Just a mile or so from the hall, some men in a car had driven past, calling them "KKK," "baby killers," cursing, circling, waiting in the bushes. The *rectora* had turned them back with a blow of the whistle. Some had begun to run. Others did not, could not, and the group scattered. They returned, crying, shattered, the cocoon lanced in some way. The story came to me in jagged pieces. I cried with them, feeling as though I had abandoned them to danger.

Several hours passed in the bare hall while the *rectora,* in a cellular phone consultation with the pilgrimage organizers, decided what to do. The women gathered in their groups to cry, pray, discuss what had happened, or just sit or lie together. Multiple interpretations of "the incident" emerged: a jarring reminder of reality; just another "big blister"; dark spirits lurking in the shadows; a violation; a protection from or warning against something worse down the road if we had traveled that way; an ambush—"they knew exactly what they were doing, and here in a small town, they saw us coming"; persecution—"just like the first Christians"; a test of faith—"will you take a bullet for being a Catholic?"—the crucifix (*guia*) we always carried at the front of the line would have given us away; or just drunk kids—"drive-by shootings happen all the time." A policeman came by later, his lean, slight, and uniformed body eyed warily by the women. He told Maria that it was no big deal, and besides, with no license plate number, he couldn't *do* anything; and "anyway, they didn't actually *shoot* at you, did they?" He left quickly, scurrying across the scuffed floor under the women's stares, which betrayed their anger.

We were bussed to the edge of the San Ildefonso Pueblo. I was to join them after all. "We're on tribal land here," Maria said, "This is protected territory. These are our roots—the Hispanic and Native cultures are mixed. We can walk from here." We stopped briefly at the church. It was empty, but someone had left the door open for us. Kneeling, the stiff joints creaking, the women offered Hail Marys for various intentions. One by one, the voices of thanksgiving and petition arose from the group, "for my sister and her new baby," "for the safety of all the pilgrims," "for the families we have left behind this week," "for my best friend who will be buried this afternoon back home," and mine, unplanned, "for the men my sisters encountered this morning when I was not with them—for peace, tolerance, and understanding." Outside the church, we rested in the pale sunshine before the next miles. Shelley, who had been to the hospital with me last night, offered me a gift: "Would you like to carry my rosary for a while? It has been in my family for generations. There's lots of beautiful prayers and stories on it." She had seen that I was limping badly and told me that it would give me strength through the miles today. When I hung it around my neck, the carved crucifix dangled to my knees. I tucked Jesus into the belt of my waist pouch, and the deep brown, worn wooden beads and dull brass links swung against my body as I walked.

Later that day, we came to the banks of the Rio Grande. It should have been dry, according to the pilgrimage organizers, and we were supposed to be able to walk across. But more than a muddy trickle ran through the riverbed, and despite jokes about walking on water and parting the sea, there really was no way for us to get across. Our accompanying truck and van had already been sent on another route. We were still giggling and reveling in this unplanned rest stop when a man in an old pickup truck came by. We jokingly stuck out our thumbs for a ride, and he obligingly took three loads of shrieking and laughing women bumping and splashing through the mud and water and deposited a waving bunch on the other side. With our hands stretched out, we sang our blessing song[10] and gave him one of the small colored plastic rosaries from the boxful we carried for distribution to those we met along the way.

Despite the jolliness of the afternoon, our arrival in Pojoaque was somber and disappointing. There was no hot water for our showers at the local school, and a funeral reception was taking place in the parish hall where we were to sleep and eat, so we had to wait for several hours in a small, cramped room. We were all grumpy, yet many women pointed out that *every Friday night* of pilgrimage *every year* is like this. It's the last full day of walking before we reach Chimayo, and everyone is hurting and exhausted. But as the veterans also predicted, spirits lifted after Mass and dinner, and excited chatter about our arrival in Chimayo replaced complaints and sulky silence.

The men's group from the south also spent the night in Pojoaque. They slept in a high school down the road from the parish hall, but we saw them at Mass—across the center aisle, and at dinner—at separate tables in a divided room. The *guadalupanas* and *peregrinos* were not to speak to each other, we were told by our *rectora,* nor were we even supposed to acknowledge or look at them. The boundaries between genders were still clear. Yet we heard their deep voices singing the same songs we had so lightly sung all week, their utterances in unison with ours in prayer and blessing for our hosts. Some of the women had husbands or sons in the group, and the families connected with quick glances. Without words, a mutual recognition of exhaustion and anticipation filled the space between us all.

We get to "sleep in" until 3:00 A.M. tomorrow, but I can hear some of the women talk about getting up earlier to do their hair and makeup so we can walk into Chimayo by 10 A.M. "wearing no pain." I will wear a long, white cotton skirt I have saved for the occasion, together with my blue pilgrimage T-shirt.[11] The pilgrims from all five directions, men and women, will be wearing these shirts as we converge en masse at Chimayo. The evening ends with all four groups coming together to "share" one last time—a kind of "scheduled communitas," it seems to me. We form a circle in the center of the hall, pull up our pillows, sleeping bags, and basins, and one by one, each speaks of what she has learned and loved on pilgrimage. Tiny stories of journeying emerge: expectations and experiences, pledges to return next year, testimonies from the veterans and the new girls, stories of aunts, friends, or mothers who inspired them to go on pilgrimage, promises made, and vows kept, amid much laughter and many tears.

We arrive at Chimayo on Saturday morning after hours and miles in relentless cold rain. I am aching, limping, and thrilled. My toe is bandaged to three times its size, and it sticks out at an odd angle beneath the mud-drenched sock from my soaked sandals with worn-down soles. People line the way into the town and down to the *santuario;* hands applaud and hold flowers and reach out to touch us as we walk by. It looks like a crowd to me, although others say that the weather has kept the usual throngs away this year. Our group is the first to arrive, and we huddle together in the candle-warm church and sing and clap as the pilgrims from the other directions arrive, group by group.

They look like us, clad in dripping blue T-shirts and bright rain ponchos, muddy shoes, straw hats, and waist pouches and holding tattered song and prayer books. Eventually, we settle, and the onlookers crowd into the back of the church to hear the priests and bishops speak and to watch us walk one by one up to the front of the church to receive and kiss a small metal crucifix dangling on a black cord that is then hung around our necks.

Then, filing past the tiny room that contains the famous Chimayo healing sand, we assemble again on wet metal benches in the open-air church for Mass. The rain has stopped, and the sky is its brilliant New Mexico blue once again, but I am chilled to the bone and cannot stop shivering. I feel dizzy as the pain from my foot travels up into my leg. I try to concentrate on the procession of the five *guias* (the crucifixes that each group carried as a guide along the way) and the Tewa drum and song that brings them in. The drum resounds in my head and fills the space between my bones. Aunt Grace, who has not left my side since our arrival, puts her arm around me and gives me a butterscotch candy.

During the week, all the groups have collected petitions and scoops of earth from the communities they passed through. Upon arrival at Chimayo, the leader from each group places the slips of paper on which petitions and prayers are written in a basket on the altar in the *santuario*. Outside, the director of the pilgrimage from the Archdiocese of Santa Fe pours the earth collected from all five directions onto the wet ground in the shape of an encircled cross. As the shades of dirt mix together, he talks about how the unity of the New Mexican land and its diverse people is achieved through pilgrimage. Speeches are made—the usual, the expected, but empty for me. One by one, in a last directed communal movement, we get up and file by the five *guias*, bending on one knee to the ground to kiss the feet of each crucified Jesus. I watch all those in line ahead of me and doubt that if I kneel I will be able to rise again. I do, and my long, white skirt drags in the mud. I stand, unmoved and stained by my regrounding.

I return to my seat chattering with the cold, and someone from the crowd hands me a coat. Aunt Grace takes my icy, pale hands in her warm, brown ones, rubbing them, whispering below the gospel reading to me that everything will be fine. Halfway through the Mass, Aunt Grace asks me if I am feeling okay. I shake my head "no." The next moment, two sets of strong arms lift me up and help me walk out to the parking lot. My feet barely brush the ground. Embarrassed to be leaving mid-Mass, yet more afraid that I would faint if I stood up for the Eucharist, I meet no eyes as I am shuffled away from the other pilgrims. Inside the van, I slip into darkness, a butterscotch candy dissolving in my mouth.

I awake, and it is over. Mass has ended; someone is opening the door to gather their bags. I stumble out into the sunshine, still weak, and reach for the side of the van to steady myself. Blinking, I see duffel bags, backpacks, and cots being gathered from the luggage trucks; families introduced; hugs and tears of good-bye; hundreds of pilgrims in their blue T-shirts rejoining their families, back into real time, driving off in all directions. The scene is quick, without lingering. Someone takes my arm. Over here. Meet my husband or my brother or my daughter, wedding rings and watches slipped back on. Hands grasped, promises made to keep in touch, "we'll see you next year." Ann finds me and leads me to her son's car. He has already retrieved our bags, which are soaked through from riding where the tarp had blown off the luggage truck in the morning's rain. Climbing into the back seat, my head slumps against the window, and I catch one last glimpse of our pilgrimage earth turning to mud in the new rain.

Talking Softly and Walking Loudly: (Dis)closure of Voice in Pilgrimage Narrative

In writing this chapter, I am highly conscious of what and how I say and do not say. What is quieted in this account? What is silenced? There is another side of the story, yet untold—a "biography in the shadow," if you will (Behar 1993, 320). In the above narrative, I casually mention the health problems I had struggled with all year—a throwaway line, only meant to impress upon the reader my disappointment at facing the possibility of missing out on the pilgrimage if I could not walk. Indeed, the issue of my health is much less accidental. According to medical professionals, I have ankylosing spondylitis (AS), a progressive, systemic type of arthritis that cuts a path of pain and immobility from the pelvis to the neck and that circles around the ribs and collarbone. The disorder is conventionally treated with a program of exercise and stretching and a wide range of anti-inflammatory and immunosuppressive drugs, including chemotherapy and antimalarials. But embodied for me, the disease means living with the betrayal of my body, a radical kind of *dis*embodied intimacy with my physical self, and a life of fighting and fielding its demands.

In the nine months prior to the pilgrimage, I had been on numerous medications and had suffered spinal pain, severe weight loss, intestinal difficulties, migraines, bleeding, and a rabid discouragement with physicians' inability to control the disease. When the application for the pilgrimage arrived in December, I was gray and exhausted. As I signed on to be a pilgrim, the distance between my body in its present state and the strength I imagined that I would need to walk seemed cavernous. June drew nearer, and I kept switching medications, hoping that I would find *something* that I could tolerate. Just two weeks before I left for New Mexico, I had settled on a combination of drugs that my doctors and I thought would be better.

Nevertheless, quiet, private worries and fussing about acceptance and revelation filled my mind. Should I make some sort of full disclosure about my poor health to my fellow pilgrims—if only to inform them in case I happened to run into any trouble on the road? I didn't know how to tell them, and few would guess my actual condition by looking at me. But what if my telling was interpreted as a request for healing? I worried that by doing so I might turn the women's sacrificial energies away from whatever vows or intents they had originally held. I was well versed in the transforming effect of anthropologists' presence on the people they are studying, but I worried about "contaminating" the whole scene. In my most self-absorbed moments, I glumly thought that I would gather no data or experiences other than those that focused on the women's reactions to me as a "sick pilgrim."

I needn't have worried. Throughout the week, I heard stories of illnesses, deaths, and tragedies that put my own troubles in a humble perspective. Nonetheless, in choosing *not* to reveal my illness to my fellow pilgrims, a situation emerged in which I was conscious of my own silence. That silence screamed paradox and irony. There I was, a young woman with a chronic disease, on pilgrimage with dozens of Catholic women who believed, *really* believed, in miraculous healing. With them, I was adrift in rosaries and blessings and prayers, and I reveled in the intensity and ineffability of emotion and experience. But fundamentally, I was (and remain) an "unbeliever" of sorts, peripheral, distanced, and disconnected from the New Mexican Catholic world of healing sand and miracles. With all my heart and every inch of my body, I was *present* and *centered* on that pilgrimage. I *walked loudly*. Yet, I *talked softly,* submerging my voice in anonymous yet universal descriptions of "the women," preferring largely to present my experiences simply as "pilgrimage," relegating my doubts and differences to metaphorical parentheses.[12]

Perhaps the *guadalupanas,* in their own ways, also "talked softly" in their motivations and "walked loudly" in their movements. My "fellow pilgrims" appeared to be largely homogeneous in terms of ethnicities, culture, and class; commonalities not (im)posed by the act of pilgrimage (Turner and Turner 1978, 39). They also shared preexisting Catholic beliefs, such as the power of repeated rosaries and Mass and of healing through sacrifice. These beliefs were *not* contested but rather confirmed, authenticated, and idealized through participating in the pilgrimage. For these women, pilgrimage was an occasion for "full-time" Catholicism, emphasizing suffering, prayer, and healing, meant to enhance, guide, and define in its idealness the everyday Catholic life of the other fifty-one weeks of the year. In fact, all the women I walked with were regular churchgoers and heavily involved with other Catholic activities and organizations; the pilgrimage was the pinnacle and the start of the cycle of a year of faith and practice.

Yet together with this apparent reinforcement of the "official" structures and beliefs of the Church, it is noteworthy that *not once,* in either Ann's letters, the leaders' instructions, or the women's conversations while on the road, was the official purpose for the Pilgrimage for Vocations—to increase the number of priests and nuns—ever mentioned. Our shirts said so on the back, and the archdiocese sponsored it all, but during the entire week, women spoke of every other motivation—vows, healing, peace, faith, promises—*except* vocations.

This makes, I believe, for a kind of quiet, unspoken competition and contestation between the "lay" participants and the "official" Church structures.

I suggest that there were no *loud* conflicts or contestations over the meanings of either the walking or the destination. Even the discussions and multiple interpretations of the incident in Los Alamos served in the end to *reconnect* the group and heal its fractures from the frightening experience (compare Eade and Sallnow 1991). I would, of course, be naive not to imagine that the women I walked with experienced some kinds of doubt, difference, or even dissent in their own minds. But these were silent, or silenced; the homogeneity of the external motion and motivations was unmistakable.

However, the comradeship and communitas I experienced emerged from the intense physicality of the venture—from the shared movement—and *not* from common motivations. Ann and the other women prompted me both quietly and overtly in both movement and motivations. Yet, once in motion, on the road, no one asked my *why* I was walking. My dashes of doubt and frustration were interior, as were those of the other women. On we walked in a single line, in silence, song, and soft talk.

When I set out, I anticipated that participating in the pilgrimage would provide me with access to the women for future research projects in New Mexico. In this way, I imagined that the pilgrimage would "define and relieve" the *extra*ordinary nature of the radical Otherness that the faith, beliefs, and practices of the women represented to me. And at the same time, I hoped that my participation in the pilgrimage might "define and relieve" for me the terrible "ordinariness" that being chronically ill had become (see Graburn 1977, 23). On one level, I *was* seeking a kind of healing, renewal, even peace with my body, hopes that I spoke to no one about along the way. That I remained for the most part healthy while walking and then became ill at the center remains a mysterious irony to me. Pilgrimage took me on parallel journeys of discoveries of both self and Other. Other than a sunburn, a few blisters, and sore muscles, I expected *not* to be transformed in any significant way except, I hoped, in my understanding of the other women.

For me, and perhaps for others, the "AH-HA" moment, "that place" that Ann spoke of, was not located in Chimayo but rather en route. Like me, the other women seemed to focus more on the annual journeying *on the road* and not on what one might find at the shrine. When they spoke about past pilgrimages, the shrine at Chimayo itself was never mentioned except in terms of how many miles *away* it might be. Their memories—and my own—were of the *journey:* sacrifice, prayers, friendships, communities, weather, meals, blisters, and the pain of the walking. Yet the center itself was not unmoved. To the shrine, they/we brought petition papers and scoops of earth collected during our travels and laid them down, thereby subtly transforming and mobilizing the sacred center. The other women too *walked loudly.*

There was meaning in the movement and triumph in the arrival, but then, after the final Mass, a hurry to get back home to the structures and roles of daily life. At the center, priests and organizers took over the direction of both movement and meaning, instructing us to kneel and kiss the *guias,* receive a crucifix, hear the Mass. When this was over, no charismatic magnetism of the shrine itself kept the pilgrims a moment beyond the final "amen." From five directions they arrived, and in many more they quickly dispersed.

Making Known in the Breaking of the Bread: Epistemology and Methodology after the Fact

Looking back over my story, questions remain. When, if ever, did I stop "dancing on the periphery of experience" and take steps as a pilgrim (Kohn 1994, 20)? There is no one moment. Do the generalizations I make, the descriptions I ascribe to "the women," and the interpretations and sentiments I end the day's journal entry with render me guilty of imposition, appropriation, or merely orchestration of voice? Or is the movement from "I" to "we" symbolic of the overlap between methodology and epistemology—between doing and making known—central to the participant-observation that is at the core of all ethnography? In my tacking between silence and voice, my own and that of others, have I demonstrated the crux of the paradoxical nature of anthropological methods? Or have I merely confused and conflated the essential dialectic of experience and interpretation? And what of the politics of (self-)representation and revelation? My experience of this pilgrimage brings these issues of disclosure and closure at all stages of ethnography into sharp relief.

So I told a story. Using the vehicle of narrative, I have moved my own fieldwork experiences to center stage in the presentation of *an* ethnography of pilgrimage. Arguably, such reflexivity is a productive means of transforming social experience in the field into anthropological knowledge (Hervik 1994, 79). I emphasize thick ethnographic descriptions grounded in lived experiences, which are then transformed into an interpretive story. The narrative structure perhaps best holds together the contestations, improvisations, changes, contradictions, ambiguities, revelations, doubts, and vulnerabilities that characterize my own experiences as well as those of the other pilgrims (Ellis and Flaherty 1992, 4–5).

The women and I: we become enmeshed in these stories. The tales we tell of the days on the road are connective tissue, defining the sinews of experience, shaping the muscles of memory. These accounts mobilize the relationship between the individual and the pilgrimage landscape and weave the two together inseparably. Although we may begin to understand pilgrimage through individual stories, these can only lead us to and from the collective journey. Narrative reveals that pilgrimage is not lived linearly nor alone. It is lived through the subjects' voices and eyes, and these instruments are "always reflexive, nonlinear, subjective, filled with flashbacks, after-images, dream sequences, faces merging into one another, masks dropping and new masks being put on" (Ellis and Flaherty 1992, 7). The journeying subjects, in motion and in context, shape the destination of a pilgrimage as a meaningful site of experience and knowledge.

But this site and its meanings have many levels. We become netted in the stories—layer upon layer of revelations of identities, of transmission of experience and its transformation into anthropological knowledge. Jesus walks and reveals his identity to his traveling disciples through the breaking of bread; the ethnographer reveals and hides her identity to her pilgrim subjects through participation, walking lots and talking some. These revelations are cryptic, and these identities encoded in action. The ethnographer then breaks open her experience and offers it in leveled pieces to an academic audience through stories that incarnate events, flesh out memory, and embody hermeneutics.

Postscript

Six years later, and I have not walked in pilgrimage to Chimayo again, despite annual invitations from Ann, Aunt Grace, and many others. I have been to New Mexico many times since 1997 to continue the research on Kateri Tekakwitha, as I had planned. I have also returned to the *santuario* twice, both times by car, as a kind of well-informed tourist traveling with a local friend. Chimayo is in fact a beautiful shrine and grounds, and in these later visits, I have found solace at the quiet altar and hope in the jars of healing sand I keep in my home. My own illness has progressed, and walking any real distance has become more difficult. My sister *guadalupanas* age as well, yet they continue to walk to Chimayo every year and inspire me still.

I was in Albuquerque in April 2002 and accompanied Ann and Aunt Grace to a preparation meeting for that year's pilgrimage. The same warm smiles were as welcoming as if I had never left. Guilt, sadness, anger, and bittersweetness all washed over me. Yet I smiled to myself at my thought that, like before, I found the litany too long, boring, and out of tune. But still, I waited in line with all the others to have my turn to kneel at the foot of the *guia*—the same cross I had helped carry en route to Chimayo in 1997—and spend a few moments in prayer. I rose in pain and tears, remembering the rain and the mud and the same movement years ago. My memory has dried now, the experience is a precious fossil of a time long past of motion and grace.

Notes

1. Each group still has a *rector* or *rectora* who leads the pilgrims and makes decisions regarding organization, logistics, and other pragmatic matters. In addition, each group has a spiritual director who leads prayers and is generally responsible for the spiritual well-being of the group. The positions are voluntary and change from year to year.

2. In the Pilgrimage for Vocations, male pilgrims are known as *peregrinos,* the Spanish word for "pilgrim." Female pilgrims are called *guadalupanas,* named after the lay Catholic women's devotional groups that are often dedicated to Our Lady of Guadalupe, the dark-complexioned apparition of the Virgin Mary who appeared to a Mexican peasant in the sixteenth century. See note 9 (below) for further discussion of Our Lady of Guadalupe. While many of the women I walked with shared with me their devotion to Our Lady of Guadalupe, the name *guadalupana* for the purposes of this pilgrimage means simply, as Ann says, "women pilgrims" and is used to emphasize the focus on the laity in this event rather than on devotion to any particular saint.

3. The United Church of Canada was formed by the merger of Methodist, Presbyterian, and Congregational Churches in 1925. The United Church is known for its liberal views and has, since its inception, been linked to issues of social gospel (McManners 1992, 413–14).

4. In describing myself and inscribing other women, I found that much of the Turnerian discourse leapt to mind. Turner's theory has been criticized for its structuralist determinism and its concomitant lack of space for contestation and diversity. For example, Eade and Sallnow argue that the determinism of the Turnerian model limits its usefulness in that it imposes a spurious homogeneity on an essentially heterogeneous phenomenon (1991, 2–4). While I am largely in agreement with the criticisms offered by Eade and Sallnow, among others, nevertheless, I believe that the vocabulary that Turner offers does indeed describe some elements of pilgrimage. The stripping of identity in the form of jewelry and wedding rings, the sameness apparent in the coming together en masse of the blue T-shirt-clad pilgrims at Chimayo, the disjunction of time and space while on pilgrimage, and the intense community instantly formed en route all lend themselves to expression in a Turnerian dialect.

5. A rosary is a string of beads used to keep count in saying prayers. A chaplet is a smaller version of a rosary. The chaplets that we were given at the beginning of the pilgrimage and that we gave to people along the way included a small medal of Our Lady of Guadalupe. The prayers to be said with each bead express devotion to her.

6. The *Angelus* is a prayer that recalls the Annunciation and is meant to be said three times a day. Its text is based on Luke 1:26–38, in which the angel Gabriel announces the birth of Jesus to Mary. The five groups of pilgrims all stopped en route and said this prayer at the appointed times. As we knelt for prayer, our spiritual director advised us to imagine all the pilgrims from all the directions praying together. The prayer is as follows:

Spiritual Director (SD): The angel spoke God's message to Mary
Pilgrims (P): and she conceived of the Holy Spirit

> Hail, Mary, full of grace. The Lord is with thee. Blessed art thou amongst women, and blessed is the fruit of your womb, Jesus. Holy Mary, Mother of God, pray for us sinners, now and at the hour of our death. Amen.

SD: I am the lowly servant of the Lord
P: Let it be done to me according to your word

> Hail, Mary . . .

SD: And the word became flesh
P: And lived among us

> Hail, Mary . . .

SD: Pray for us holy Mother of God
P: That we may become worthy of the promises of Christ
All: Let us pray.

> Lord, fill our hearts with your grace; once, through the message of an angel you revealed to us the incarnation of your Son; now, through his suffering and death, lead us to the glory of His resurrection. We ask this through Christ our Lord. Amen.

7. This is part of the chorus of "Four Strong Winds" (Ian Tyson/Warner Brothers Music):

> Four strong winds that blow lonely, Seven seas that run high,
> All these things that don't change, Come what may.

8. This is the text of "Footprints in the Sand" (anonymous):

> One night a man had a dream. He dreamed he was walking along the beach with the Lord.
>
> Scenes from his life flashed across the sky and he noticed two sets of footprints in the sand, one belonging to him and the other to the Lord.
>
> When the last scene of his life had flashed before him, he recalled that at the lowest and saddest times of his life, there was only one set of footprints.
>
> Dismayed, he asked, "Lord, you said that once I decided to follow you, you'd walk with me all the way. Why at the troublesome times of my life, the times that I've needed you most, would you leave me?"
>
> The Lord replied, "My precious child. I love you and I would never leave you. During your times of trial and suffering when you saw only one set of footprints, that was when I carried you."

9. The Virgin of Guadalupe is believed to have appeared to an Indian peasant in 1531 on a site previously consecrated to an Aztec goddess (McManners 1992, 420). She is depicted as having a swarthy complexion and black hair. Devotion to Our Lady of Guadalupe is the most popular form of veneration of Mary in New Mexico. See Wolf (1958) and Taylor (1987) for the history of Our Lady of Guadalupe in Mexico; and Rodriguez (1994) for current ethnographic research on Our Lady of Guadalupe as a symbol of Indian and Hispanic Catholicism and the devotion to her by women in the American Southwest.

10. We sang this song after each meal to all those who had prepared and served us

food. We asked them to kneel, stretched out our hands, and sang the following two times:

> May the blessing of God be upon you.
> The blessing of the Father and the Son
> And may the spirit of love, the spirit of peace,
> Be with you all your days

Afterward, we asked them for their blessing and went down on our knees with heads bowed to receive it. Some sang the same song back to us; others prayed silently or, at the pueblos, in the native tongue; some touched our shoulders or handed us prayers and petitions written on scraps of paper collected from their community. Also, our *encuentros* (planned meetings at the side of the road where members from the communities along the way provided us with a short rest and a snack) ended with a mutual blessing and distribution of rosaries and chaplets to our hosts.

11. The T-shirts are a significant part of the pilgrimage. Each year they are a different color and design and are emblazoned with the "theme" (a biblical passage) and date of the pilgrimage. Comments about the style and designs of the shirts and reminiscences about past pilgrimages accompany the wearing of the previous years' shirts. Comments such as "Oh, that was a nice shirt that year. Remember how cold it was when we walked from the north?" weave material and memory. Although the current year's shirt is not to be worn until the last day and the arrival at Chimayo (except for any prewalk blessings, as I discovered a week ago!), it seems to be expected that previous years' T-shirts become this year's pilgrimage wear.

12. See Behar and Gordon 1995 on issues of voice and its submergence and universalization; Clifford and Marcus 1986; and Clifford 1988.

References Cited

Abu-Lughod, Lila. 1991. "Writing against Culture." In *Recapturing Anthropology: Working in the Present*. Ed. Richard G. Fox. 137–62. Santa Fe: School of American Research Press.

Behar, Ruth. 1993. *Translated Woman: Crossing the Border with Esperanza's Story*. Boston: Beacon.

Behar, Ruth, and Deborah A. Gordon. 1995. *Women Writing Culture*. Berkeley: University of California Press.

Clifford, James. 1988. *The Predicament of Culture: Twentieth-Century Ethnography, Literature, and Art*. Cambridge, Mass.: Harvard University Press.

Clifford, James, and George E. Marcus, eds. 1986. *Writing Culture: The Poetics and Politics of Ethnography*. Berkeley: University of California Press.

Dubisch, Jill. 1995. *In a Different Place: Pilgrimage, Gender, and Politics at a Greek Island Shrine*. Princeton, N.J.: Princeton University Press.

Eade, John, and Michael J. Sallnow. 1991. Introduction to *Contesting the Sacred: The Anthropology of Christian Pilgrimage*. Ed. John Eade and Michael Sallnow. 1–29. London: Routledge.

Ellis, Carolyn, and Michael G. Flaherty, eds. 1992. *Investigating Subjectivity: Research on Lived Experience*. London: Sage.

Graburn, Nelson H. H. 1977. "Tourism: The Sacred Journey." In *Hosts and Guests: The Anthropology of Tourism.* Ed. Valene L. Smith. 17–31. Philadelphia: University of Pennsylvania Press.

Hervik, Peter. 1994. "Shared Reasoning in the Field: Reflexivity beyond the Author." In *Social Experience and Anthropological Knowledge.* Ed. Kirsten Hastrup and Peter Hervik. 78–100. London: Routledge.

Kohn, Tamara. 1994. "Incomers and Fieldworkers: A Comparative Study of Social Experience." In *Social Experience and Anthropological Knowledge.* Ed. Kirsten Hastrup and Peter Hervik. 12–26. London: Routledge.

Kraker, Daniel. 1997. "Soul Attractions: 10 Sites for Modern Seekers." *Utne Reader,* July–August, 76–77.

McManners, John, ed. 1992. *The Oxford Illustrated History of Christianity.* New York: Oxford University Press.

Rodriguez, Jeanette. 1994. *Our Lady of Guadalupe: Faith and Empowerment among Mexican-American Women.* Austin: University of Texas Press.

Taylor, William B. 1987. "The Virgin of Guadalupe in New Spain: An Inquiry into the Social History of Devotion." *American Ethnologist* 14:9–33.

Turner, Victor, and Edith L. B. Turner. 1978. *Image and Pilgrimage in Christian Culture: Anthropological Perspectives.* New York: Columbia University Press.

Wolf, Eric R. 1958. "The Virgin of Guadalupe: A Mexican National Symbol." *Journal of American Folklore,* no. 71:34–39.

3   Pilgrimage to "England's Nazareth":
       Landscapes of Myth and Memory
       at Walsingham

SIMON COLEMAN

Over the past century, the rural English landscape has become a wide-spread national symbol of an apparently unchanging and ancient heritage. Hastrup and Olwig are surely correct to assert that the only place such land-scape actually remains untouched by trusts, tourists, and tea shops is on canvas (Hastrup and Olwig 1997, 8), but it still embodies a resonant countryside aesthetic (Harrison 1991) produced for, and to some extent by, the romantic gaze of urbanites in search of renewal and inspiration (Urry 1995, 213; Okely 1997, 194; see also Darby, 2000). Furthermore, the very notion of Englishness is sometimes associated with a vision that is definitively rural and painterly. An example is Constable Country, a heritage representation (marketing a part of rural England through the work of the painter) that has recently been analyzed by Judith Okely (1997). In many such representations, landscape is much more than nature improved and depicted by humankind: it is also a way of equating the rural with the historical. To engage with Constable Country is to invoke an ideal of a past that can be imagined to take material and spatial form in a particular part of the countryside.

In studying these issues, anthropology can of course do more than merely deconstruct ideologies of rural landscape that depict it as unchanging heritage. Anthropology can also challenge the notion, derived from art history and some elements of geography, of seeing landscape as a fixed cultural image and resource (see Hirsch 1995, 2). Ethnographic approaches can show how static ways of depicting and analyzing surroundings that invoke the idea of landscape being viewed, consumed, and objectified from a fixed perspective are unable to deal with processual, subject-centered ways of constituting place through movement and interpretation (see Gell 1995). Landscapes are lived as well as represented (although of course there is an interplay between the two), and multiple paths and perspectives are available to the traveler as well as the viewer.

My essay invokes these themes by examining the dynamic construction and reconstitution of a particular part of rural England, and moreover, one located geographically close to Okely's Constable Country. The ancient and tiny village of Walsingham is situated in north Norfolk, an area of the eastern portion of England that remains relatively remote from much of the rest of the country, surrounded by narrow country lanes that have so far proved resistant to the building of freeways. Despite the presence of intensive agriculture in the region, Walsingham and its surroundings are picturesque in a way that mostly conforms, often highly self-consciously, to stereotypes of English rurality, and this is a quality that is sometimes exploited in television and feature films. A very gently rolling landscape leads to the sea, some five miles away, and a small river meanders through surrounding fields.

Even the casual visitor, however, soon comes to realize that this is no ordinary village. Statues of the Virgin Mary adorn shop windows and front rooms of houses in the High Street; the roads in and around the village are frequently clogged by slow-moving processions of people chanting the Ave Maria; a number of signs and posters inform the visitor that they have arrived at "England's Nazareth," a name intriguingly juxtaposing the national and the biblical. These are indications that Walsingham is not merely a village emblematic of the English rural past; it is also the foremost site of Christian pilgrimage in the country, attracting perhaps a quarter of a million people (both tourists and pilgrims) to its sights. The community of "locals"—from agricultural workers to shrine officials—is constantly augmented, especially in the months of spring and summer, by communities of faith: groups of Anglican and Roman Catholic pilgrims from parishes round the country, who often return annually in groups during the pilgrimage season from late spring to early autumn.

I want to show that such pilgrimage does not merely involve an intensified form of prayer; it also involves for the pilgrim (and even for the tourist) complex and varying forms of engagement with the physical environment provided by the village and its landscape: from the fields to the shrines, the narrow lanes to the pubs. In his analysis of Jerusalem as a contested pilgrimage site, Bowman (1991) also refers to the relationship between pilgrim and place, noting that the holy city is a location where pilgrims who have developed or inherited certain images of the city can embody those images and engage with them as aspects of the material world. The imaginary becomes reified in the reconstruction of holy sites by pilgrimage groups and individuals, and sacred places "serve primarily as *loci* where the pilgrims are better able to body forth the subjects of their meditations and their imaginations" (99; see also Coleman and Elsner 1995).

Walsingham is a complex site in which the imagination is given material form in multiple ways. Key to such imaginings, I argue, is not merely the fixed gaze of the viewer, however, but also forms of movement and performance that reconstitute the place in the very process of performing pilgrimage. Such movement recapitulates to a greater or lesser extent the complex theological, historical, and mythical narratives offered by the site and its officiants—narratives that, as we shall see, evoke biblical myth through a view of English history and landscape—and it does so in ways that can involve embodied experience as much as cognitive reflection. Frequently, official narratives can be subverted by pilgrims as they engage creatively with the landscape and buildings of the village and its surroundings, yet in such subversion pilgrims may describe themselves as getting close to the "true meaning" of the original pilgrimage and the place.

A common thread that runs through many experiences of profound engagement in the site involves the notion that performing pilgrimage provides a way to blend the autobiographical and the canonical. In moving through the sacred and historically charged landscape of Walsingham, pilgrims often see themselves as bringing together and reconciling elements that have previously been difficult to integrate: personal history, shrine history, national identity, and biblical truth can combine in powerful ways. Part of my argument will be that pilgrimage in this context provides the opportunity for people to engage with resonant symbols of faith and identity by breathing life into personal and institutional history simultaneously, reframing both in mutually constitutive ways. However, the varieties of modes of engagement that are evident reveal some profound and significant differences in the ways pilgrims and even shrine officials relate to such symbols of faith and belonging and indeed relate to very different practices of appropriating tradition, history, and myth.

Materializing the Medieval: Replication, Mimesis, and Metonymy

Before I discuss the ways in which Walsingham is constituted through contemporary pilgrimage practices, I need to say something of the site's origins and recent revival. In the process of doing so, I hope to indicate some of the ways in which multivalent mythical, theological, and historical narratives are created out of the landscape and material culture of the place. In fact, very little is known of the foundation of Walsingham as a place of pilgrimage. According to an anonymous fifteenth-century ballad, however, the site goes back some nine hundred years to pre-Norman times. The Virgin Mary is said to have appeared in a vision to a local aristocratic lady called Richeldis, who was urged to build a Holy House in Walsingham, modeled on the exact dimensions of Christ's childhood home in Nazareth. According to this story, biblical narrative and sacred space were appropriated in tangible terms at the very beginning of the site's emergence, giving them geographical and historical resonances in a Norfolk village that came to be known as "England's Nazareth." The story, at least as interpreted from a contemporary viewpoint, also makes a point about nationality: origins are sought in the Anglo-Saxon period, not the era of foreign, Norman rule. Furthermore, the date appears to grant to England the first-ever Marian shrine in Europe. Pilgrims still associate Richeldis's vision with the establishment of England as "Our Lady's Dowry," a land specially favored by the Virgin.

Walsingham flourished as a pilgrimage site in the Middle Ages, being rivaled in the British Isles only by Canterbury. Within the Holy House was placed a statue of the Virgin and Child, while adjacent or near to it there were established some of the usual appurtenances of a successful pilgrimage destination: an Augustinian priory in the center of the village, a Franciscan friary, and numerous apparently extortionately expensive inns. Its importance also made it vulnerable to the depredations of Henry VIII, however, and it was almost completely destroyed in the sixteenth century.

In the post-Reformation period, the village as a site of pilgrimage lay largely dormant for many centuries. However, the nineteenth century in England saw Catholic emancipation, the emergence of the Anglo-Catholic Oxford Movement, and forms of antiquarianism that came to value the past in contrast to an industrializing present. All of these factors came into play in the modern revival of Walsingham as a pilgrimage center. Of the medieval site, what remained were mostly some impressive ruins (with the appearance of "follies," yet authenticated by genuine age), including the remains of the east window of the Augustinian priory and a small, fourteenth-century building called the Slipper Chapel, situated a mile and one-half from the village. The chapel had provided the last stop for medieval pilgrims before they arrived at the shrine.

In 1896 a wealthy benefactress, Charlotte Boyd, became interested in the site. According to Jennings (1992, 7), Boyd had visited Glastonbury Abbey earlier in life, "and moved by the desolation, she 'saw' her life's work before her—the restoration of monastic buildings . . . to their full 'Anglican' use."

Boyd could not persuade the owners of the priory remains to sell, but she did purchase the chapel and paid for the restoration of its medieval glory (previously, it had been used as a cowshed by a local farmer). Soon afterwards, she converted to Roman Catholicism.

At the same time, Father Wrigglesworth, the priest at the Roman Catholic church in the nearby market town of King's Lynn (itself a stopping post for medieval pilgrims to Walsingham) decided to restore some of the medieval pilgrimage. As with Boyd, his historical and spiritual interests had clear affinities (as an ardent amateur photographer, he had prepared slides illustrating the history, shrines, and teaching of the Roman catacombs). In Wrigglesworth's new church, he had a facsimile of the Holy House of Nazareth built. This was modeled on a shrine at Loreto, reputed to contain the actual Holy House of Nazareth, miraculously transported to Italy by angels. Wrigglesworth also began a series of small-scale pilgrimages in a minirevival of medieval practice.

Such activities aroused notice in select religious circles. A certain Reverend Oswald H. Blair, writing in 1904, appears to be beside himself with excitement in describing the restoration of the chapel (quoted in Walsh 1904, 330): "Little Walsingham! The heart throbs when the dream of a lifetime is realized and we reach what was once the Lourdes, the Loreto of England." Blair's rhetoric here echoes that of other twentieth-century Roman Catholic and Anglican writers in consciously placing Walsingham among the big European pilgrimage sites, medieval and postmedieval. However, Charlotte Boyd died in 1906, and Roman Catholic involvement in Walsingham itself remained muted until 1934, when a Mass was said at the Slipper Chapel, which was also restored for worship. An inaugural pilgrimage was led to the chapel, with possibly as many as nineteen thousand people attending (Gillett 1946, 75). Since then, the Roman Catholic shrine has continued to expand, a Chapel of the Holy Ghost being consecrated in 1938 and a large, barnlike Chapel of Reconciliation in 1982. Crosses were carried from all parts of the country and added to the shrine, forming the Stations of the Cross, in 1948.

The Roman Catholics may have been the first to restore activity at Walsingham, but they were soon caught up and surpassed by High Anglicans, led by the charismatic and eccentric, Tractarian-influenced local priest, Hope Patten. Possibly even more than Boyd or Wrigglesworth, Patten was fascinated by the Middle Ages and the possibility of their "restoration" in the present. In 1921 he had been appointed vicar of Walsingham, at that time a poorly paid spiritual outpost. He had a statue of Our Lady of Walsingham carved from figures depicted on a medieval seal from the Augustinian priory and organized pilgrimages to the village for small groups, while also maintaining frosty relations with a local bishop who was rather worried by the dizzying altitude of

Patten's High Anglicanism. In 1931 Patten was able to remove pilgrimage activities from the bishop's jurisdiction by relocating the focus of pilgrimage to land in the village bought privately by a benefactor. Here, he had his own replica of the Holy House built. The shrine was opened October 15, 1931, and incorporated the statue of Our Lady of Walsingham. Extensions were added in later years, as more and more pilgrims came to the site.

We see how the revival of the site as a place of pilgrimage transformed it spatially and liturgically: a single shrine and tradition were split into two parts, one might almost say moieties, each echoing but also transforming the other, both claiming faithfully to represent not only the true tradition of the church universal but also that of medieval pilgrimage to the site. Although a spirit of ecumenism now prevails, at least officially, in the contemporary shrines, in the early days of restoration some fifty or sixty years ago these evocations of biblical myth and medieval history were carried out in a spirit of competition and mutual avoidance. The High Anglican Patten seems at times to have taken a certain mischievous delight in the competition between the two shrines and even took the opportunity to give it a twist, invoking biblical geography. In his regular newsletter to friends of the shrine, *Our Lady's Mirror,* he writes in the summer of 1935: "The Romans, too, have been active and their pilgrimages to the Slipper Chapel are very frequent. . . . One supposes the conditions are not unlike those in the Holy Land, where the Orthodox and the Latins, the Armenians and other Easterns, all claim the Holy Sites and live together, treading on each other's toes more or less frequently!" (Patten 1935, 1).

A year later, Patten (1936, 4) talks of how Roman Catholics still mistake the Anglican shrine for the Slipper Chapel and recounts a story of how three devout ladies lit candles at his shrine, before discovering to their presumed horror that they had performed their devotions in the wrong building. On discovering their mistake, they apparently wrapped up their candles in a sheet of paper and took them to the Slipper Chapel, determined not to worship in the shrine of the enemy. A similar sense of humor seems to pervade the claim, recounted to me by a Roman Catholic priest who has lived in Walsingham for many years, that in the old days the Slipper Chapel toilets were deliberately designed to resemble Patten's Anglican shrine.

The stakes of such competition were high, not least because both sides claimed that their restorations of the shrine had much more than parochial significance. Both were constructing a pilgrimage tradition that was consciously national in its appeal. Patten, for instance, encouraged cells devoted to Walsingham to be set up around the country and abroad, while the Roman Catholic shrine came to boast Stations of the Cross incorporating crosses taken to the site from all parts of England.

Competition in the appropriation of medievalism was also evident. Modes of reinvoking the Middle Ages that were used can be divided into three basic forms: liturgical mimesis; architectural replication; and metonymic appropriation. By "liturgical mimesis," I refer to the ways in which both Anglo-Catholics and Roman Catholics employed liturgical forms that allowed them to echo medieval practice, ranging from the celebration of Mass to the use of processions, that appeared to provide the opportunity "literally" to walk in the footsteps of earlier pilgrims. Patten in particular was a past master at this and evoked antique practices by the use of such props as gorgeous purple robes and quasi-medieval heraldry.

Such mimesis was clearly reinforced, as noted, by the construction or restoration of ancient shrines: Wrigglesworth's Holy House in King's Lynn and Patten's version in Walsingham itself were models of the supposed original (while the Slipper Chapel could claim to be the real thing). Both of these replications of the Holy House translated biblical space to Norfolk at the same time as referring to the site's medieval past.[1]

Despite the power of replication, however, Anglicans led by Patten found another way in which to seek connections with the Middle Ages: they claimed to have found the site of Richeldis's original Holy House in the course, ironically, of constructing its replica. When the foundations of the new Holy House were being excavated in the 1930s, a well was discovered. Having consulted the somewhat ambiguous archaeological evidence available at the time, Patten decided that this was the holy well of the original site. The well was reconstructed in a place adjacent to Patten's reproduction of the Holy House, implying that the house occupied the original space of Richeldis's building. His action was not merely an appropriation of a link to the past on an alleged historical level, it was also significant in terms of the spatial and liturgical dynamics of the village: while the Slipper Chapel and Roman Catholic Holy House were peripheral to Walsingham, the well was much closer to the present village itself, within sight indeed of the Augustinian priory. Patten also took the discovery as a sign, a vindication of his own standpoint in opposition not only to Roman Catholics but to the many skeptics located in the Church of England. There is an extraordinary passage in an elegy written by Sir William Milner on Patten's death in 1958 where Milner writes of what supposedly happened the night before the installation of the image in the restored Holy House in 1931: "A strange thing happened the night before, when Fr. Patten was in the new building, and was conscious of the presence of several figures, in the dress of the Augustinian Canons, visiting the various altars, consulting a paper which one of them held in his hands, and then nodding their heads at evident pleasure at each altar, newly consecrated that day" (Milner 1958, 20).

Such visions were not uncommon with Patten. The unpublished memoir of one of his fellow workers (Oldroyd n.d., 9) notes that he occasionally went into "trances" during which "he would re-enact historical scenes especially bloody martyrdoms as though he were actually taking part in them." Oldroyd also remarks, perhaps a little sardonically, "I felt he must have read a lot of historical novels at some time." Certainly, Patten seems to have combined an almost shamanic relationship with the past with a desire to validate his imagination in material ways. What is significant about this is not merely the appropriation of the past in a building, but the way in which the very process of restoration provided its own legitimacy on spiritual as well as archaeological grounds. Patten was not only claiming to have literally encompassed a site of medieval miracles, he also located his restoration in the quasi-mythical tradition of the original foundation of the shrine. Richeldis had a dream or vision of the Virgin Mary, while Patten himself had a vision of those who guarded the medieval shrine and clearly approved of the historical accuracy of his reconstruction.

As if the reconstruction of the Holy House and the discovery of the well were not enough, Patten provided yet another means of materially blurring the boundaries between imaginative revelation and metonymic connection with the past. Into the very walls of the Holy House, he built a collection of what is now more than 170 stones taken from the monasteries dissolved by Henry VIII. The fabric of English medieval Catholicism was literally reconstructed within the walls of Patten's shrine. In bringing the stones together, the shrine both celebrated multiple places destroyed by the ravages of the past and bolstered the spiritual authenticity of a single place, Walsingham, as the sacred center in which such places could be unified in the present.

Performing the Past in the Present

In the present, pilgrimage has come to dominate the center of the village. Where once resident agricultural workers could find butcher's, baker's, and saddler's shops in the High Street, they now encounter what some locals describe as "tea and tat shoppes," dispensing liquid refreshment or religious souvenirs and sometimes both. Only by walking away from the middle of the village to areas rarely visited by tourists or pilgrims can one find council houses displaying no trace of archaizing influences. The effectiveness of this self-conscious and distinctly modern way of creating a medieval feel is well expressed by the following description of the place by a journalist in a local newspaper, written in 1937 but still relevant today (*Eastern Daily News* 1937): "Part of yesterday I spent in the Middle Ages for I passed through Walsingham, pausing to visit the Shrine of Our Lady. Walsingham itself is truly Mediaeval in atmosphere."

The image of the medieval that can be re-created at Walsingham has been attractive to Anglo-Catholic and Roman Catholic revivalists in a number of ways over the past century, quite apart from the association of Mary with England. The medieval period is romantically remote from the present and yet is taken to have a contemporary message: the need for religious awakening to Catholicism combined with the desire to think back to a spiritual Golden Age when the Church was unified, unriven by the present sectarian conflict. The fact that so little is actually known about medieval Walsingham provides a historical and quasi-mythical blank space in which multiple readings of the past can be inscribed. Because nothing of note has happened regarding pilgrimage between the medieval period and the present, the juxtaposition of the two remains uncluttered by intervening historical events.

In physical terms, the landscape surrounding the village is often seen by visitors and pious residents as adding to the medieval feel, providing a generalized sense of a rural and bucolic England, untouched by the modern age, that complements the mythological medievalizing of twentieth-century revival. Claude Fisher, a journalist and Roman Catholic who came to live in Walsingham for many decades and joined its considerable band of local historians, described a scene from the pilgrimage in the following terms (1979, 68): "A half-score of early 1930s Ayrshire cows seen from the Fakenham Road with their horns (then fashionable), grazing round the sunlit glories of the Slipper Chapel, with the little river Stiffkey meandering below, and acres of golden corn beyond the chapel, created a scene worthy of the brush of a Constable and was a picture no townsman was ever likely to forget." Besides evoking the painterly qualities of Constable Country, Fisher notes here a key element of pilgrimage of the 1930s and indeed of the present: the fact that so many who visit the place see it through urban eyes. Rurality for such visitors not only indicates that they are in a place very different from the everyday (appropriate to the liminal space and time of pilgrimage), it also implies the ability to reach into a past world that can speak to the present.

Contemporary pilgrimage to Walsingham involves more than merely viewing the scenery, however. The village provides a complex set of stages for the performance of pilgrimage. The Anglican and Roman Catholic shrines offer parallel ways in which to replay the story of Walsingham and Nazareth, but, increasingly, the boundaries between Anglican and Roman Catholic shrines have been blurred, and some joint pilgrimage activities take place. Many factors have contributed to such changes. Patten died in the late 1950s and was succeeded by administrators who entertained some skepticism towards Patten's archaeological claims and a greater openness to Roman Catholicism; Vatican II has liberalized both Roman Catholic and Anglo-Catholic traditions; Roman Catholicism has become an increasingly mainstream part of British spirituality since the Second World War, as has the Anglican shrine itself; many more people come to Walsingham than have done so in the past, and for some, the boundaries between tourism and pilgrimage have become attenuated if not impossible to detect.

If the past is appropriated at Walsingham today as much as it ever was, the processes of appropriation have shifted in some very significant ways. Certainly, debates still rage over the historical authenticity of parts of the shrines, in particular the Holy House and well that Patten built, but these debates have tended to go underground—pronounced in pubs or by people buttonholing visitors in the street—rather than constituting official discourse.

For some visitors, the place still provides the means by which to insert themselves into collective and well-defined identities—Roman Catholic or Anglo-Catholic. Many of these visitors are part of annual parish visits and are led by their local priest, who is seen as a guide and interpreter of the sites. Such pilgrims tend to focus on one or the other of the shrines, although visits to "the opposition's" shrine may occur in free time. Particularly for committed High Anglicans who come in parish visits, pilgrimage provides a rare occasion to meet large groups of Christians of a like mind.[2]

Such parish pilgrims, as I call them, display characteristic ways of appropriating the traditions of Walsingham. Pilgrimage provides a means of replicating the piety of the medieval age and in particular provides a reminder that exactly the same practices have been going on for centuries. Walsingham incarnates the past, as a museum case ideally prevents decay or transformation. Stability and continuity are reflected in pilgrimages through the village and the chosen shrine. The same activities are carried out often by the same people at the same time each year, so that within the great tradition of the medieval pilgrimage a parish can create a little tradition of its own continuous and regular, if temporary, appropriation of Walsingham: such self-referential mimesis becomes a kind of ritual within a ritual. Here, for instance, is an Anglo-Catholic pilgrim describing her parish's pilgrimage, which has been ongoing for some forty years. "We have Benediction; yesterday we had requiem mass, and the choir sang the Russian [hymn]—we always have that, that's beautiful. This morning we've had sprinkling, and during the mass we had healing. . . . After that we always have the sprinkling, and tonight it's the candlelit procession." Such a catalog of activities is the result of coordination between shrine officials and parish pilgrims and provides minor variations on core themes and activities within a standardized pilgrimage repertoire. Many such pilgrims value the opportunity to worship in a context that places their own practices on a wider and more historically resonant stage. Thus, another Anglo-Catholic describes the value of Walsingham as a place: "There's a sort of feel of a place, which is not because people are particularly sensitive but because after a while you realize that what you do back in [a town in the north of England] in, say, a church that was built at the end of the last century has been going on in some of these churches for seven or eight centuries, and it makes you feel that you are part of something which is more than just [the town], just local, just the way *we* do it, just the way people have been doing it in my lifetime."[3] The practices of such pilgrims perhaps come closest to a straight embodiment of themes of replication, mimesis, and metonymy in their appropriation of the past—themes that link them to the early twentieth-century revivalists. The story of Richeldis is to be taken as literally as possible, and Patten's well is often seen as providing a tangible link with a sanctified past.

Other pilgrims, however, reflect some significant transformations that have occurred in relation to Walsingham over recent decades, including the liberalization of Catholicism and the massively increased influx of visitors who are less committed to the maintenance of theological and liturgical boundaries between faiths. In effect, Walsingham has become desectarianized and made more open as a site of religious "heritage" and spiritual as well as secular tourism. Such "heritage" pilgrims perhaps regard themselves as committed Christians, but a visit to Walsingham may be valued as an opportunity, rarely repeated, to engage in traditions that remain foreign to the rest of their lives. Anglicans choose to visit Roman Catholic services and vice versa; both may go to the two Orthodox churches that also happen to be in the village; even some relatively Low Church Anglicans admit to coming to the place—for what one called a kind of "religious holiday." Many such pilgrims confess to a profound ignorance of the historical details of the place or its traditions: all that matters is that it provides a forum for exploration—of the medieval past, of group dynamics among one's fellow travelers, of new liturgies, of novel forms of behavior—whether that means going to the pub or praying to the Virgin. As one Anglican pilgrim puts it, "I know almost nothing about it. I mean I know it's called England's Nazareth, and it's something to do with the Holy House, but I still don't think I could define what the Holy House is."[4] The official routes and narratives offered by the shrines may be deliberately avoided by these pilgrims, even if they are traveling with others. Interviewees have talked of going to the beach or wandering round the countryside as part of a personalized pilgrimage, or praying alone in the Holy House rather than going to a sprinkling. Sitting in the pubs may also be viewed explicitly as means of encouraging fellowship in a "Merrie England," "Chaucerian" way, rather than attending a Mass. Walsingham even has a following among the gay Catholic community, as its festivals are seen as opportunities to "camp it up" in a carnival atmosphere.

If tradition is being appropriated here, it is not a case of attempting to gain authenticity through a metonymic or simple mimetic link with the past; rather, tradition—embodied in a building, a landscape, a ritual, a procession—is a generalized and unspecific resource, a means of engaging with the unfamiliar and the liturgical "other." The carnivalesque space and time of pilgrimage provide the opportunities for creative, sometimes playful, sometimes ironic appropriations of the place and its narratives. Some pilgrims even welcome the sense they had of being ideologically alienated by shrines that do not, for instance, support the ordination of women or that devote so much attention to the Virgin, since they know that the borrowing of Walsingham's traditions for the weekend does not mean they have to take such traditions home with them.

Such visitors to the site tend to deny that a fixed set of truths—historical or symbolic—are embodied or incarnated at the shrines of Walsingham: rather, it can best be seen as a physical vehicle through which to construct forms of authentic experience. To quote one priest, commenting on the story of Richeldis: "Really, it's the tradition. And may or may not be true. . . . Even if it isn't true, it doesn't matter. . . . But it's as convenient a peg to hang anything on as anything else."

Of course, we saw how Patten engaged in an exercise of the historical imagination, but for him such historical reconstruction could be validated by metonymic links with the past as "revealed" by archaeology. The "heritage" pilgrims I am describing do not require such links to authenticate their experience. For them, the use of the imagination and the mixing of performance genres are the point of the exercise of engaging with the liturgies, landscape, and buildings of Walsingham. Let me quote at some length the words of one Roman Catholic pilgrim, talking of a visit to the village with a group of fellow theology students. She describes a performance of the Stations of the Cross put on by two of her party, who had previously been drama students:

> This particular weekend it had been snowing, and I think it had snowed the day before and there was ice and still a bit of snow around. . . . And [the people who were arranging the pilgrimage] organized these Stations of the Cross all around the streets and country lanes. . . . And . . . instead of having visual markers as you would do in the gardens, they acted out the scenes of the Stations without announcing them first. . . . I thought 'Oh, this is a bit different from hot, dusty Palestine. . . . It's going to be a bit funny walking around all these slushy, cold Norfolk, country lanes, pretending that we're dying of the heat in Jerusalem.' But what they actually did was cleverly use the conditions

we were actually in—the cold, the damp, and snow—to make the points, to incorporate them into the devotions. And there was one point . . . on the corner of the road. . . . The man who . . . was playing the part of Jesus—he was only wearing shirtsleeves . . . and he fell over in the mud, and just got covered. . . . And he got up and angrily said, 'Oh, I've had enough of this, I'm not going on with it. . . .' And everybody was just terribly awkward and thinking, 'Oh no, what's going to happen next?' And just as he was saying this, one of the students who was standing in the crowd of us . . . he just walked out of the group standing there, and took off his coat . . . and put it on him, and suddenly we all realized that was Simon of Cyrene taking the cross. . . . It was extraordinarily effective.[5]

The effectiveness of this performance seems to lie in its geographical and liturgical variations on standard enactments of the Stations. Convention is made to refer indexically to the unique group of pilgrims present—a group that may never gather again in the same way, unlike the parishes described earlier. The landscape of Walsingham along with the effects of the season are incorporated into the occasion: instead of seeing this semi-improvised liturgy as simply replicating a biblical event, the pilgrims choose to demonstrate how the meaning of such an event can be translated to English conditions. In this way, biblical myth is both "naturalized" in its new context and made to live through modified enactment. The performance of the Stations thus presents an ambiguous Janus face to convention: it takes place at one remove from the Anglican or Roman Catholic site geographically and liturgically, yet it is sufficiently close to be encompassed by the space and time of a pilgrimage to Walsingham. The village and its surrounding environment provide not merely a flexible stage for pilgrimage performances but also easy if vicarious access to a quasi-biblical but distinctly English landscape.

Many variations of such symbolically charged experiences are recounted by pilgrims. A common theme of these accounts is the ability of the landscape and spaces of Walsingham to provide a resonant three-dimensional frame within which experience appears to be amplified and given new significance. In the context of pilgrimage, of course, participants move through this frame and choose their degree of involvement in actions that take place within its bounds (and at times, as we have seen, they extend the conceptual space of Walsingham to include places far removed from the village). In the following description, a lapsed Roman Catholic describes a powerful moment in his own experience of pilgrimage when his perspective moved from one of observing from afar into active engagement. He talks of how members of his extended family who are devout Roman Catholics arrange a pilgrimage to Walsingham each year, in which as many members of the family are incorporated as possible. This man felt torn between attachment to his family and alienation from

Roman Catholicism and its history at Walsingham. He therefore deliberately arrived late one year and stood waiting for his family at a point halfway down the Holy Mile, the road between Walsingham and the Roman Catholic Slipper Chapel:

> And in the distance, I saw this pilgrimage in between autumn hedgerows. And my family doesn't dress up a lot, they're sort of a very dowdy lot, and they could have been from *any* era really. It looked absolutely wonderful, magnificent, and they were really processing, in a pilgrimage, along the lane in between the two hedgerows . . . and deeply moving actually, and I felt very happy . . . observing them. And they were my lot too, and I felt very comfortable with that, not being totally part of them, but being close to them. . . . Then I walked down across a field and joined halfway.[6]

The frame Walsingham provides here is one that provokes the imagination through its generic qualities. The countryside and the clothes worn by the family blur the boundaries between the past and the present, and the account presents a familiar social group in almost transcendent terms. The description ends, of course, with a gesture of reconciliation, as the observer chooses to become an active participant in the scene he has previously been regarding from a fixed and alienated position.

Transforming Landscapes

The contrast in modes of engagement between parish and heritage pilgrims that I have been describing here is not a simple binary opposition. Numerous mediating positions exist between the two. However, one way to think about it is in terms of Okely's (1997) discussion of the different modes of appropriating Constable Country by local residents of the village where she worked and lived. Okely notes how middle-class informants were contemptuous of the idea of owning mere reproductions of Constable's depictions of the local landscape and preferred to produce their own representations in paint. Working-class residents, however, chose reproductions of the countryside and had no aesthetic interest in the concept of an original work of art. Although I would not draw class boundaries quite as starkly as Okely, there is no doubt that parish pilgrims tend to be more working-class than the more playful heritage pilgrims, particularly among Anglicans. The important contrast here is between viewing a cultural resource as an unchanging symbol of continuity and seeing it as the launching point for liturgical and interpretative creativity. At Walsingham, both forms of engagement involve blending the self with canonical tradition. While one mode valorizes the exemplary and essentially replicable nature of sacralized history, the other interacts with tradition in a way that involves a more fluid, mutually transformative process.

My claims here have some resonances with Connerton's (1989) analysis of forms of recollection in commemorative ceremonies and bodily practices. Part of his discussion illustrates ways in which ceremonies can appear to deny temporal distance in invoking the past. He also notes how, as a story told becomes a cult enacted (43), ceremonies provide ways in which to form meaningful narrative sequences out of experience. I have tried to show how pilgrimage to Walsingham allows participants to locate experience in narratives that are performed as well as told but also permits variations in the degree to which commemoration need imply replication. The pilgrimage landscape of Walsingham is akin to a "theatre of memory," in Samuel's phrase (1994), and it is one where links to the past can be established as much by staged performance as by history or archaeology.

Notes

1. McDannell (1995), referring to the replication of Lourdes in Notre Dame, has noted how nineteenth-century Catholics accepted reproduction and facsimile as a part of their aesthetic lives. Halbwachs (1941) has also, famously, discussed the way sacred topography can be altered to suit contemporary concerns.

2. Nowadays, they not only have to run the theological gauntlet of evangelicals who brand them as idolaters but also liberals who oppose the High Anglican opposition to women priests.

3. Interview with the author, Walsingham, 1997.

4. Interview with the author, U.K. Midlands, 1993.

5. Recorded interview with the author, Walsingham, 1993.

6. Interview with the author, East Anglia, U.K., 1993.

References Cited

Bowman, Glenn. 1991. "Christian Ideology and the Image of a Holy Land: The Place of Jerusalem Pilgrimage in the Various Christianities." In *Contesting the Sacred: The Anthropology of Christian Pilgrimage.* Ed. John Eade and Michael Sallnow. 98–121. London: Routledge.

Coleman, Simon, and John Elsner. 1995. *Pilgrimage Past and Present in the World Religions.* Cambridge, Mass.: Harvard University Press.

Connerton, Paul. 1989. *How Societies Remember.* Cambridge: Cambridge University Press.

Darby, Wendy Joy. 2000. *Landscape and Identity: Geographies of Nation and Class in England.* Oxford: Berg.

Eastern Daily News. 1937. June 28.

Fisher, Claude. 1979. *Walsingham Lives On.* London: Catholic Truth Society.

Gell, Alfred. 1995. "The Language of the Forest: Landscape and Phonological Iconism in Umeda." In *The Anthropology of Landscape: Perspectives on Place and Space*. Ed. Eric Hirsch and Michael O'Hanlon. 232–54. Oxford: Clarendon.

Gillett, Henry M. 1946. *Walsingham: The History of a Famous Shrine*. London: Burns, Oats, and Washbourne.

Halbwachs, Maurice. 1941. *La Topographie Légendaire des Évangiles*. Paris: Presses Universitaires de France.

Harrison, Carolyn. 1991. *Countryside Recreation in a Changing Society*. London: TMS Partnership.

Hastrup, Kirsten, and Karen F. Olwig. 1997. Introduction to *Siting Culture: The Shifting Anthropological Object*. Ed. Kirsten Hastrup and Karen F. Olwig. 1–14. London: Routledge.

Hirsch, Eric. 1995. "Landscape: Between Place and Space." In *The Anthropology of Landscape: Perspectives on Place and Space*. Ed. Eric Hirsch and Michael O'Hanlon. 1–30. Oxford: Clarendon.

Jennings, D. 1992. "Walsingham and Its Contribution to English Marian Devotion Principally from 1897 to the Present-Day." Undergraduate diss., St. John's Seminary, Wonersh, U.K.

McDannell, Colleen. 1995. *Material Christianity: Religion and Popular Culture in America*. New Haven, Conn.: Yale University Press.

Milner, William. 1958. "Reminiscences." *Our Lady's Mirror,* Autumn, 18–22.

Okely, Judith. 1997. "Picturing and Placing Constable Country." In *Siting Culture: The Shifting Anthropological Object*. Ed. Kirsten Hastrup and Karen F. Olwig. 193–220. London: Routledge.

Oldroyd, L. n.d. "Recollections of Hope Patten." Unpublished notes in author's collection.

Patten, Hope. 1935. "Notes." *Our Lady's Mirror,* Summer, 20.

———. 1936. "Notes." *Our Lady's Mirror,* Summer, 4.

Samuel, Raphael. 1994. *Theatres of Memory: Past and Present in Contemporary Culture*. London: Verso.

Urry, John. 1995. *Consuming Places*. London: Routledge.

Walsh, William J., ed. 1904. "The Apparitions and Shrines of Heaven's Bright Queen." In *Legend, Poetry and History*. Vol. 1. New York: Carey-Stafford Company.

4　Santiago de Compostela in the Year 2000: From Religious Center to European City of Culture

SHARON R. ROSEMAN

On November 20, 1995, the Council of Ministers of the European Union decided that the Spanish city of Santiago de Compostela would be one of nine locations to share the honor of being named a "European City of Culture" in the year 2000.[1] To many Europeans, Santiago de Compostela was not a surprising choice, given that it is a prominent Christian pilgrimage site and has thus been a favored destination for travelers since the early Middle Ages. However, since its inception in 1984, the competition to be named a European City of Culture has been fierce, as cities vie with each other to receive the financial and other benefits that go along with the designation. Consequently, officials in Santiago de Compostela prepared an elaborately argued bid for bureaucrats of the European Union (EU) promoting the city's candidacy.[2] The bid outlined the reasons why Santiago would be an appropriate choice as one of the European "cities of culture," particularly during the year that would mark the beginning of a new millennium.

In this chapter, I examine the discourses about Santiago de Compostela, pilgrimage, culture, and Europe that are contained within this bid. My analysis of this document is interrelated with three bodies of social scientific research: a constructivist approach to the study of pilgrimage journeys and sites (e.g., Eade and Sallnow 1991a); a focus on the current expansion of "cultural" or "heritage" tourism that sometimes includes examples of the marketing of religious pilgrimage sites to a wide variety of potential visitors (see, e.g., Crain 1996); and reevaluations of the "culture concept" over the last fifteen years in anthropology and related disciplines.

This case study of the framing of the Santiago bid to be named a European cultural capital illustrates one instance of the crafting of a discourse about a pilgrimage site and thus generally supports the position of authors, such as Eade and Sallnow (1991b), who emphasize the processes whereby the characteristics, personal meanings, and ideological significance of pilgrimage journeys and destinations are continuously constructed (often in competing ways). My study also coincides with social scientists' evaluations of the recent elaboration of particular cities and regions as significant "heritage" or "cultural" touristic destinations (e.g., Chang et al. 1996). As part of my approach, however, I also briefly summarize past attempts to "sell" Santiago de Compostela in order to emphasize that the "construction" of Santiago de Compostela is not a new phenomenon and that there is a continuity underlying recent discursive transformations. One has to consider that particular pilgrimage sites only grew to prominence during previous historical periods because of the manner in which religious concepts of the sacred were employed as a way of highlighting the drawing power of these sites. Moreover, these conceptualizations of the sacred have both influenced and been reconstituted in nominally secular texts, one example being the bid examined in this chapter. Other examples would include a number of the travel guides prepared for free distribution and for sale to both religious and nonreligious tourists who come to the city. In the Santiago bid in particular, however, rather than focusing solely on long-standing tropes, such as those related to the sacred body of St. James or the sanctified quality of the cathedral site, the authors introduce a series of discourses that speak directly to the suitability of Santiago de Compostela as a European city of "culture" in the year 2000. As I outline below, the authors of the bid maintain that the history of this city and of the Galician region as a whole has bestowed on this place a significant heritage beyond the pilgrimage site and also a tradition of cultural pluralism. As part of the competition within Western Europe (and elsewhere in the world) to attract tourists in a multifaceted market, this manner of selling Santiago de Compostela can be viewed as parallel to the attempts of many other governments to market their cities as significant heritage or cultural sites (e.g., Chang et al. 1996; and Richards 1996). For anthropologists, however, this elaboration by governments and the private sector of the distinctiveness and value of local, regional, and national "cultures" in order to market touristic places cannot be analyzed without considering our own disciplinary debates over the concept of culture itself.

The argument that follows is organized into several sections. In the first section, I further sketch how my analysis of a particular set of discourses about a long-standing pilgrimage site is linked with the anthropological literature on pilgrimage, cultural tourism, and the debate over the culture concept. In the subsequent section, I turn to the case of Santiago de Compostela, first providing an overview of the history of Santiago de Compostela that demonstrates that the significance of the pilgrimage site has been constructed throughout history by advocates who worked actively to ensure its reception of various honors and resources and thus its continued renown. Then, I examine one such construction—the 1995 bid prepared by the city of Santiago de Compostela for the EU City of Culture competition.

Debating Pilgrimage and Culture

As discussed in chapter 1 of this volume, there has been a resurgence of interest since the early 1990s in comparative pilgrimage studies as well as in research on pilgrim-tourists, religious tourism, ethnic tourism, and the history of human journeying (see, e.g., Coleman and Elsner 1995; Dubisch 1995; Eade and Sallnow 1991a; Jackowski and Smith 1992; Morinis 1992; Nolan and Nolan 1992; Pitchford 1995; Rinschede 1992; Smith 1992; and Vukonić 1992). Pilgrimage researchers Eade and Sallnow (1991b) and Coleman and Elsner (1995) have drawn attention to the importance of the four coordinates of person, place, text, and movement in shaping the development of pilgrimage sites. Frequently, these coordinates tend to overlap, as in the case of Santiago de Compostela, where "the power of the living person [Saint James] is sedimented and preserved after his death in the power of place" (Eade and Sallnow 1991b, 8).

As in pilgrimage, the four coordinates of person, place, text, and movement powerfully inform accounts of tourist voyages and destinations. However, in examining literature on Santiago de Compostela published since the 1990s (including guidebooks, Catholic Church publications, and the bid for the City of Culture competition), one finds that a new coordinate can be added to this list—that of culture. And this emphasis on the cultural history of Santiago de Compostela coincides with social scientific examinations of, and theoretical debates about the implications of, heritage or cultural tourism.

Although heritage policies and development usually refer to the preservation and protection of physical objects (such as buildings) and the character of specific geographical areas, Meethan (1996, 25) notes that these actions involve the reconstitution of the "old" and the associated re-creation of new "narratives of material culture." With respect to the emergence of heritage tourism, there was an associated "shift of focus from prestige buildings and monuments to the vernacular and a concomitant dilution of the elitist aspects of history as scholarship, its spreading appeal to a mass audience, and the emergence of heritage as a form of mass consumption" (325).

Heritage tourism is now often subsumed under the broader category of cultural tourism in policy documents, such as those of the European Commission (see Richards 1996, 261). And like "heritage," the term "culture" has been expanded over the last several decades to mean more than the elitist "high" culture of museums, concerts, and art galleries. Today, "cultural tourists are interested in the lifestyle of other people . . . their history, and the artifacts and monuments they have made. Thus this category also includes what some have called ethnic and historical tourism. . . . Cultural tourism may be contrasted with recreational tourism—stereotypically focused on sun, sand, sea and sex" (Boissevain 1996b, 21–22).

Alongside this broad definition of cultural attractions, one finds that the label "cultural tourist sites" is attributed to a wide range of places: one category comprises cultural tourist sites that have been long-standing sites of the aforementioned "high" culture, such as Florence (Richards 1996; van der Borg, Costa, and Gotti 1996); a second group can be defined as former manufacturing centers that are involved in the narration of the cultural and historical significance of their industrial pasts (Chang et al. 1996; Meethan 1996); and a third group includes geographically and politically marginalized areas that are developing their cultural tourism through an emphasis on distinctive ethnicities and regional characteristics (see, e.g., Crain 1992, 1996, 1997; and Nogués Pedregal 1996). A fourth type of cultural tourist site could clearly encompass pilgrimage destinations, such as Santiago de Compostela, that combine features of the first and third categories listed above.

Among analysts of this expansion of cultural tourism in Western Europe and other advanced capitalist nations, there is widespread agreement that it involves an accommodation to two changes: the restructuring of the global economy whereby these nations are losing their manufacturing base and relying more on expanding their service sector; and the necessity of diversifying the range of attractions and services that one offers to increasingly sophisticated tourists who may be seeking something more than beach resorts (e.g., Urry 1990). This process of diversification has increasingly involved the role of various levels of government, either directly through financial investment in projects that expand a locality or region's "cultural capital" (Meethan 1996, 323) or indirectly through the establishment of policies that encourage similar endeavors by local entrepreneurs. However, much of this economic and cultural development directed toward a potential tourist market is achieved through partnerships between the public and private sectors (Chang et al. 1996).

As Chang et al. (1996) summarize, while some authors interested in this form of touristic development have demonstrated that it leads to the accentuation of the local and regional specificity of distinct sites (e.g., Boniface and Fowler 1993), other researchers have proposed a globalization thesis arguing that the emergence of similar facilities and attractions (e.g., sanitized waterfronts, craft and music festivals) throughout the world has led instead to both cultural homogenization and increasingly reduced local control over economic development (see, e.g., Crick 1989; Greenwood 1989; and Short et al. 1993; see also Greenwood 1977 for an earlier perspective).

However, Chang et al. (1996), among others (e.g., Boissevain 1996a), reject an either/or analysis of heritage and cultural tourism, noting that "although heritage tourism may be the chosen strategy, different destinations tend to accentuate themes peculiar to their culture and location as a way to differentiate themselves from competitors" (Chang et al. 1996, 287). In this quotation and in some of the other research that I cite, as in the advertisements and other promotional literature produced to highlight cultural tourism attractions, one finds an often unproblematic use of the term "culture" that is the indirect result of the influence of many decades of writing by academic anthropologists and scholars in related disciplines (see also Handler 1988). The proliferation of the use of the term "culture" by different actors for a variety of reasons implies that the anthropological focus on this concept has had an extensive influence even when many of the consequences of this influence are unintended. Somewhat ironically, just as some are embracing the concept of culture in economic and political struggles for resources and recognition, some anthropologists and historians of anthropology are in the process of critically interrogating, and in some cases even rejecting, many of the implications of the concept (see, e.g., Abu-Lughod 1991; Alonso 1994; and Clifford 1988).[3]

Disturbed by the epistemological implications connoted by the culture concept that was developed by ethnographers and ethnologists over the course of the twentieth century, and following the emergence over the last two decades of a renewed anti-neocolonialist critique within anthropology, Abu-Lughod (1991) argues that the notion of culture implies a false homogeneity and boundedness circumscribing groups of people and thus de-emphasizes differences within groups. She goes on to suggest that "evidence" of cultural difference can be used to dominate subaltern peoples, since rigid separations "inevitably carry a sense of hierarchy" (138). Although her argument "against culture" is convincing to some extent, Abu-Lughod also acknowledges that notions of cultural distinctiveness have become important political tools for a variety of constituencies. One could say that among those constituencies are members of economically and politically marginalized populations within wealthy and powerful nations, such as the United States, as well as activists in postcolonial and nonstate nations who wish to assert their "difference" as a way of articulating the inherent legitimacy of their home territories as nations. One would have to include as well the attempts of individuals in both economically marginalized regions and long-standing centers of power to market their home areas as attractive destinations for tourists (see, e.g., Crain 1992, 1996; and van der Borg, Costa, and Gotti 1996).

In the case of the contest to become a European City of Culture (or for that matter, an Olympic site), however, these individuals have to respond to a mandate that they articulate the appropriateness of their place as standing for something broader than local regional distinctiveness. As in other discursive commentaries on the need to develop European, rather than or in addition to, national, regional, or local identities, I argue below that the Santiago de Compostela bid includes a postmodern and, one might say, "postcolonial" concept of culture. Moreover, this conceptualization of culture shares many similarities with the constructivist approach of anthropologists such as Abu-Lughod (1991) and Eade and Sallnow (1991b), who are concerned with rendering a new idea of culture that can accommodate pluralism, ongoing transformation, and the frequent crisscrossing of boundaries.

Constructing "Culture" in Santiago

Clearly, the constraints of the EU City of *Culture* competition provide a major reason for the detailed elaboration of the notion of culture in the Santiago de Compostela bid. However, as I discuss above, like other cultural tourism proposals, the idea of European culture developed by the authors of this bid goes beyond references to the "high" culture of fine art, classical music, museums, and monuments that one has grown to expect in European tourism literature. This broadening of the discourse about Santiago de Compostela coincides with a general strategy of *turismo integral,* or "multifaceted tourism," elaborated in Spain in the early 1990s to attempt to attract tourists who are interested in more than the beaches and sunshine with which Spain had previously been associated by foreign tourists. This campaign was marked in 1992 by the replacement of the previous slogan "Spain: Everything under the Sun" with the new phrase "Spain: Passion for Life" (Crain 1996, 28–29).

In developing their particular version of Santiago's potential for cultural tourism, the authors of the bid draw on a broad notion of human cultures as comprising particular "ways of life" and worldviews; their use of the culture concept resonates with the usual anthropological use of the term. I have found that the same conceptualization is utilized by other interlocutors who are concerned with defining Galician culture in particular. In this section, I briefly

assess the context in which this all-encompassing notion of culture has become prevalent in nonacademic discourse. I also suggest that, in their efforts
to define "European" identity, the authors of the Santiago de Compostela bid
have actually gone beyond the essentialist idea of primordial, bounded cultures that Abu-Lughod (1991) and other authors have criticized.

Since 1981, Santiago de Compostela has been the symbolic capital of the
Comunidad Autónoma of Galicia—one of ninenteen semiautonomous regions
established according to the terms of the 1978 post-Franco Spanish Constitution.[4] The growing assertion by Galicia and other regions in Spain of their
right to increased levels of administrative and fiscal independence in relation
to the central government is the culmination of over a century of cultural and
(in some cases) linguistic revitalization activity. Nationalist Galicians, like
Catalans and Basques, strive to highlight how different their history and society are from those of other parts of Spain and Europe (see, e.g., Roseman
1995, 1997). During the 1980s, this discourse of distinctiveness increasingly
developed a definition of cultural difference. This adoption of the culture
concept by nationalist Galicians is part of a larger trend whereby "culture"
has replaced other terms that have been used widely in popular and academic
arenas to denote unique boundaries—terms such as "ethnicity," "folk,"
"race," and to some extent "religion" (see, e.g., Stolcke 1995). The modernist sense of the term "culture," like these other terms, tends to embrace some
of the implications of rigid lines of division existing between people in different social categories that Abu-Lughod (1991) and others have described
(see, e.g., Clifford 1988; and Turner 1995).

As in other postcolonial and nonstate nations, in Galicia there has been a
tendency for political actors to codify their histories, languages, religious beliefs, and consequently their cultures as part of a definition of nationality (see,
e.g., Fox 1990; Handler 1988; Handler and Linnekin 1984; Linnekin 1990; and
Trosset 1993; see also Turner 1995). As Anderson (1991) notes, these activities
by twentieth-century nationalists involve their employment of a similar rhetoric and technologies to those used by the powerful nation-states, such as
France during the eighteenth and nineteenth centuries.

However, as I demonstrate below, the emerging implications of Spain's
entry into the multistate European Community (now also including the EU
structure) have meant that some nationalist Galicians, like Catalans and
Basques, have begun to locate themselves and their territory as symbolically
within Europe, rather than Spain.[5] Their political agenda of trying to achieve
more autonomy from the Spanish state in many ways coalesces with the aim
of European unity activists who wish to promote "European" rather than
nation-state identities. And the recent elaboration of an idea of European

unity and a European culture has resulted as well in a fascinating discursive transformation. Rather than borrowing the same language of primordialism and strict boundaries that were used to define nations in the past, some European unity activists (including EU officials) refer to a concept of culture that is similar to that being developed in postmodern anthropology—a concept that emphasizes plurality, multiple subjectivities, transformations, and the crossing of borders (see, e.g., Behar 1993; and Tsing 1993).

Below, I argue that the authors of the Santiago bid contribute to such a discourse. Their conceptualization of European "culture" is neither rigid nor essentialist. Although, not surprisingly, references are made to Santiago as a center of Galician culture, the focus is on why Santiago de Compostela *is* already a European cultural capital. I contend that this articulation of a postmodern culture concept is meaningful for the task of promoting supranational, rather than either national or local, identities. Furthermore, coinciding with the emphasis on the coordinate of "movement" in the anthropological literature on tourism and pilgrimage, one of the most interesting aspects of the European culture concept developed in the Santiago bid is the fact that the concept is based on the idea of journeying and, more specifically, on the medieval pilgrimage route to Santiago. European unity is symbolized by the pilgrimage route that involved thousands of culturally diverse Europeans traveling along the same "road" and the ideal that there emerged a spirit of tolerance and unity among them. Before presenting some examples from the Santiago bid to illustrate this discourse further, I provide a short summary of the history of the city and the pilgrimage itself.

Historical Sketch: The Emergence of Santiago de Compostela as a Religious Center

Many Galicians viewed the attribution of the City of Culture designation to their capital to be the culmination of a process of cultural and political revitalization of Santiago de Compostela as a city of consequence on an international scale. During earlier periods in history, through the advocacy of various church and secular authorities, this city named for the apostle St. James was awarded similar honors and an accompanying fame.

Christian narratives recount that James, the brother of Jesus, had traveled to the Iberian Peninsula to preach; when he was executed by Herod upon his return to Jerusalem, his body was placed in a boat at Jaffa. Escorted by other apostles, James's relics landed on the Atlantic coast of Galicia (at the town of Padrón) where several miracles occurred to human individuals and animals who came into contact with the sacred body of Santiago. For example, it is recounted that a noblewoman named Lupa was converted to Christianity upon seeing that the wild oxen pulling the cart containing the body of James were tamed; she also immediately provided a family tomb for his remains (Stokstad 1978).

It was in the early ninth century that relics said to be those of James and two of his disciples were discovered on a hilltop near what is now the city of Santiago de Compostela. A hermit named Pelayo was directed to the spot by an abnormally bright star and the appearance of an angel. The most proximate bishop, Theodomir, was called to examine the scene, and he pronounced the tomb to be that of St. James. Pope Leo III confirmed Bishop Theodomir's assessment, and the pilgrimage began soon afterward, with the blessing of King Alfonso II (then monarch of what is now Asturias, León, and Galicia) who built a church on the spot of Pelayo's discovery (Stokstad 1978; Hogarth 1992).

However, at no time was Santiago de Compostela's eventual renown as a pilgrimage site automatic or accidental. For example, in the mid-twelfth century, the efforts of the energetic Bishop Diego Gelmírez resulted in Santiago becoming not only a renowned destination for pious Christians but also an archdiocese in control of the centers of Salamanca, Braga, and Avila. The historical accounts (e.g., Filgueira Valverde 1982) are clear: Santiago's ascendance as the third in a triad of key Christian shrines in the early medieval period was not simply the result of word-of-mouth accounts but rather stemmed from the organized activities of individuals like Gelmírez: "In contrast to the venerable shrines in Jerusalem and Rome, the tomb and church of St. James at first would have appeared very humble indeed if it were not for the talents of the monastic propagandists. The large number of pilgrims to Spain did not arise out of spontaneous piety alone. . . . Even the archbishop of Santiago, Gelmírez, travelled through France and Italy in the early twelfth century preaching the pilgrimage to his cathedral" (Stokstad 1978, 16–17).

Later in the twelfth century, Archbishop Suárez de Deza, a native Galician, became an equally effective promoter of the city and the shrine site with "the climax of his reign [being] . . . the establishment of the Jubilee, a Holy Year still celebrated whenever the feast of St. James falls on Sunday" (Stokstad 1978, 88). Archbishop Suárez was able to persuade King Ferdinand II to make a pilgrimage to Santiago on the occasion of the first Holy Year celebrations in 1182. Another reason for the early success of Santiago as a meaningful shrine for all European Christians was that St. James had been regarded as the patron saint of the Spanish military efforts during the seven centuries of warfare between Christians and Moslems on the Iberian Peninsula. Consequently, one of the common nicknames for the saint used by devotees in the past (but now downplayed) was *Matamoros* (Moor slayer) (e.g., Rodríguez López 1993).

In 1480, the "Catholic monarchs" Ferdinand and Isabel made Santiago the seat of the territorial government (of the Audiencia Territorial de Galicia), although it was later moved to the city of La Coruña. These monarchs also founded a hospital for pilgrims and established a university in the city. Santiago's popularity as a pilgrimage destination never completely waned but certainly declined in relative terms through the tumultuous seventeenth and eighteenth centuries, despite the extensive building work that was done on the cathedral and on other buildings in the city during that period. The revocation of the lands of Spanish monasteries and convents after 1835 (after the passing of the Exclaustration Act) resulted in many of the buildings in the city falling into states of disrepair (Stokstad 1978, 161–62).

Santiago's reemergence as a focal Catholic site in the modern period can be traced back just over one hundred years ago to the moment when the relics of St. James were relocated and then accepted as valid by Pope Leo XIII in 1884.[6] Owing to Francisco Franco's National Catholicism and his promotion of the Spanish tourism industry, the entire old city core of Santiago was named a "national monument" in the 1940s. Later, the old pilgrims' hospital was transformed into a *parador*—one of many government-run luxury hotels still operating in Spain. In addition, like kings and archbishops in earlier points in history, Franco himself publicly promoted Santiago on the occasion of the 1965 Holy Year celebrations (Nolan and Nolan 1989, 137; see also Starkie 1957).

In the 1990s, Santiago was a growing city with a population of just under 100,000 residents. Its economy was based mainly on the pilgrimage-tourism industry, employment in the Galician autonomous government bureaucracy, and the university. By 1997–98, more than 40,000 university students were being added to the city population from October to June. Santiago is also a commercial center for surrounding rural communities, and there is some light industry in the outskirts (Guisan 1990).

Increases in income and leisure time during the last few decades have meant that many Europeans have been able to visit Santiago de Compostela. However, as in previous centuries, active publicity about the city and the pilgrimage route is crucial to its sustained popularity. Santiago continues to attract visitors because of the active solicitation of international recognition by government and church officials and their subsequent reference to these honors when advertising the city abroad.

In 1984, UNESCO labeled the city an international site of "Cultural Patrimony for Humanity," and in 1993, one of St. James's Holy Years, the same designation was applied to the pilgrimage itself. That year, the governments of the city of Santiago de Compostela, the Autonomous Community of Galicia, and Spain provided extensive funds to raise the profile of the pilgrimage and that of the region as a whole, both within Spain and internationally. These efforts were so successful that continued financial and other support was committed after that year ended, with the goal of extending what amounted to a large-scale cultural renewal and tourism development project until 1999, the next Holy Year (see Rodríguez Campos 2002, 41–42). This series of initiatives was slated to run until the year 2000 and to be linked to plans for the EU City of Culture activities. In addition, promotion of the pilgrimage to Santiago has started to depict it as a spiritual search for European, rather than Christian, identity and comradeship. Indeed, this transformation of the pilgrimage coincides with the trend for New Age spiritualists to follow the famous "French Way," with the goal of going beyond Santiago de Compostela to seek out the coastal village of Fisterra—the destination said to have been the goal of pre-Christian pilgrims attempting to reach "the end of the earth."

The foregoing brief history demonstrates a consistent pattern in which Santiago de Compostela has been actively constructed and promoted as a "center" over the centuries. Now, I turn to examine one of the more recent instances of this discursive process.

"The Idea of Europe Was Born along the Road to Santiago" (Goethe): The Constitution of European Culture

The influence of anthropological terminology and concepts is impossible to ignore in the bid for Santiago de Compostela to be named a European City of Culture in the year 2000 (Concello de Santiago 1995). Terms such as "ethnocentrism" are used repeatedly, and one also finds such phrases as "culture and subsistence" and "Nature and Culture." Furthermore, the word "anthropological" is employed philosophically as a key word, as in the following examples: "Ritual and the connection with the anthropological" and "the anthropological in all cultures." What is most interesting, however, is the way in which the authors of the bid transform modernist anthropology in their formulation of the reasons why Santiago is an appropriate choice not just as a City of Culture but in fact as a *European* City of Culture. At one point, they state that the EU cultural capital will be the "City that Europe designates as an emblem of tolerance, conviviality, and creation" (*a Cidade que Europa designa como o emblema pola tolerancia, a convivencia e a creación*).[7] Moreover, Galicia and Santiago are said to represent this emblem because of the long history of pilgrimage to the city and its connection with European unity: "Galicia participated in the Middle Ages in the most advanced European cultural production . . . and is at present inserted in the process of construction of the European

Union, that, in an intense and ideal form, symbolizes the Jacobean [Pilgrimage] Route" (Concello de Santiago 1995, 138).

As these quotations indicate, in the Santiago bid European culture is constituted in terms of the following two themes: (1) cultural pluralism and transformation; and (2) solidarity and tolerance. Each theme can be illustrated best with some examples.

Cultural Pluralism and Transformations

In characterizing the idea of "Europe" as a pluralistic society, the Santiago bid talks about the medieval pilgrimage to Santiago de Compostela as one of the key instances when people crossed borders and met people who were from different backgrounds. This process changed the city, making it a cosmopolitan center: "from all the corners of Europe pilgrimages to the tomb of the Apostle . . . ended up constituting a phenomenon . . . that brought to the city of Compostela art, culture, philosophy, fashions, commerce, etc." (Concello de Santiago 1995, 118).

The notion that the city became a center in which a pluralistic European culture could flourish because of Santiago's status as a Christian pilgrimage destination is repeated numerous times in the bid, as in the following statement: "The influence of the pilgrimage way [*camiño*] in Compostela throughout history is indubitable. . . . The city is once again becoming the focal point for Europe. . . . Compostela is thus recuperating the role that it played over the length of the medieval period as a catalyzing center of thought, art, knowledge, and culture, which in another time arrived only via the pilgrimage way" (Concello de Santiago 1995, 120).

Every domain of life in Santiago de Compostela and along the pilgrimage route is characterized as having been influenced by the culturally diverse backgrounds of the pilgrims: music, art, dance, philosophy, and so on. Even the cuisine of Galicia and Santiago are said to be "syncretic" because of this history of cultural exchange: "Here all the cuisines of Occidental Christianity converge. . . . The pilgrims brought manners from distant lands" (Concello de Santiago 1995, 129).

Santiago de Compostela is also characterized as an ecumenical and philosophical, rather than a purely Christian, center. The authors of the bid outline how, in the year 2000, they will mount exhibits that demonstrate the connection between domains such as art and religion across the world, "demonstrating that indissoluble link between art and religion in all the zones of the world: in Christian, Buddhist, Islamic, Jewish, and Hindu traditions, in classical mythologies and in primitive cultures" (Concello de Santiago 1995, 139). Individuals are said to have come to Santiago in search of personal transformation and fulfillment, out of "the necessity of many people to satisfy their spiritual arenas, to express their religious sentiments, and to fulfill processes of intellectual and personal growth, to seek out knowledge and wisdom" (139).

This contact between people from different parts of Europe made Santiago de Compostela a place of cultural transformation. In effect, the transformations of European culture as a whole are said to be reflected metonymically in the architecture of the place, "a city with a structure that was typical of a medieval burg, that constructed and reconstructed itself over the course of centuries, retaining vestiges of each style" (Concello de Santiago 1995, 119).

During each period in history, as in Europe as a whole, "Santiago de Compostela enlarged and declined, according to the sign of the times" (Concello de Santiago 1995, 119). For example, the late nineteenth-century *Rexurdimento,* or cultural rebirth of Galician culture, transformed the Catholic Compostela into what became the cradle of anti-Francoist political resistance in the 1960s and 1970s. And in the 1990s, Santiago had become "not simply a monumental city encased in the past; it is a city in which modern life and contemporary buildings are also protagonists" (120). The bid gives examples of "modern" sites for pilgrims and other travelers to the city that parallel the cathedral and other religious monuments, including the Galician parliament, the newly built Audiencia de Galicia (which contains a gallery and concert hall), and the Galician Center for Contemporary Art (opened in 1995).

The bid also emphasizes that Compostela is a "green city" that is surrounded by treed hills and contains numerous cultivated parks. The focus of the EU and European cities on providing protection of environmental spaces is presented in the bid as coinciding with the way in which human societies are transformed partly in response to cyclical and radical changes in the territories in which they are located. And because social systems are influenced by the environment, it is possible to draw "infinite anthropological associations with other cultures far away." In effect, by considering the ecological connections between culture and ecosystems, "it is possible to reflect on the permeability of cultures" (Concello de Santiago 1995, 138).

As one can see with this last remark, the authors of this text are not simply talking about Santiago, Galicia, and Europe as having been in constant transformation. They are offering a concept of culture that highlights change, diversity, and interconnectedness:

As for the concept of the "present," if we are capable of grasping a universal realm of reference rather than one that is strictly local or regional, we [must] consider the experience of historical process. There does not exist "a present" culturally speaking but rather many evolving realities, simultaneous in "time" but diverse in their [experience] of the velocity of change. The [concept of] "distinct cultural presents" permits us to visualize history, just as the present vision of the sky tells us of the reality of the past of the stars that we see and that we know have already expired. (Concello de Santiago 1995, 137)

There is also an emphasis in the bid on the fact that cultures are constructed by human actors and that European culture has flourished and will continue to be strengthened if there are social spaces in which creative activities can be freely carried out. Some of the concepts associated with the plan to highlight "Spectacle" and "Creation" in the proposed year 2000 celebrations can be seen in the following phrases: "People's participation in Creation"; "experience of culture as a social act"; and "Compostela is the result of creative activity" (Concello de Santiago 1995, 140–41).

According to the bid, recognition of these processes would draw European artists into the city to collaborate with Galicians during the year 2000 and would achieve the goal of "provoking artistic and cultural production" (Concello de Santiago 1995, 141). As a City of Culture, Santiago de Compostela would be transformed into a "European Cultural Space." However, the audiences are also recognized as creative. Therefore, mention is made of the "Creation of the Spectators" of the planned series of artistic events and of the way in which artists will be in contact with these spectators in order to confront their perceptions of the works of theater, dance, visual art, and other media (140–41).

This emphasis on contact between European artists and between these artists and spectators is not surprising. European unity advocates feel that if Europeans are to develop meaningful identities as members of a unified, multistate political union, it is crucial that they participate in such events (Borneman and Fowler 1997). Programs of the EU, such as the City of Culture competition, have been initiated partly in order to achieve this goal. What is interesting in light of the pilgrimage literature is the fact that references to European solidarity in the Santiago de Compostela bid resemble the Turnerian notion of communitas.

The Route of European Solidarity

An additional theme that runs through the Santiago bid is that the medieval pilgrimage to the city resulted in the development of tolerance, understanding, and a feeling of solidarity among people from different parts of the continent.[8] One has to keep in mind that this claim, like the notion of all pilgrims experiencing "communitas," is the articulation of an ideal. However, as Coleman and Elsner (1995, 202) point out, some pilgrims do share this ideal and experience a heightened sense of spiritual freedom and comradeship with other pilgrims. I have met some travelers with both religious and nonreligious motivations who experienced a sense of European unity with other tourists along the route to Santiago. Other travelers certainly did not. Furthermore, since today many pilgrims travel to Santiago de Compostela and other Galician shrines in rented coach cars with large groups of people from their home communities, it is not uncommon to find that they do not even meet other pilgrims while in the city.

However, what is important in the context of the Santiago bid is the way in which the ideal of "solidarity" is used to characterize pan-European culture, for the pilgrimage to Santiago is conceived of as a *"Camiño de Solidariedade"* (Concello de Santiago 1995, 142) that breaks down social barriers and cultural differences.

If one examines the text carefully, it becomes apparent that the notion of solidarity articulated in the bid concerns more than simply Europeans coming together. This articulation of solidarity is a transformation of Christian ideas of fellowship and grace. A curious set of linking propositions frames the emphasis:

> Culture is also about the emotions.
>
> Emotionality translates into a desire for perfection and justice.
>
> Justice implies solidarity.
>
> European Culture [capitals in original] will [continue] to materialize as a culture of solidarity. (Concello de Santiago 1995, 142)

The reference to justice is linked to a discussion of how Santiago de Compostela, as a city that has been granted the status of a World heritage site by UNESCO and a European cultural capital in the year 2000, will contribute toward the protection of the cultures of developing countries. The authors of the bid state that they "reject ethnocentrism, that they wish to plant in the European cultural consciousness the valorization of 'difference,' and that they want to mobilize . . . processes leading toward [relations of] solidarity with others" (Concello de Santiago 1995, 137). This commitment to helping the less fortunate was also extended to Europeans who would not have the resources to participate in the year 2000 celebration. The bid promises to provide human and financial resources to help make it possible for members of disadvantaged social classes and groups within Europe to attend the year 2000 events in Santiago.

In their discussion of solidarity, the writers of the bid are able to draw together the themes of pluralism, creativity, and human cooperation as fundamental to a new culture concept: "The concepts of cultural Production and Solidarity [capitals in original] can be used to formulate an identity. Culture is the axis that permits the pursuit of the knowledge of difference and that . . . through expressivity it is possible to reach understanding between peoples and persons, resulting in a spirit of help and cooperation" (Concello de Santiago 1995, 137). However, this culture concept is developed in the context of the history of the Santiago pilgrimage. It was in the last decades of the twentieth century that EU officials decided to seek out cities that could prove that they were "emblems" of tolerance, cultural pluralism, cooperation, and creativity—notions that have been developed as "secular" values underlying European unity politics.

Conclusion

The Cities of Culture competition is one among numerous programs designed to achieve the European Union's goal of promoting European identities among citizens in member states. It is also a response to an overt awareness on the part of government officials at every level that some of the most viable "products" that Europe has to "sell" to both internal and non-EU visitors in this period of late capitalism are its history and culture (Ashworth and Tunbridge 1990; Guisan 1990; Laurier 1993; Richards 1996; Williams and Shaw 1991a, 1991b). As the example of the Santiago bid demonstrates, this focus on maintaining and stimulating touristic and associated industries within the EU provokes a contest over not only economic resources but also the constitution of broad conceptual categories, such as history, religious traditions, nationalisms, the environment, and "Europe" itself.

My analysis of the bid produced to convince the EU to choose Santiago de Compostela as one of nine cities to be a cultural capital in the year 2000 also has the aim of contributing to the broader literature on pilgrimage and tourism. I agree with Eade and Sallnow (1991b) that it is important that we carefully examine the different discourses that are being elaborated at particular pilgrimage sites and acknowledge the diversity of motivations that draw people to these places. The suggestion put forward by these researchers that different case studies can be compared with regard to the content of such discourses is also helpful. Furthermore, I contend that the religious circumscription of sacred places, bodies, texts, and movement (Coleman and Elsner 1995; Eade and Sallnow 1991b) has influenced the apparently secular description of why certain sites draw tourists. In the case of the Santiago bid to the EU, however, the most important symbolic coordinate is the newer one of "culture."

While Galicians sometimes utilize an essentialist notion of culture to promote their legitimacy as a nation separate from Spain, the authors of the bid develop a radically different terminology to describe why Santiago de Compostela should be a European City of Culture as a way of marking the beginning of the twenty-first century. As I have demonstrated, their articulation of the culture concept in this text resembles postmodern anthropological emphases on plurality and shifting boundaries. Finally, in contrast to the earlier image of a Europe divided into rigidly bounded states, the notion of culture put forth in the Santiago bid also accommodates a political agenda that promotes a fluid and emerging supranational European unity.

Notes

1. The official name is "European City of Culture." Nevertheless, the widespread colloquial usage of phrases such as "European cultural capital" (*capitalidade cultural europea,* in Galician) penetrated official documents, including the Santiago bid for the candidacy (see Concello de Santiago 1995). The other eight cities are the following: Prague (Czech Republic), Cracow (Poland), Brussels (Belgium), Reykjavik (Iceland), Helsinki (Finland), Avignon (France), Bologna (Italy), and Bergen (Norway).

2. They also mounted an impressive multimedia exhibit in the old city core, which I had the chance to visit in July 1995. This exhibit was organized to provide visual images to accompany the same text used in the written bid. Upon request, visitors to the exhibit, among whom were included many pilgrims and tourists as well as Galicians, were provided with copies of the bid free of charge.

3. An additional example of a situation in which groups of people are elaborating and insisting upon essentialist notions of cultural distinctiveness for particular purposes is the vibrant "politics of difference" or "diversity" that is being played out on university campuses in the United States (and to a lesser extent in Canada and Western Europe). Members of minoritized populations utilize the culture concept to demand affirmative action scholarships and hiring programs as well as changes to curricula (Roseman 1995).

4. The Autonomous Community of Galicia passed its own Statute of Autonomy in 1981, which established the regional government, or *Xunta,* as a new level of administration. Along with the Basque Country and Catalonia, Galicia was considered to be a "historical nation" and was able to pursue a "fast track" to semiautonomy. The region continues to be composed of the four provinces of A Coruña, Lugo, Pontevedra, and Ourense; many of the functions previously handled by the central government bureaucracy in Madrid, however, were gradually handed over to the Galician *Xunta* during the 1980s and 1990s. A significant aspect of this transition has been the revitalization of the Galician language as a code used in education, road signs, and government (see Roseman 1995).

5. This process of asserting a non-Castilian (or even non-Spanish) identity could be observed during the 1992 Olympics held in Barcelona. The Catalans who were hosting the Olympics insisted on flying their own flags and using their own language during official events. An advertisement for the Olympics publicized throughout the world in

widely circulated periodicals, such as *Time,* reproduced a map that outlined Barcelona and Catalonia within Europe, not Spain. In a related trend, there is a recent push for the EU to use the concept of cultures (rather than regions) in order to provide a way for the smallest of minoritized populations to assert their identities. The Flemish government, with support from the Basques, Bavarians, and others, was successful in convincing the EU to initiate "Europe of Cultures—2002." This strategy is explicitly linked by EU officials to EU expansion; commission member Flor Van de Velde stated that "Europe of the Regions [one of the official EU committees] is far too heterogeneous for the regions. We are striving for a much wider idea, based on culture and the economy. Cultural identity and not the nation-state should be the basis for Europe's future" (*The European,* 1996, 11; see also Shore, 2000).

6. Detailed information on the results of church-sponsored archaeological excavations in both 1878–79 and 1946–59 can be found in Guerra Campos (1982).

7. This and all further translations into English are my own.

8. However, as discussed in chapter 1, note 7, this claim is disputed by Sumption (1975).

References Cited

Abu-Lughod, Lila. 1991. "Writing against Culture." In *Recapturing Anthropology: Working in the Present.* Ed. Richard G. Fox. 137–62. Santa Fe: School of American Research Press.

Alonso, Ana María. 1994. "The Politics of Space, Time, and Substance: State Formation, Nationalism, and Ethnicity." *Annual Review of Anthropology* 23:379–405.

Anderson, Benedict. 1991. *Imagined Communities: Reflections on the Origin and Spread of Nationalism.* London: Verso. (Originally published in 1983.)

Ashworth, Gregory J., and J. E. Tunbridge. 1990. *The Tourist-Historic City.* London: Belhaven.

Behar, Ruth. 1993. *Translated Woman: Crossing the Border with Esperanza's Story.* Boston: Beacon.

Boissevain, Jeremy, ed. 1996a. *Coping with Tourists: European Reactions to Mass Tourism.* Oxford: Berghahn Books.

———. 1996b. Introduction to *Coping with Tourists: European Reactions to Mass Tourism.* In Boissevain 1–26.

Boniface, Priscilla, and Peter J. Fowler. 1993. *Heritage and Tourism in the "Global Village."* London: Routledge.

Borneman, John, and Nick Fowler. 1997. "Europeanization." *Annual Review of Anthropology* 26:487–514.

Chang, T. C., Simon Milne, Dale Fallon, and Corinne Pohlmann. 1996. "Urban Heritage Tourism: The Global-Local Nexus." *Annals of Tourism Research* 23:284–305.

Clifford, James. 1988. *The Predicament of Culture: Twentieth-Century Ethnography, Literature, and Art.* Cambridge, Mass.: Harvard University Press.

Coleman, Simon, and John Elsner. 1995. *Pilgrimage Past and Present in the World Religions.* Cambridge, Mass.: Harvard University Press.

Concello de Santiago. 1995. *Compostela: Ciudad Europea de la Cultura en el Año 2000.* Santiago de Compostela: Concello de Santiago.

Crain, Mary M. 1992. "Pilgrims, 'Yuppies,' and Media Men: The Transformation of an Andalusian Pilgrimage." In *Revitalizing European Rituals*. Ed. Jeremy Boissevain. 95–112. London: Routledge.

———. 1996. "Contested Territories: The Politics of Touristic Development at the Shrine of El Rocío in Southwestern Andalusia." In *Coping with Tourists: European Reactions to Mass Tourism*. Ed. Jeremy Boissevain. 27–55. Oxford: Berghahn Books.

———. 1997. "The Remaking of an Andalusian Pilgrimage Tradition: Debates regarding Visual (Re)presentation and the Meanings of 'Locality' in a Global Era." In *Culture, Power, Place: Explorations in Critical Anthropology*. Ed. Akhil Gupta and James Ferguson. 291–311. Durham, N.C.: Duke University Press.

Crick, Malcolm. 1989. "Representations of International Tourism in the Social Sciences: Sun, Sex, Savings, and Servility." *Annual Review of Anthropology* 18:307–44.

Dubisch, Jill. 1995. *In a Different Place: Pilgrimage, Gender, and Politics at a Greek Island Shrine*. Princeton, N.J.: Princeton University Press.

Eade, John, and Michael J. Sallnow, eds. 1991a. *Contesting the Sacred: The Anthropology of Christian Pilgrimage*. London: Routledge.

———. 1991b. Introduction to *Contesting the Sacred: The Anthropology of Christian Pilgrimage*. Ed. John Eade and Michael Sallnow. 1–29. London: Routledge.

The European. 1996. April 11–17, 11.

Filgueira Valverde, José. 1982. *Historias de Compostela*. Vigo: Edicións Xerais de Galicia. (Originally published in 1970.)

Fox, Richard, ed. 1990. *Nationalist Ideologies and the Production of National Cultures*. Washington, D.C.: American Anthropological Association.

Greenwood, Davydd J. 1977. "Culture by the Pound: An Anthropological Perspective on Tourism as Cultural Commoditization." In *Hosts and Guests: The Anthropology of Tourism*. Ed. Valene L. Smith. 171–85. Philadelphia: University of Pennsylvania Press.

———. 1989. "Epilogue to Culture by the Pound: An Anthropological Perspective on Tourism as Cultural Commoditization." In *Hosts and Guests: The Anthropology of Tourism*. Ed. Valene L. Smith. 2nd ed. 181–85. Philadelphia: University of Pennsylvania Press.

Guerra Campos, José. 1982. *Exploraciones Arqueológicas en Torno al Sepulcro del Apostol Santiago*. Santiago de Compostela: Edición del Cabildo de la S. A. M. Iglesia.

Guisan, María del Carmen. 1990. *Galicia "2000": Industria y Empleo*. Santiago de Compostela: Universidad de Santiago de Compostela.

Handler, Richard. 1988. *Nationalism and the Politics of Culture in Quebec*. Madison: University of Wisconsin Press.

Handler, Richard, and Jocelyn Linnekin. 1984. "Tradition, Genuine and Spurious." *Journal of American Folklore*, no. 97:273–90.

Hogarth, James, trans. 1992. *The Pilgrim's Guide: A 12th Century Guide for the Pilgrim to St. James of Compostela*. London: Confraternity of St. James.

Jackowski, Antoni, and Valene L. Smith. 1992. "Polish Pilgrim-Tourists." *Annals of Tourism Research* 19:91–106.

Laurier, Eric. 1993. "'Tackintosh': Glasgow's Supplementary Gloss." In *Selling Places: The City as Cultural Capital, Past and Present*. Ed. Gerry Kearns and Chris Philo. 267–90. Oxford: Pergamon.

Linnekin, Jocelyn. 1990. "The Politics of Culture in the Pacific." In *Cultural Identity and Ethnicity in the Pacific.* Ed. Jocelyn Linnekin and Lin Poyer. 149–73. Honolulu: University of Hawaii Press.

Meethan, Kevin. 1996. "Consuming (In) the Civilized City." *Annals of Tourism Research* 23:322–40.

Morinis, E. Alan, ed. 1992. *Sacred Journeys: The Anthropology of Pilgrimage.* Westport, Conn.: Greenwood.

Nogués Pedregal, Antonio Miguel. 1996. "Tourism and Self-Consciousness in a South Spanish Coastal Community." In *Coping with Tourists: European Reactions to Mass Tourism.* Ed. Jeremy Boissevain. 56–83. Oxford: Berghahn Books.

Nolan, Mary Lee, and Sidney Nolan. 1989. *Christian Pilgrimage in Modern Western Europe.* Chapel Hill: University of North Carolina Press.

——. 1992. "Religious Sites as Tourism Attractions in Europe." *Annals of Tourism Research* 19:68–78.

Pitchford, Susan R. 1995. "Ethnic Tourism and Nationalism in Wales." *Annals of Tourism Research* 22:35–52.

Richards, Greg. 1996. "Production and Consumption of European Cultural Tourism." *Annals of Tourism Research* 23:261–83.

Rinschede, Gisbert. 1992. "Forms of Religious Tourism." *Annals of Tourism Research* 19:51–67.

Rodríguez Campos, Joaquín. 2002. "Ideas on Atlantic Culture in the Northwest Iberian Peninsula: 'Myths' and 'Realities.'" *Journal of the Society for the Anthropology of Europe* 2:35–44.

Rodríguez López, Antonio. 1993. *Guía de Santiago de Compostela.* Madrid: Ediciones El País.

Roseman, Sharon R. 1995. "'Falamos como Falamos': Linguistic Revitalization and the Maintenance of Local Vernaculars in Galicia." *Journal of Linguistic Anthropology* 5 (1): 3–32.

——. 1997. "Celebrating Silenced Words: The 'Reimagining' of a Feminist Nation in Late Twentieth Century Galicia." *Feminist Studies* 23 (1): 43–71.

Shore, Cris. 2000. *Building Europe: The Cultural Politics of European Integration.* London: Routledge.

Short, J., L. M. Benton, W. B. Luce, and J. Walton. 1993. "Reconstructing the Image of an Industrial City." *Annals of the Association of American Geographers* 83:207–24.

Smith, Valene L. 1992. "Introduction: The Quest in Guest." In "Pilgrimage and Tourism: The Quest in Guest," ed. Valene L. Smith. Special issue, *Annals of Tourism Research* 19:1–17.

Starkie, Walter. 1957. *The Road to Santiago: Pilgrims of St. James.* New York: E. P. Dutton.

Stokstad, Marilyn. 1978. *Santiago de Compostela in the Age of the Great Pilgrimages.* Norman: University of Oklahoma Press.

Stolcke, Verena. 1995. "Talking Culture: New Boundaries, New Rhetorics of Exclusion of Europe." *Current Anthropology* 16 (1): 1–24.

Sumption, Jonathan. 1975. *Pilgrimage: An Image of Medieval Religion.* London: Faber and Faber.

Trosset, Carol. 1993. *Welshness Performed: Welsh Concepts of Person and Society.* Tucson: University of Arizona Press.

Tsing, Anna Lowenhaupt. 1993. *In the Realm of the Diamond Queen: Marginality in an Out-of-the-Way Place*. Princeton, N.J.: Princeton University Press.

Turner, Terence. 1995. "Anthropology and Multiculturalism: What Is Anthropology that Multiculturalists Should Be Mindful of It?" In *Multiculturalism: A Critical Reader*. Ed. David Theo Goldberg. 406–25. Oxford: Blackwell.

Urry, John. 1990. *The Tourist Gaze: Leisure and Travel in Contemporary Societies*. London: Sage.

van der Borg, Jan, Paolo Costa, and Giuseppe Gotti. 1996. "Tourism in European Heritage Cities." *Annals of Tourism Research* 23:306–21.

Vukonić, Boris. 1992. "Medjugorje's Religion and Tourism Connection." *Annals of Tourism Research* 19:79–91.

Williams, Allen M., and Gareth Shaw. 1991a. "Tourism and Development: Introduction." In *Tourism and Economic Development: European Experiences*. Ed. Allen M. Williams and Gareth Shaw. 2nd ed. 1–12. London: Belhaven.

———. 1991b. "Western European Tourism in Perspective." In *Tourism and Economic Development: European Experiences*. Ed. Allen M. Williams and Gareth Shaw. 2nd ed. 13–39. London: Belhaven.

5 Stories of the Return:
Pilgrimage and Its Aftermaths

NANCY L. FREY

In this chapter, I focus on the return journey as an important and understudied arena of human movement and provide a model for its study based on my research on the contemporary Camino de Santiago pilgrimage (the "Camino"). The following statement by sociologist Judith Adler guides the theoretical approach of this chapter:

> The broad theoretical concern shared by those who hope to understand modern forms of travel glossed as "tourism" as well as modern and earlier styles of travel glossed as "religious," is with human *mobility,* deliberately shaped with expressive and communicative, rather than simply instrumental purposes in mind. All human mobility involves mutually defining contact between social groups, accompanied by a traffic in information and goods, and struggles for control of these processes. But the specific theoretical concern of students of tourism and religious travel alike, is with mobility structured to test and sustain complex cultural constructions of self, social reality, space, time, or even ultimate reality (God, eternal Truth, etc.). (Adler 1994, 3; emphasis in original)

From Adler, I utilize several key points: (1) the categories pilgrimage and tourism are more effectively understood as similar forms of human mobility, rather than binary oppositions; (2) as forms of human mobility, tourism and pilgrimage are expressive, stylized, and analyzable types of meaningful human action; and (3) human mobility also questions and functions to maintain sociocultural beliefs and practices. Understood in this way, the emphasis in research on pilgrimage and tourism shifts away from a definition of difference based on a binary opposition toward an understanding of the meanings of human movements and the way in which these movements influence the individual and society. The latter issue focuses on outcomes: how do travel experiences not only "test and sustain" but also affect (transform or change) participants in the short term and the long term, once the return lap is made? Using the Camino, I will first show how the categories of pilgrim and tourism are used and understood along the contemporary pilgrimage route and then focus on the outcomes of (these self-defined) pilgrims' journeys.

The failure of the Camino to fall neatly into the categories of pilgrimage as a "serious" religious and sacred journey or of tourism as "frivolous" travel (see Pfaffenberger 1983, 61; Smith 1992; and Graburn 1977, 1983) led to my emphasis on the meanings of human movement and the outcomes of journeys. The Santiago pilgrimage, in its reanimated form, defies easy definition, sharing elements of both tourism and pilgrimage. Eade and Sallnow suggest that it is "necessary to develop a view of pilgrimage not merely as a field of social relations but also *as a realm of competing discourses*" (1991, 5; emphasis in the original). Their emphasis on the multiplicity of discourses found at pilgrimage sites (and, I would add, tourism sites) is clearly applicable to the modern Camino de Santiago. Additionally, it is clear from my research that participants are deeply affected by the pilgrimage and that the experience continues to influence their daily lives after their return home.

Since the 1980s, the Camino de Santiago has experienced an unprecedented reanimation. Each year, in progressively increasing numbers, thousands of people re-create the medieval journey, walking and bicycling hundreds of miles across Spain's ever-changing landscapes and architecturally rich north to reach the tomb of Saint James in Santiago de Compostela. Calling themselves pilgrims, wearing the Santiago pilgrim's scallop shell, carrying a Pilgrim's Passport, following the yellow arrows that mark the historically reconstituted medieval routes, passing through the many villages and towns along the way, as well as visiting hundreds of Romanesque, Gothic, Renaissance, and Baroque churches and monuments, the participants elect to do this long, often arduous journey under their own power, rather than to reach Santiago by motorized transit. The "Camino," or "Way," is the term used to identify the network of thousands of miles of roads and trails that extend across Europe and lead to Santiago. The modern reconceptualization of the Camino takes pilgrims over two-thousand-year-old Roman roads, stone and dirt paths, paved highways, tractor roads, and forest tracks. The most popular starting point among contemporary pilgrims is the border between France and Spain, and walking the route takes from twenty to thirty days (cycling, from ten to fifteen).[1] The population of pilgrims along these routes is constantly in flux. Many pilgrims construct their journeys according to their available vacation time. Some may only have a week or two and elect to make the journey in stages, as a "part-time pilgrim," doing one- or two-week stages over many years. Others decide to start the journey from a point closer to Santiago, such as León. Still other pilgrims walk or cycle from their homes in France, Germany, Belgium, Holland, and other European countries, making journeys that extend from weeks to months in length.

Hailing from more than sixty countries, modern Santiago pilgrims have little in common with pilgrims at other popular centers of pilgrimage in Europe (such as Lourdes in France or Fátima in Portugal). As Turner and Turner observe, "the most characteristic modern pilgrimage is blended with tourism, and involves a major journey, usually by modern means of transportation, to a national or international shrine" (1978, 240). The fact that Santiago pilgrims voluntarily eschew modern transport marks an important difference between this and other pilgrimage centers, and it hints strongly at the fact that participants' movement choices are expressive, communicative, contesting, sustaining, and possibly related to transformation of their life worlds.

Surprisingly, modern pilgrims to Santiago are often urban, middle-class, educated Europeans who, rather than having a religious motive, are often on the road for a host of cultural, spiritual, athletic, and personal reasons. Curiously, 60 percent of Santiago pilgrims are male. While many pilgrims are at least nominally Catholic, there are also large numbers of Protestants, as well as agnostics, an occasional Buddhist, and those interested in various individualized New Age or esoteric spiritualities. Many pilgrims have difficulty articulating the reasons for their journey. Pilgrims are often attracted to the metaphorical pilgrimage as an inner journey and want to actualize the physical journey to help them access those inner "destinations" that are distant in daily life. Other pilgrims specifically plan and make the journey as a break from their daily lives; as a way to cope with death of a loved one; as a transition from other serious losses, such as divorce, separation, or unemployment; to fulfill a religious vow; or to have a period of reflection and decision making. Often motives are multilayered and evolve over the course of the journey. Some pilgrims find themselves on the route out of curiosity or as a result of the desire to understand the Camino's popularity.

One's religious practice or motive is often secondary to the more important element of the pilgrimage: how the pilgrim physically makes the journey itself. That is, the *how* often takes primacy over the *why* of the journey among Santiago pilgrims. This statement refers to most pilgrims. Among some pilgrims, especially those actively involved in religious practice, one's religious motive is very important in the definition of an "authentic" pilgrim. Additionally, the Pilgrim's Passport (*Credencial del Peregrino*), issued by the cathedral in Santiago, does specifically state that one's motive for making the pilgrimage should be religious. However, there is very little control of this factor. Moreover, the cathedral personnel do little to test the authenticity of religious motivation other than asking pilgrims to write their motive upon arrival in Santiago. Pilgrims often go to the Pilgrims' Office in Santiago because they want to receive the Compostela, an official-looking certificate written in Latin that confirms the completion of the journey, which some call the diploma. In order to receive the Compostela, the pilgrim must present the Pilgrim's Passport full of the stamps that he or she has received each day, demonstrating that the journey has been authentic and that the pilgrim has walked at least one hundred kilometers or cycled two hundred kilometers. The Pilgrims' Office grants the Compostela using a very ample definition of "religious" motivation with three general categories: religious, religious-cultural, and spiritual. Under the heading "spiritual," pilgrims have written "personal" and "educational" and been granted the Compostela. Later, when compiling statistics, the office simply lumps these three categories together as religious and claims that 97 percent of pilgrims are religiously motivated, while only 3 percent claim only cultural or athletic reasons. Both the Pilgrim's Passport and the Compostela are prized mementos of the journey, although some pilgrims complain about the "tourist" quality of the passports.

Among those who walk and cycle, people who travel by bus and car are often labeled tourists even if they have a religious motive because they do not make the long, arduous journey. For those who elect to walk and cycle, pilgrimage is a physical act that occurs on the ground, not just a spiritual exercise. After much thought, one twenty-six-year-old Swiss woman left her apartment, family, and job as a kindergarten teacher in order to reflect on her life and to fulfill a childhood dream of walking from her home in Switzerland to Portugal along the Camino de Santiago. A year after completing her four-month pilgrimage, she wrote to me in 1996:

> And to compare the pilgrimage with other travels, I think the main difference is that the pilgrimage for me changed me as a person, made me more confident, made me accept and love myself more and open up to new ideas and patterns. It was an inner and outer way where other travels are mostly outer ways. The inner way isn't as important. You travel somewhere to educate yourself, see new things, culture, people, environment but I've never heard of anybody say: "I'm going on 3 weeks holiday to search for something more, to answer some questions—such as you do as a pilgrim."[2]

Thus, one's movements—how they are conducted, selected, enacted—play an important role in how others (pilgrims, villagers) perceive and judge one's journey, which often influences the individual's performance of the pilgrimage. Pilgrims generally believe that through movement on foot or by bicycle along the road one can have encounters or experiences that lead to change. Such experiences and the ensuing personal growth are believed to be impossible for those who travel by car or bus. Human-powered movement and discovery are positively linked.[3]

Like this young Swiss woman, pilgrims to Santiago usually understand their journeys as pilgrimage and not tourism, though many struggle with these terms. Acquiring one's identity as a pilgrim is usually a process that takes place over the course of the journey (Feinberg 1985; Haab 1996) and may not even occur until the participant returns home. Additionally, the process is frequently comparative and involves defining oneself in relation to other travelers, namely tourists. On the pilgrimage, the tourist is the antithesis of the pilgrim. Unlike pilgrims, tourists are thought to be people who do not have face-to-face contact with villagers, do not appreciate the spaces of the Camino, and do not suffer the heat and pains of the road. Pilgrims frequently complain about interactions with tourists at common points of contact, such as monuments or the cathedral in Santiago. Tourists in these spaces, especially those in groups, are often described as noisy and pushy. Pilgrims report feeling uncomfortably like objects of attraction as cameras are whipped out by curious onlookers eager to snap the photo of the "authentic sweaty pilgrim." Pilgrims often feel that their long, hard journeys make them special and superior to tourists. And pilgrims often conspicuously mark themselves as different from other travelers by prominently displaying the scallop shell, which is worn around the neck, on the backpack or bicycle pannier. Even when walking around a village or city at day's end, some pilgrims continue to wear the shell.[4] Many participants describe feeling like a pilgrim in particular moments (the closer one gets to Santiago, when recognized as a pilgrim by outsiders, during physically trying moments) and like a tourist in others (while visiting cities and churches). Some pilgrims describe feeling like "frauds" because they act like a pilgrim (wearing the scallop shell, carrying the Pilgrim's Passport, staying in pilgrims' refuges) but do not feel like a pilgrim on the inside. While some have an awareness of role-playing, others revel in "being a pilgrim," flaunting the symbols and expecting to be treated specially by villagers. One concern among many pilgrims and those heavily involved in the pilgrimage's infrastructure is that the pilgrimage already has or will turn into a form of "cheap tourism," populated by cheap, greedy holiday makers who "do" the Camino as an inexpensive way to travel. In France and Switzerland, the Camino is expressly advertised this way.

Most pilgrims have had other types of travel experiences and use these as reference points to understand the pilgrimage. An Italian physical therapist in her thirties living in London explained that at times she felt like a pilgrim while walking but emphasized that she was a "pilgrim with money." She based her ideal model on the mid-nineteenth-century Russian pilgrim ("homeless wanderer") who searches for spiritual succor with a knapsack, dried bread, and a Bible in the breast pocket (French 1974). Other participants, who have done other types of long-distance journeys, comment that many of the experiences of trial, self-awareness, and easy contact with other travelers are familiar. What is unique about the Camino is the ethos of the pilgrim and the special attention placed on his or her successful completion of the journey, as well as an infrastructure designed to help the pilgrim, which includes well-marked roads that cross rural and urban spaces, and people disposed to offer unanticipated assistance. Moreover, the journey is one-way, and almost all participants share the same goal. Other long-distance walks (such as the Pacific Crest and Appalachian Trails in the United States) are two-way and do not have the historical landscapes of cathedrals, wayside churches and hermitages, monasteries, and hilltop villages that constantly remind the walker or cyclist that he or she is participating in an act with a long history. The Santiago pilgrimage is like "walking in the shadows of the past," as one man put it.

Comparing his experience as a pilgrim to Santiago in 1994 with a walking trip to Rome in 1997, a Dutch man wrote me from Italy on the second journey: "here, in my tent, smelling the old acquainted scent of socks worn daily in tight, warm walking shoes, I thought of giving you the following information." Besides being dubiously honored by my association with smelly socks, I was interested to know how his thoughts on the pilgrimage had evolved. In 1994, needing to take a serious look at his life, he had taken a six-month leave from his position in the field of mental health and walked to Santiago from his home in Holland. Returning home, he quit his job. Three years later, not wanting to walk the Camino again, he decided to walk to Rome over a three-month period. After describing the present journey, he remarked, "I don't call it a pilgrimage this time. Just a trip with visits to churches and other historical places. There is, by the way, not a Camino that leads you to Rome. That makes it different, more alone and not being recognized as a possible pilgrim. That also makes it easy to call yourself a pilgrim on the Camino." On the Camino, it is easy to call yourself a pilgrim because one is easily recognized in this role by outsiders and strangers and is encouraged to conform to it.

What appear to be superficial debates about one's identity as a pilgrim actually reveal the multiplicity of motives for modern pilgrims' journeys. After listening to countless stories of lives in transition, of intentionally sought-out physical and mental hardship, of pride in the accomplishment, of the primacy of the individualized "spiritual" over the institutionalized "religious," of unexpected encounters with human warmth and natural landscapes, of friendship and a past imbued with nostalgia, it became clear to me that these pilgrims are often not on the road to heal the body but rather are searching for ways to heal or discover the self or the "soul," a term commonly used by those following the Camino. Pilgrims often describe their daily lives and society as dislocating, materialist, and alienating. The Camino, on the other hand, represents a series of meaningful contacts—human, physical, geographic, emotional—involving all of the senses. The pilgrimage provides a welcome alternative to the stresses of the quotidian. The contrast between these different spheres of experience, as well as the realization that it is possible to live one's life differently, leads some to seek, often unexpectedly, transformation of self and society as a result.[5] Thus, the question of how pilgrims take their travel experiences home seemed fundamental for the holistic understanding of the reanimation of the Camino. The choice to avoid modern means of transportation also implies a rejection of certain aspects of modern life and effectively indicates what many pilgrims feel is lacking in their daily lives. This choice also conditions the types of experiences that pilgrims undergo along the way. Elements in these experiences consistently valued by pilgrims include having "real" face-to-face, meaningful contacts, experiencing the "genuineness" of the rural people, feeling less materialist, learning to live with less yet feeling enriched, valuing one's body and its achievements, and being in contact with nature (see Graburn 1995).

In both academic and travelers' narratives of journeys, when the geographic destination is reached, the journey, or the account of it, most often ends. The pilgrimage or travel experience is usually treated in isolation and bracketed between the departure from home and the return as if there were no continuity between the experiences. Reaggregation, or reintegration, as a central part of rites of passage, is essentially ignored. As anthropologist Ann Gold observes, in her exceptional study of the return of Rajasthani (India) Hindu pilgrims to their daily lives, most pilgrimage studies focus on the "journey's destination—the riverbank, the temple town, the lake, or mountain shrine with little attention to its closure or return lap. The student of pilgrimage, then, interviews and observes pilgrims as pilgrims in the context of their journey's goal, but not of its end" (1988, 1). Gold marks the end of the journey as home, the place where pilgrims almost always return and begin again the daily rhythm of living. She is not the only researcher to address the importance of the return in pilgrimage. Especially in the case of Islamic pilgrimage, or *hajj*, in which the return pilgrim from Mecca and Medina assumes a new social status and title (*hajji*) as a result of the devotional act, researchers have discussed how the homecomers, with their knowledge acquired at the holy Islamic center, can influence social practices and understandings (Ferme 1994; Campo 1995). Most often, though, in the Christian context, there are few rites of return or reincorporation that greet a return pilgrim or returnees in general (compare Schutz 1945; and Meintel 1973).

This lack of attention to the return has both theoretical and methodological components. In general, scant attention has been placed on the theme of ritual aftermaths. The dominant Western post-Enlightenment organizing paradigm of progress and the view of life as a line have influenced the reading of pilgrimage as a linear narrative (compare Lee 1949; see also Harbsmeier 1986). As Gold (1988) observes, the focus is on the pilgrim's journey and action at the goal. The return seems to be culturally constructed as unimportant, uninteresting, or simply unnoticed, since it is not a direction in which Western thought usually turns. Instead, metaphors of breaking new ground, forward progress, and discovery are privileged. In contrast, expressions like "going backwards" and "going in circles" are pejorative in tone.

The metaphor of life as a line, found in secular thought, parallels a Christian worldview in which one's finite earthly journey follows the one-way metaphorical path toward the celestial heaven or toward Christ.[6] In contrast, Hindu pilgrimages (*tirthas*) often emphasize circumambulation around a sacred center, with many overlapping local, regional, and national circuits. Diana Eck comments that "Tirtha . . . is a word of passage. It refers not to the goal, but to the way, the path one travels" (1981, 325). Rather than the finite linear Christian journey, Hindu pilgrimage "is a process of ending the endless journey of life and death" (Saraswati 1985, 101). Here, going in circles is a meritorious act, not something to disparage. In contrast to Hindu sacred geography, which literalizes the metaphor of life as a circle, Christian sites tend to be scattered randomly on the countryside, linked by zigzagging lines, and are reached by a linear journey (see Nolan and Nolan 1989). The pilgrimage to Santiago is a good example. The pilgrimage roads begin from scattered points and all lead to the same goal, which in the Middle Ages was thought to be the end of the earth, a metaphorical heaven (Alonso Romero 1993, 7–8). Now the pilgrimage is marked by conspicuous yellow arrows that guide the pilgrim clearly in a one-way direction to Santiago. Rarely do modern pilgrims consider returning home by foot and bicycle, as they came.

The lack of emphasis on the return can also be understood as a methodological problem: how does one do an anthropological study of a moving population that shares a common destination but not a common home? One of the challenges for ethnography in the twenty-first century will be to create effective "multi-sited ethnography," using Marcus's term, in which the focus of study is the "circulation of cultural meanings, objects, and identities in diffuse time and space" (1995, 96). Studies of both pilgrimage and tourism lack adequate models to address the return from, and outcomes of, journeys. This problem arises in part from the dispersion of travelers once they return home (assuming the mode of travel is not a community-based journey). Despite convincing processual models of pilgrimage and tourism, the analyses appear to begin and to end with the process of journeying to the destination, rather than to focus on the reincorporation of travelers into their social groups at home.

Before discussing the literal turning around and going home, I focus first on the fluidity and the relativity of the end: where does the journey end, and when does the return home begin? It was clear from my research that pilgrims often come to different kinds of "endings" in their journeys that do not correspond to the geographical destination. Some participants "arrived" at certain points on their inner journeys that made the geographical end in Santiago irrelevant. For example, a French computer programmer in his late forties, who first made the pilgrimage as a physical challenge, returned home and later felt dissatisfied with the outcome. He realized that he had simply replicated the rhythm of his daily life "as a race" from which he had hoped to flee. After these reflections about the first journey, on the second pilgrimage he felt that he reached a point along the way when his goal and his desire merged, and he achieved the sense of "learning to be" rather than racing to the finish. When we met, he was still ten days away from Santiago. He said that since he had reached this inner realization he was now "just walking." The inner work and goal had already been reached. Similar to this Frenchman, pilgrims often begin to anticipate the end and the return before reaching their destination. For some, the approach to Santiago is tinged with ambivalence and anxiety. These pilgrims express regret that there is not enough time left on the journey to complete their inner work, or they explain that they simply do not want to end the adventure. These feelings lead some to change their rhythm and speed to put off the arrival, while others are eager to reach the long-anticipated and imagined goal with triumph and pride (see Haab 1996, part 2; 1992). These same feelings are mirrored upon arrival in Santiago.

While some pilgrims try to create a transitional period between the Camino and home—a time of reflection—most participants immediately return home, and the structures of society quickly bracket the experience. Many find themselves back at work within twenty-four or forty-eight hours of taking off their boots and backpacks, with little or no time to reflect on the journey's impact. Others are eager to return and share with their families the joys and stories of the journey. Usually, though, the return is tinged with the sadness of saying good-bye to new friends and to an experience that for many is "extraordinary" (as one Englishwoman in her forties put it) or "one of the most marvelous trips of my life" (as a Spanish man in his late twenties said). Some pilgrims, especially Catholic, may see the arrival in Santiago as the beginning of a spiritual journey to be continued in daily life.

Other pilgrims do, though, extend their journeys or plan a period of "closure" (a personalized rite of reincorporation), anticipating that the return home will be difficult.[7] The most common post-Santiago destination is the spit of land that forms a dramatic geographic end point, located on the Atlantic coast eighty kilometers west of Santiago: Finisterre, the medieval end of the earth. Most often arriving at this ruggedly beautiful site by bus, pilgrims search for and often find closure in reaching a point where forward progress is no longer possible. Many wait for the sun to set into the flat horizon of the endless sea, imagine a connection to their Celtic ancestors, and experience a symbolic death and rebirth by bathing in the Atlantic or burning their clothing in rites of purification. Others simply gaze and contemplate.

In order to study the return with a dispersed population of thousands, I decided to follow the same methods used by pilgrims seeking to maintain connections to the Camino: corresponding with pilgrims in fifteen countries; visiting other pilgrims at their homes in such countries as Spain, England, and Germany; attending Friends of the Camino meetings and conferences of Jacobean studies; and returning to the Camino as a refuge attendant, or *hospitalera*.[8] Since my work involved a "multi-sited ethnography," I chose not to study the pilgrimage from a fixed point, in Santiago or at a particular point along the way. Working in six refuges over a three-month period, as well as living in Santiago for six months meeting pilgrims as they arrived, allowed me to meet a diverse group of pilgrims and to understand the production of the pilgrimage at many sites and on various levels of experience. The Camino pilgrimage is not "of" a single place but a collectivity of many places. In order to understand how the Camino continues to influence pilgrims' daily lives, I wrote to pilgrims at intervals of three months, six months, and a year after their return home. Rather than use questionnaires, I asked several open-ended as well as individualized, personal questions about the journey based on my previous relationship and talks with each pilgrim. I have maintained a correspondence with a more limited group since 1994. In addition, I have both formally and informally interviewed hundreds of pilgrims who did the Camino prior to 1980 and in the years since then to see what role, if any, the pilgrimage plays in their lives.

Anthropologist E. Alan Morinis suggests that "The return to the everyday is a component of almost every pilgrimage. While the sacred place is the source of the power and salvation, it is at home once again that the effects of power are incorporated into life and what salvation is gained is confirmed. The return journey and the reincorporation of the pilgrim into social life are the test of the pilgrimage. Has there been change? Will it last?" (1992, 27; see also Coleman and Elsner 1995, 207). Morinis assumes in this statement that the "function" of pilgrimage is to produce change and that it is only once the pilgrim is at home that the effects of the sacred are realized and cemented. While pilgrimages may be oriented toward change, they are also made to renew or express faith and local identity and even to maintain the status quo. A change of health or an inner state may be desired, but a pilgrim may also simply demonstrate gratitude through his or her journey.

Most often, going home is viewed with ambivalence by Santiago pilgrims. Many describe a period of adjustment common to people (such as anthropologists after fieldwork, exchange students, Peace Corps workers, children after summer camp) who return home after extended stays in other countries or communities. As Meintel suggests, "the most important 'shocks' to be encountered by those who enter another culture or subculture are those of self-discovery. Revelations about oneself may become clear only upon return home; moreover they may also be engendered by everyday social experiences in one's own cultural setting" (1973, 47). Depending on how deeply the person felt impacted by the Camino, the adjustment may be difficult and may result in personal, professional, and familial changes. The returned pilgrim may unexpectedly find himself or herself viewing daily life with different eyes and realize that perhaps the changes are coming from within, those of Meintel's "self-discovery." Daily life may not seem as relevant, exciting, and open as being on the road. Moreover, the abrupt experience of return rarely allows most people to process the weeks and miles. Feeling "disoriented" is common; the speed of motorized transit is alienating and may even create a feeling of vertigo. Most participants cannot remember any other time in their lives when they passed thirty days without getting in a car or a bus. Many miss the clear sense of direction that the Camino provides.

While many pilgrims find themselves disoriented, others feel prepared to "conquer the world" when they turn around to go home. The vast majority of pilgrims describe their pilgrimage experiences as positive, rewarding, and surprising. Most would consider repeating the pilgrimage, having gained spiritually, personally, physically, and socially more than they ever imagined. A Spanish painter from Barcelona told me how he regained his desire to paint while making the pilgrimage after a two-year depression and divorce. Along the Camino, he produced hundreds of watercolors and later held an exhibition in Santiago. He not only continued to paint but began to participate occasionally in meetings and activities of the Friends of the Pilgrims association in Barcelona, and he has repeated the pilgrimage three more times in successive years since 1993. The pilgrimage may translate for some pilgrims into a renewed sense of appreciation for and commitment to their family or a desire to pursue a personal project or to follow through on or make a decision.

Sociologist Alfred Schutz, commenting on the first response of the homecomer to the return, suggests that "Home shows—at least at the beginning—an unaccustomed face" (1945, 369). Not only does home often appear different to the returned pilgrim but the returnee may also present an "unaccustomed face" to those who await his or her return. Friends and family may comment on or notice differences in the returned pilgrim. A Spanish chemistry student in his twenties wrote to me a month after returning, "Now that I have returned my friends tell me that I have changed a lot (I hope for the good) and on a personal level the Camino has given me many things, all of them very good (even, at times, from the bad you learn)." What friends and family notice may be visual differences (tan, weight loss, muscle tone) or even more subtle changes that are often an exteriorization of what has been garnered on the inner journey. A new bodily confidence, a glow or shine in the face, a positive attitude, and a sense of renovation are common. A fifty-eight-year-old American woman, who walked from León alone for two weeks, wrote six months after completing the pilgrimage, "When my husband, son and Spanish friends greeted me with a bouquet of wildflowers at the Alicante airport [in southeastern Spain] where I flew from Santiago—they met a different person housed in the same body!" In addition, pilgrims return home with material objects from the Camino—photos, the dirty backpack or bicycle pannier, often the shell and a walking stick, numerous stories, and the Compostela and the Pilgrim's Passport. In many of the homes I visited, the pilgrim had framed the Compostela and placed it in a public space within the house. Many pilgrims, though, sense that while friends, family, and coworkers may be interested, curious, or supportive on return, no one really understands what the homecomer is talking about. This sense of lack of comprehension may lead the returned pilgrim to feel a sense of isolation and to seek out ways to maintain contact with the Camino. A common experience for pilgrims in the immediate postreturn period is a time of transition between these two realities: the Camino and home life.

One of the most profound ways that the Camino continues to persist is on the level of memory. Memories are not only visual but often fully sensual. Especially during the first year after returning, pilgrims often describe sudden unexpected "flashbacks." A twenty-eight-year-old Swiss law student wrote that "in the shower, on the tram, at work I suddenly feel the wind, the temperature, the smell. They are very precise memories." Pilgrims often describe how these memories, more than just a pleasant mental return, serve to bring back the feelings of the Camino, recapture what was gained, and remind them of what was important—a type of reorientation to the road. Three years after completing the pilgrimage in 1994, a Belgian business consultant in his fifties wrote, "I am missing the good times on the Camino! In retrospect, it was one of the best periods of my life. Things were so simple: clear objective, little or no constraints, wonderful friends, meetings, walking and resting. . . . I wonder if you've published your thesis . . . please send it to me so that I can remember the good times and the freedom of the Camino." He asked me to help him go back to the Camino through memory to revisit not only the places but the sensations and to feel the freedom again. The Camino is for this man and many other people, as one author puts it, "a place in our souls which we visit when, in other worlds and circumstances, we cannot put on our boots and backpacks and begin another day on the Road to Santiago" (Davidson 1994, xi). Many pilgrims have described returning to the pilgrimage route by car and passing over the spaces they covered walking and being stunned by the clarity of their memories of incidents, events, people, pains, and desires. The landscapes become uniquely marked by stories and experiences of the journey and are often remembered in the body, a type of corporeal memory. A Spanish psychologist put it well when she commented that the experience "was recorded on my body" (*fue grabada en mi cuerpo*).

In terms of what people do with these memories, I have noticed several general trends that I would describe as integration, compromise, and compartmentalization. Victor Turner, writing on pilgrimage and death, remarks, "The plain truth is that pilgrimage does not ensure a major change in religious state—and seldom in secular status—though it may make one a better person, fortified by the graces merited by the hardships and self-sacrifice of the journey" (1992, 37). Here, a potential outcome of pilgrimage is to become "a better person" through the work of the physical journey. But many pilgrimages, especially the modern ones, as Turner also points out, do not involve an arduous journey or self-sacrifice nor, again, is change a goal. Perhaps we need to clarify what is meant by "change." The work of the pilgrim after the return home varies according to the participant and his or her own life world. There are a large group of pilgrims that actively, at least in the short term, try to integrate aspects of the pilgrimage into their daily lives. While some are successful, many flip-flop between a sense of failure and one of achievement on the "pilgrimage of life." The motives and meanings of the journey emerge along the way, and for many participants these continue to evolve over time after the return home. Many pilgrims, and increasingly more each year since the late 1980s, repeat the pilgrimage: to renew the feelings, to meet friends once again, to continue the path of self-discovery, to try new routes, and to revise how the first pilgrimage was made, as well as to avoid the present of their quotidian lives.

The metaphor of trying to live one's life as a pilgrimage is commonly used by returned pilgrims and might mean "to look for silence," to "live in the here and the now," to go more slowly, to simplify one's life, to keep walking and remain physically fit, to be more oriented toward others, to continue the search in daily life, and to be more compassionate. A lawyer from Madrid in his thirties, who decided to reconsider his professional life upon return, wrote, "the important thing is to take each step, live each moment, enjoy each person, and to always be in movement with your eyes open." For some, the journey continues as a spiritual path of prayer, a budding interest in religion, a springboard to other pilgrimages and journeys, and even a conversion. For others, the journey continues as a path of personal growth or leads to other humanitarian interests or a new career. Many feel a strong sense of gratitude towards the Camino. The American woman who felt that she was a different woman in the same body after walking two weeks in 1995, wrote the following in 1997:

> I wanted to pass on one of the continuing threads resulting from my original walk, León to Santiago '95. My journal reflects observations on the need to simplify, shed extra "baggage" of all sorts in my life and the exquisite beauty and freedom of traveling "light." We sold our 10 year old Volvo in June—expecting to buy something with less than 200,000 miles for me to drive "around town." My husband has a "good car" for his commute of 120 miles daily. Sticker shock hit, $20,000 for a car!!! Slowly but *intentionally* we moved to a decision to try being a one-car family (again—long ago, it worked). We live in town and I can walk to most things I want and can use the "family car" for longer points on weekends, days he goes out late. It's freeing. It feels good. I would not have embraced this idea had it not been for the walk. Hurrah for health and the environment!!!

The American woman's case shows how the pilgrimage can continue working its way into people's lives unexpectedly. In "A Journey without End: Reflections on a Pilgrim's Progress," the author, a cultural anthropologist, reflects on the journey to Santiago she made ten years previously: "in a most disconcerting way, I was finding myself transformed by this ancient journey, one that took me not only across the landscape of Spain but also across the landscape of my soul" (Aviva 1996, 65).[9] Though her life led her in many directions after finishing her doctorate, ten years later she returned to the Camino with renewed interest, remembering it as a place of truth and discovery: "This time, however, I do not know what road I travel, except that there are many hidden beneath this one—and, perhaps, beneath the many is the One" (72).

What these people describe complicates Turner's (1992) vague idea that one is made a "better person" or Morinis's (1992) assumption that salvation is confirmed through pilgrimage. An outcome of the journey may be that one feels like or strives to be a better person, but that is not necessarily the case. Similar to Aviva, there are those for whom the Camino continues to have a persuasive impact, at times with success and at other times with failure. A young man of French and English background studying in Paris wrote several months after returning from his second pilgrimage, in which he walked from the French capital, "the ex-pilgrims hurtle forward on the time-track each day one more day of living, sometimes 5 km of living; sometimes 25 km; sometimes 40; sometimes none." Many want to bring back home this "energy" garnered while making the Camino but oftentimes find it difficult. Some returned pilgrims recall continuing to search for yellow arrows in their hometowns or cities and find themselves disoriented and lost on an inner level as well. A Canadian university student wrote five months after returning, "it is a time of great transformations and changes but I have no idea what they are. As a result I feel fragile and vulnerable. They are odd feelings for me to admit as I have always fought for the impression of confidence, faith in myself, passion. I believe they are there, and truly mine, I just have to reclaim them." Others find that integrating the Camino's discoveries into home life would compromise work or family relationships in ways that the returned pilgrims were not ready or willing to accept, owing to the associated sacrifices. It can become a painful inner struggle to make these two realities compatible. As a French psychologist in his forties told me, "Once your eyes have been opened [to the hypocrisies of one's life and the possibilities for change] it is impossible to close them again."

Another general trend, despite the description of the pilgrimage as very positive, is "compartmentalization." Maureen, a character in David Lodge's novel *Therapy,* walks to Santiago and has a sexual encounter upon arrival there with the main character, a man who has made part of the pilgrimage to pursue her. Maureen's comment, rejecting his marriage proposal, sums up well the pattern of compartmentalization: "'It's been wonderful,' she said. 'But it's like the whole pilgrimage, a kind of kink in time, when the ordinary rules of life don't apply. When I go home, I'll be married to Bede again'" (Lodge 1995, 316). Rather than seeing continuity between the two realities of experience (the pilgrimage and home life), a number of pilgrims treat them as distinct. As an inversion of daily life, what occurs on the Camino is understood as "out of time and place." Affairs among pilgrims are not uncommon, and experimentation of many types is frequent. Some pilgrims conclude that these experiences are bounded within the space of the Camino, and there they remain. Often suggesting that the Camino is not "real life" and what occurs during the pilgrimage pertains only to the journey, such pilgrims tend to see the Camino as an island of experience. While the Camino is often remembered as very positive, it does not represent for these individuals a point of personal change. It may lead to friendships and to repetition of the Camino but not as an inner way that guides future actions. A Spanish man in his late twenties commented on the disappointment he felt after having a reunion with his new friends from the Camino: "you know that for me making the Camino was, among other things, a liberation, or better, the confirmation of a liberation. For my friends the experience is different. For them the Camino has been above all a holiday, a beautiful parenthesis in the middle of the quotidian, and once over, nothing has changed." Many pilgrims enjoy playing the part while on the road and taking the "fringe benefits of being a pilgrim" (as one Dutch man put it), but they find little motive to continue the metaphor of life as a pilgrimage after the journey unless it has made an impact on them at some inner level.

Others, especially (retired) men, become "serial pilgrims," repeating the pilgrimage one to three or more times a year, year after year. With barely time to contemplate the outcome of the journey, they are on the road again, often presenting themselves as "experts" or taking great pride in the fact that they have done it five, ten, or fifteen times. When I asked them why they repeat, many spoke of the friendships, the places they know, and the people they have met. These serial pilgrims rarely mention any type of personal change. The idea of being "addicted" to the Camino is alluded to frequently among pilgrims, and sometimes the notion of addiction is used jokingly to refer to the way people get hooked (*enganchado*) to the pilgrimage or, in the pejorative sense, to describe those who incessantly repeat. One negative aspect of the serial pilgrims is that, instead of moving toward the pilgrims' generally understood ideal of humility, insight, and respect for others, they tend to believe that their own authenticity is increased, that they have rights of ownership over the Camino and its refuges, and that they are entitled to special treatment because they are pilgrims. Being a pilgrim becomes a very comfortable habit for some, often those who consider themselves the most "authentic."

One final pattern I have noticed in the postpilgrimage period involves those few people who feel that the Camino has had little or no impact on their lives. I have observed this reaction usually among men who are experienced long-distance travelers or walkers and who are accustomed to many of the sensations that pilgrims often experience for the first time, including the types of easy contacts among fellow travelers, the sense of freedom, the power and challenge of solitude, and the changes in perception of time and space. As one American, a self-defined "long-distance walker" who was thinking about repeating the Camino or looking for another walk in Italy, reflected, "I am in love with the *route*. I think it is wonderful that long-distance routes exist where a soul can take off on foot, walk-walk-walk and think about his or her life, sort things out in his or her mind, get a little freer of the past" (emphasis added). The Camino is just another route, albeit a special one, for this man on his continuing journeys.

The pilgrimage also has lasting social implications for the lives of many returned pilgrims. Another testament to the Camino's influence has been the formation on a wide scale of Friends of the Camino associations located in the countries and communities of the returnees. Many pilgrims feel at a loss upon return, since they live in societies where there is little if any social or ritual recognition for the homecomer. Consequently, to fight isolation as well as to continue their connection to the pilgrimage, returnees have formed associations. Although these began to form in the 1950s in France and Spain with the aim of preserving the patrimony of the Camino and developing the study of the Middle Ages, in the early 1980s the associations began to have a new emphasis: providing assistance and information for potential pilgrims. There was also a shift in the membership of the associations from primarily students of medieval studies to those who had made the pilgrimage on foot or by bicycle. The associations provide a public space for returned pilgrims to share the experience of the return with fellow pilgrims, help future pilgrims, and publish their experiences in association bulletins, as well as to continue their connection to the Camino through leadership roles, friendships, and participation in association activities. These new pilgrims' associations began first in England and then spread to Germany, Belgium, Holland, and Spain and later to Switzerland, the United States, France, and even Brazil. In each country, several associations may exist, and membership numbers in the thousands. In Spain alone there are over thirty associations, twenty of which are members of the "Spanish Federation" of associations formed in the late 1980s, which receives funding from the national Ministry of Tourism as well as the Council of Europe.

Pilgrims also continue the pilgrimage after the return home through weekend retreats, reunions, and gatherings. In the mid-1990s in Spain, two priests began to hold weekend meetings with a spiritual-religious emphasis twice a year for returned pilgrims to process their experiences along the way and help reincorporate the Camino into daily life. In addition, the strong friendships formed on the Camino by crossing linguistic, age, class, and geographic barriers are often maintained by yearly reunions and letters. Alternatively, reunions and gatherings of pilgrims who have not previously met one another are occasionally held in local areas. For example, an American woman told me she was planning a gathering ("it can't be a reunion because we've never met each other") in her hometown "of people who have shared an experience—to most of us, an extra-ordinary experience!" She further comments, "If there are only a few gathered, I'm sure it will be worthwhile."

The formation of new social relationships through the Camino is often one of the most highly valued elements of the pilgrimage. These pilgrims are effectively creating the types of connections and the sense of belonging that many found lacking in their personal lives before making the pilgrimage. In addition, pilgrims often feel a sense of gratitude and loyalty to the Camino as a whole. The gifts received along the way are numerous and are distributed throughout the journey. Moreover, the sense of gratitude may be related to acts of kindness, but often it is expressed for intangible gifts over the course of the journey: for sunsets, places that allow insight, unexpected encounters, and even pain. Consequently, a number of pilgrims strive to return something to the Camino. This reciprocity is sometimes carried out directly through volunteering in a refuge, assisting in an association, helping another pilgrim, or donating money to the Camino. A more indirect form of reciprocity for the gifts of the Camino involves contributing to other humanitarian causes. As a direct result of the pilgrimage, participants have been involved in fund-raisers for charities, worked in orphanages, and even gone to India to work with Mother Teresa. While these activities are more the exception than the rule, they signal the role that the pilgrimage can play in influencing some people's lives and the belief that life "on the Camino" can be transferred to the "real world."

As a result of the pilgrimage, an informal transnational community of "Santiago pilgrims" has formed, linked by a shared experience, rather than by motive, religion, ethnicity, or locality. The nature of this shared experience is essentially founded on movement, described by one German seminary student as "going the human speed." Interpreting travel on the Camino and its meanings reveals that these pilgrims implicitly reject, at least temporarily, consumer society and technology that privileges speed in favor of a reality that is person-oriented and "closer to the ground."

Notes

This essay is based on my larger work, *Pilgrim Stories: On and Off the Road to Santiago* (1998).

1. One aspect of the reanimation has been the development of the construct "to do the whole Camino," meaning traveling the stretch from Roncesvalles in Spain or St. Jean-Pied-de-Port in France and following the more or less historical reconstruction of the routes to Santiago that pass through the major cities of Pamplona, Burgos, León, Astorga, and Ponferrada and many intervening villages and hamlets.

2. All quotes are taken from letters in my possession, unless otherwise noted. All translations are my own.

3. There is a complicated discourse on authenticity among pilgrims of various types (walkers and cyclists, most generally) that has arisen with the reanimation, a discourse that establishes hierarchies of difference and relates to how pilgrims believe the Camino ought to be performed in order for it to be "truly" experienced. See Frey (1998).

4. See Teas (1988, 36) on youth travelers in Nepal and the relationship between austerity and status; also see Adler (1985) and Cohen (1973).

5. Two public institutions that have recognized the potential of pilgrimage to change an individual are the Belgian juvenile penal system and the Belgian organization Oikoten, which seeks to rehabilitate troubled youths. Since the early 1980s, the two have worked together and sent young offenders charged with petty crimes and drug problems on the pilgrimage (one or two at a time) with a monitor, walking over four months from Belgium to Santiago. Being away from home and the environment of crime, living healthily in nature, and learning to rely on one's own strength through the Camino are intended to help motivate the young person to change in his or her daily life. These programs of rehabilitation involving the Camino are also in use in Germany and are being considered in Spain. Significantly, pilgrimages were frequently imposed as penance for crimes by civil and ecclesiastical authorities during the medieval period (Sumption 1975, 98–113).

6. This is a reference to John 14:1 in the New Testament, where Jesus states, "I am the Way."

7. I do not address here the issue of closure in Santiago, which takes many forms, including attendance at the daily Pilgrim's Mass held in the cathedral, one that is well attended by pilgrims, whether or not they consider themselves to be Catholic. See Frey (1998).

8. Part of the Camino's reanimation has also involved the recuperation of medieval models of charity. At least eighty pilgrims' refuges (*refugios, albergues*) have been opened since 1990. The refuges range from simple shelters with space on the floor for eight persons to several-story buildings complete with hot showers, room for ninety pilgrims, kitchen facilities, and bunk beds. Some refuges have been constructed with public money and are run by local or regional governments, while others are based on private donations from Friends of the Camino associations. Others are maintained by parishes and religious institutions. The refuges were originally financed locally and with pilgrims' donations, and since the mid-1990s many refuges have begun to charge a nominal fee, ranging from 3 to 5 Euros (approximately US$2.00 to US$3.50). Pilgrims may stay in the refuges if they carry the Pilgrim's Passport, a document that contributes to

the continuing reanimation and increasing bureaucratization and rationalization of the pilgrimage. Especially in the summer, volunteers (*hospitaleros*) spend between fifteen and thirty days in many of the refuges and attend to the pilgrims, orienting them to the village, helping with physical problems, providing an open ear, maintaining the cleanliness of the refuge, and offering advice.

9. Aviva wrote her doctoral dissertation on the Camino de Santiago. See Feinberg 1985.

References Cited

Adler, Judith. 1985. "Youth on the Road: Reflections on the History of Tramping." *Annals of Tourism Research* 12:335–54.

———. 1994. "The Holy Man as Traveler and Travel Attraction: Early Christian Asceticism and the Moral Problematic of Mobility." Department of Sociology, Memorial University of Newfoundland.

Alonso Romero, Fernando. 1993. *O Camiño de Fisterra*. Madrid: Xerais.

Aviva, Elyn. 1996. "A Journey without End: Reflections on a Pilgrim's Progress." *Quest* (Summer): 65–73.

Campo, Juan Eduardo. 1995. *The Other Sides of Paradise*. Columbia: University of South Carolina Press.

Cohen, Erik. 1973. "Nomads from Affluence: Notes on the Phenomenon of Drifter-Tourism." *International Journal of Comparative Sociology* 14 (1–2): 89–103.

Coleman, Simon, and John Elsner. 1995. *Pilgrimage Past and Present in the World Religions*. Cambridge, Mass.: Harvard University Press.

Davidson, Linda Kay. 1994. Preface to *The Pilgrimage to Santiago de Compostela: A Comprehensive, Annotated Bibliography*. Ed. M. Dunn and Linda K. Davidson. ix–xi. New York: Garland.

Eade, John, and Michael J. Sallnow. 1991. Introduction to *Contesting the Sacred: The Anthropology of Christian Pilgrimage*. Ed. John Eade and Michael Sallnow. 1–29. London: Routledge.

Eck, Diana. 1981. "India's Tirthas: 'Crossings' in Sacred Geography." *History of Religions* 20:323–44.

Feinberg, Ellen. 1985. "Strangers and Pilgrims on the Camino de Santiago in Spain: The Perpetuation and Recreation of Meaningful Performance." Ph.D. diss., Princeton University.

Ferme, Mariane. 1994. "What 'Alhaji Airplane' Saw in Mecca, and What Happened When He Came Home: Ritual Transformation in a Mende Community (Sierra Leone)." In *Syncretism/Anti-syncretism: The Politics of Religious Synthesis*. Ed. Rosalind Shaw and Charles Stewart. 27–44. London: Routledge.

French, Reginald M., trans. 1974. *The Way of a Pilgrim*. New York: Ballantine.

Frey, Nancy L. 1998. *Pilgrim Stories: On and Off the Road to Santiago*. Berkeley: University of California Press.

Gold, Ann G. 1988. *Fruitful Journeys. The Ways of Rajasthani Pilgrims*. Berkeley: University of California Press.

Graburn, Nelson H. H. 1977. "Tourism: The Sacred Journey." In *Hosts and Guests: The Anthropology of Tourism*. Ed. Valene L. Smith. 17–31. Philadelphia: University of Pennsylvania Press.

————. 1983. "The Anthropology of Tourism." In "The Anthropology of Tourism," ed. Nelson H. H. Graburn. Special issue, *Annals of Tourism Research* 10:9–33.

————. 1995. "Tourism, Modernity, Nostalgia." In *The Future of Anthropology: Its Relevance to the Contemporary World*. Ed. Akbar S. Ahmed and Cris N. Shore. 158–78. London: Athlone.

Haab, Barbara. 1992. "Weg und Wanderlung." In *Symbolik von Weg und Reise*. Ed. Paul Michel. 137–62. Bern: Verlag Peter Lang.

————. 1996. "The Way as an Inward Journey: An Anthropological Enquiry into the Spirituality of Present-day Pilgrims to Santiago." Trans. H. Nelson. *Confraternity of Saint James Bulletin* 55:16–32 (pt. 1), 56:17–36 (pt. 2).

Harbsmeier, Michael. 1986. "Pilgrim's Space: The Centre Out There in Comparative Perspective." *Temenos* 22:57–77.

Lee, Dorothy. 1949. "Being and Value in Primitive Culture." *Journal of Philosophy* 46:401–15.

Lodge, David. 1995. *Therapy*. New York: Penguin.

Marcus, George E. 1995. "Ethnography in/of the World System: The Emergence of Multi-Sited Ethnography." *Annual Review of Anthropology* 24:95–117.

Meintel, Deidre A. 1973. "Strangers, Homecomers and Ordinary Men." *Anthropological Quarterly* 46:47–58.

Morinis, E. Alan. 1992. "Introduction: The Territory of the Anthropology of Pilgrimage." In *Sacred Journeys: The Anthropology of Pilgrimage*. Ed. E. Alan Morinis. 1–27. Westport, Conn.: Greenwood.

Nolan, Mary Lee, and Sidney Nolan. 1989. *Christian Pilgrimage in Modern Western Europe*. Chapel Hill: University of North Carolina Press.

Pfaffenberger, Bryan. 1983. "Serious Pilgrims and Frivolous Tourists: The Chimera of Tourism in the Pilgrimages of Sri Lanka." *Annals of Tourism Research* 10:57–74.

Saraswati, Baidyanath. 1985. "Kashi Pilgrimage: The End of an Endless Journey." In *Dimensions of Pilgrimage*. Ed. Makhan Jha. 91–104. New Delhi: Inter-India.

Schutz, Alfred. 1945. "The Homecomer." *American Journal of Sociology* 50:369–76.

Smith, Valene L. 1992. "Introduction: The Quest in Guest." In "Pilgrimage and Tourism: The Quest in Guest," Ed. Valene L. Smith. Special issue, *Annals of Tourism Research* 19:1–17.

Sumption, Jonathan. 1975. *Pilgrimage: An Image of Medieval Religion*. London: Faber and Faber.

Teas, Jane. 1988. "'I'm Studying Monkeys: What Do You Do?'—Youth and Travelers in Nepal." *Kroeber Anthropological Society Papers* 67–68:35–41.

Turner, Victor. 1992. "Death and the Dead in the Pilgrimage Process." In *Blazing the Trail*. Ed. Edith Turner. 29–47. Tucson: University of Arizona Press.

Turner, Victor, and Edith L. B. Turner. 1978. *Image and Pilgrimage in Christian Culture: Anthropological Perspectives*. New York: Columbia University Press.

6   Tourism and Holy Week in León, Spain

MARK TATE

This chapter discusses the successful promotion of tourism for the ritual of Holy Week in the city of León, in northwest Spain. I focus on this promotion during the early 1980s through the activities of a penitential confraternity, El Dulce Nombre de Jesús Nazareno, which performs a procession each year on Holy Friday.

Most of the first part of this chapter examines the contents of an application submitted by that confraternity to the Office of the Secretary of State for Tourism in 1983.[1] I show how the confraternity identifies its own procession as a worthwhile experience for tourists for nonreligious reasons. In order to explain why the confraternity and its supporters formally sought to attract a nonlocal, secular audience in the early 1980s, I offer a historical perspective on Holy Week in León of the kind that has been suggested by Behar (1990) and Silverman (1979). A long-term perspective situates the recent interest in tourism in relation to a national political history and the rapid expansion of Holy Week in the 1940s. I then show why it is misleading to make the assumption that there is a categorical distinction between "insider locals" and "outsider tourists." The final section of the chapter concerns the way in which the promise of material benefits from the development of tourism in Holy Week limits the intensity of a local controversy in which it is claimed that the processions are nothing more than acts of "folklore."[2]

• • •

In 1908, *El Diario de León* printed a front-page article entitled "Our Processions." The topic of the article was the annual processions of Holy Week. The article praised the confraternities of Holy Week for their role in the processions of Holy Friday but severely criticized their *pasos,* the named statues of Christ and the Virgin Mary carried in the processions: "The truth is that the *pasos* were always ugly, bad, and anti-aesthetic . . . they neither excite piety nor move our devotion." *El Diario de León* was not alone in its criticism of the *pasos* of the confraternities at the turn of the century. In the previous year, a sixteen-page pamphlet entitled *La Semana Santa en León* (Maron 1907) was published that described Holy Week as it was performed in the city of León around this time. The author, H. Maron, characterizes the *pasos* of the confraternity El Dulce Nombre de Jesús Nazareno as "offering nothing in particular, neither in artistic nor material value" (13). He repeats the same remark about the *pasos* of the other two confraternities that performed processions on Holy Friday.

These criticisms refer to particular qualities of the *pasos.* At the turn of the century, the statues were mounted on modest wooden platforms with handles at either end, decorated to some extent with flowers, candles, and lamps and were carried on the shoulders of four male porters from churches through the streets and plazas of the city on Holy Friday. A *paso* was, and remains, the centerpiece in the performance of Holy Week processions, because its imagery of the sorrowful Virgin and the crucified Christ conveys the principal symbolic theme of the ritual: the passion, death, burial, and resurrection of Christ. It is worth noting how the criticisms of the *pasos* of the confraternities suggest by implication that their processions were failing to give to Holy Friday the kind of importance that it deserved in the wider context of Holy Week. From Maron's description, it is clear that Holy Friday was the climax of Holy Week. So the "always ugly" quality of the *pasos* at the turn of the century diminished not only the "aesthetic" and "religious" virtues of particular processions before the populace of the city but also the centrality of Holy Friday within Holy Week as a whole.

Three-quarters of a century later, in 1983, Julián Marne Martínez, the *abad,* or titular head, of El Dulce de Nombre de Jesús Nazareno, submitted an eight-page application to the secretary of state for tourism requesting that the procession of the confraternity on Holy Friday known as *Los Pasos* and a related act called *La Ronda* receive the official designation of "National Touristic Interest" (*Interés Turístico Nacional*) (Marne Martínez 1983). The application was supported by letters of recommendation from the secretary general of the civil government (Aparicio Carreño 1983), the mayor of León (Morano 1983), the vicar general of the Diocese of León (Gutierrez Tejerina 1983), the president of the provincial council (President of the Provincial Council 1983), and the secretary general of the Chamber of Commerce and Industry (Díaz Carro

1983). All of these letters shared the point of view that it was the "traditional" and "popular" character of *Los Pasos* that was attracting tourists to León during Holy Week to see the procession. In response to the application, a representative from the secretary of state for tourism visited León during Holy Week in 1984, and by 1985 the application had been approved.

I have begun this section with two historical anecdotes in order to show that a general contrast can be drawn between the Holy Week confraternity processions at the start of the last century and those of the latter part. The contrast is a particularly interesting one because the confraternity El Dulce Nombre de Jesús Nazareno is singled out at the start of the century for the poor quality of its *pasos* but by the 1980s is acclaimed by major public figures for its procession of *pasos,* which is declared to be a key source of tourism in the city during Holy Week. Throughout this chapter, I refer to this paradoxical contrast in an effort to untangle its significance. I start by showing how the application portrays the confraternity, its *pasos,* and its procession as both "traditional" and "popular."

In the documentation that accompanies the 1983 application (Marne Martínez 1983, 6), the twelve *pasos* of El Dulce Nombre de Jesús Nazareno are collectively described as "impressive." Seven hundred and twenty-six brothers of the confraternity are listed as *braceros,* or porters, of these *pasos.*[3] Under a section entitled "Artistic Value of *Los Pasos,*" the title of each *paso* is accompanied by the name of the sculptor who is known or assumed to have created the statue(s) and the year or approximate century when the statue was finished. Nine of the *pasos* date from the twentieth century, and of these, six date from the period of the Franco regime (1939–77). Three statues are dated from the seventeenth century. The documentation lists the order of appearance of the *pasos* in the procession, which also includes four sections of musicians. Two sections come from the band of cornets and drums of the confraternity, one is a military band, also of cornets and drums, and the last is the musical band from the town hall of León. Six of the *pasos* are accompanied by official escorts (*escoltas*), all but one of which come from security forces stationed in the city.[4] In sum, the statues of a majority of the *pasos* are clearly of contemporary creation and, without exception, their platforms are much larger in scale than those of their early twentieth-century counterparts. Evidently, the procession as a whole had been expanded and embellished considerably since the years when the harsh criticisms of *El Diario de León* and Maron appeared in print.

The documentation of the application (Marne Martínez 1983) also provides a historical overview of El Dulce Nombre de Jesús Nazareno and its procession. The historical sketch of the confraternity begins with its foundation in the Dominican monastery of Santo Domingo in 1611, when a "group of Leoneses" (citizens of León), motivated by "fervor for the 'Day of the Cross' [Holy Friday]," decided to establish the confraternity "to serve God our Lord and to the honor and glory of the Most Holy Name of Jesus Nazarene" (3). Notice how the founders of the present-day confraternity are portrayed as being citizens of León rather than Dominicans from the monastery. The historical sketch goes on to emphasize the continuity of the confraternity through the centuries, despite moments of crisis, such as the apparent loss of *pasos,* archives, altars, and other "patrimonial" objects when the monastery of Santo Domingo was burned by Napoleonic troops in 1809, an event that is depicted as "the greatest setback of its history."

The documentation also describes the procession route of *Los Pasos* as one of "the greatest merits of the confraternity," because of the way that the route maintains "the finest of the ancient processional itinerary" (7). The latter refers to the direction of the procession through the narrow streets and picturesque plazas of the old quarter of the city. The account also mentions that the procession passes by, and therefore recognizes and incorporates, particular "historical landmarks" of the old quarter, such as the cathedral, the basilica of San Isidoro, and four convents. It then notes that today the procession also moves through new parts of the city. These areas include some of the spacious avenues and plazas of the recently developed modern city, including the huge plaza of Santo Domingo, the universally recognized social center of the city. The fact that the confraternity had recently adjusted its procession route so that it now incorporated the new center of the city is alluded to in the application documentation as a kind of necessity, since the old quarter's streets could no longer accommodate "the enormous public" that assembles to see *Los Pasos.* Thus, the documentation of the application portrays the confraternity as embodying a nearly timeless "tradition" that connects the past with the present through the annual performance of its procession of Holy Friday, a tradition that has prevailed even through a major crisis. The tradition is not simply a religious tradition of Holy Week but even more clearly a civil-religious tradition that establishes a unity between the historical and present-day citizens of León who created and maintained the confraternity. Moreover, the confraternity's procession also forges material links between the past and present of León, since the performance of the procession is inseparable from principal landmarks in the city's central landscape, both "ancient" and "modern."

The letters of recommendation that accompany the application to the secretary of state for tourism reiterate the theme of tradition in the confraternity and its procession. "Antiquity," "continuity," "originality," and "popularity" are, for example, the words used in the letter from the secretary general of the civil government (Aparicio Carreño 1983). The letters emphasize the popular character of *Los Pasos* in terms of the large membership of the confraternity and the large size of the audience that watches the procession on Holy Friday. The letter from the mayor, for example, declares that the "popular tradition" of El Dulce Nombre de Jesús Nazareno is such that "there are few homes in the city that do not have a 'brother' from this confraternity." He is emphatic about the size of the audience and its origins: "It is massive, from all points of the province [of León] and all of Spain [and] foreign tourism is growing year after year. . . . in the present year it is estimated to have been more than thirty thousand persons" (Morano 1983).[5] The letter from the vicar general of the Diocese of León is similar: "[*Los Pasos*] awakens great interest, attention, and the assistance of numerous of the faithful and citizens both from the city and from elsewhere and also from foreign tourists" (Gutierrez Tejerina 1983). The letter from the Chamber of Commerce and Industry certifies that the "important number of persons" who come to León to see the procession has had a "notable effect on the commercial [sector] and especially on the hotel and restaurant sector."

• • •

The basic assertion of the application is that tourism has developed in León during Holy Week as a consequence of the traditional and popular character of *Los Pasos* and that its performance is therefore deserving of official recognition from the secretary of state for tourism. One unstated assumption in the application is that there is an inherent good in the relationship between *Los Pasos* and the consumptive practice of tourism. This assumption seems to be based on the notion that tourists find the traditional Holy Friday procession desirable. The application argues that *Los Pasos* embodies a performance of "long-standing tradition," imbued with an aura of authenticity by virtue of the fact that it re-creates a performance today that comes from "a long time ago." The drama of the "traditional performance" is highlighted by the particular qualities of *Los Pasos,* including its twelve *pasos* carried by hundreds of brothers, the music of drums and cornets, and the accompaniment of escorts in dress uniform. The appeal of the traditional performance to tourists is also situated spatially within the old quarter of the city, a space that is itself linked with traditional landmarks and architecture and is complemented by its modern counterpart in the new city. All these features suggest that *Los Pasos* benefits tourism by providing visitors to León with a "spectacle of tradition."

What seems to be absent from the assumed connection between *Los Pasos* and tourists is any religious motivation. It is not that mention of religion is absent from the application. As we have seen, the historical sketch of the confraternity specifically states that the original reason for its creation was "to serve God our Lord and to the honor and glory of the Most Holy Name of Jesus Nazarene." By implication, this purpose continues to guide the confraternity today. However, this statement refers to the purpose of the confraternity and its procession. No such religious connection is suggested in the application for tourists. Apart from this statement, only the letter of the vicar that accompanies the application gives any emphasis to the religious significance of *Los Pasos:* "These acts of the confraternity are distinguished by the real interest [that they create] as much from a religious point of view as a cultural and folkloric point of view" (Gutierrez Tejerina 1983). Notice, however, that although the vicar distinguishes between religious and nonreligious interest in *Los Pasos,* he does not suggest any real relationship between religious motivation, tourists, and the procession. The application seems to assume that tourists who come to León to see *Los Pasos* are not motivated by religious fervor but by a desire to experience an urban-based tradition that is religiously oriented. The connection that is made between tourists and *Los Pasos* in the application is therefore a secular one. Indeed, the entire application can be understood as the promotion of a secularized relationship between Holy Week processions and tourism, which, in light of the application's success, gained national legitimacy through the approval of the secretary of state for tourism.

Perhaps the most straightforward way to understand the purpose of the application to the state tourism office is from an economic perspective. The letter from the secretary general of the Chamber of Commerce and Industry makes it quite clear that the relationship between tourism and *Los Pasos* financially benefits the commercial and leisure trades of the city (Díaz Carro 1983). The other public figures who supported the application may also have sought to further the relationship between tourism and the procession in order to advance the needs of the service-based urban economy of León. Yet an exclusively economic explanation for the application does not account for the particular initiative taken by the *abad* of the confraternity to seek the official designation of "National Touristic Interest" for *Los Pasos*. The confraternity did not stand to gain financially from such a distinction. Neither does a strictly economic perspective account for the timing of the application: why did the confraternity and public figures perceive the early 1980s as an appropriate time to support the promotion of tourism during Holy Week? In order to answer this question, it is necessary to situate the application in a wider historical context.

• • •

As mentioned above, the application to the secretary of state for tourism indicates that *Los Pasos* had undergone significant embellishment since the turn of the century. Indeed, at the beginning of the 1980s, the publication of Cayón Waldaliso (1982) entitled *León Semana Santa Cofradía del Dulce Nombre de Jesús Nazareno* pays glowing tribute to the qualities of the twelve *pasos* of the confraternity. Cayón Waldaliso uses adjectives such as "fabulous," "truly impressive," "outstanding," "singularly attractive," and "magnificent" to describe the artistic qualities of the statues of the *pasos* (154, 158, 163, 168, 183). Cayón Waldaliso's narrative may not represent an entirely objective assessment of *Los Pasos,* since he was a brother of the confraternity, as well as its secretary, and a well-known enthusiast of the organization. Even so, from a historical perspective, his description of *Los Pasos* provides additional evidence for the paradoxical contrast mentioned at the beginning of this chapter between the processions at the turn of the century and those of the 1980s.

Cayón Waldaliso's (1982) narrative is also useful because he makes it clear that it was not until the 1940s that a process of embellishment began to take place in the *pasos* of El Dulce Nombre de Jesús Nazareno. This decade is particularly significant, since it marks the full commencement of the Franco era (1939–77), during which Catholicism became a state religion (formally declared in the Concordat of 1953).[6]

The history of Holy Week during the Franco era is a history of expansion. Before 1931, five processions took place during Holy Week. Between 1940 and 1965, eight new processions were introduced, so that each day of the week had at least one procession. Perhaps the most remarkable development of this period was the creation of four new confraternities, making a total of seven for Holy Week.[7] A number of these developments, particularly during the 1940s, took place under the direction of the Diocese of León, but many others were directed by the civilian leadership of the confraternities.

A powerful conformity to public expressions of Catholic identity was characteristic of the Franco era, a conformity that ordinary people, members of the clergy, and leaders of confraternities now refer to with the phrase "imposed religion" (*religión impuesta*). Holy Week became one of many public ritual contexts in which conformity to the official Catholicism of the Franco regime was manifested. This public demonstration of support for the Church was seen, for example, in the participation of conspicuous numbers of civil, Church, and military higher-ups in the presidency of the processions until Franco's death in 1977 when, abruptly, their numbers sharply declined, although some representation has continued.[8] While the Franco regime sought to legitimate itself by fostering the expansion of Catholic rituals, such as León's Holy Week, the particular direction of the embellishments made to processions was mainly in the hands of the civilian leadership of the confraternities. So, in the example of El Dulce Nombre de Jesús Nazareno, decisions about spending money on the renovation or creation of *pasos* were taken by the confraternity's *junta,* or governing council, rather than by the diocese or individual priests. The view of the *junta* was based on the particular and eminently *local* character of its traditional Holy Friday procession in León. Significantly, the same kind of autonomous decision making is maintained by the present-day *junta,* which continues to promote the distinctive character of *Los Pasos* relative to other processions.

By the early 1980s, El Dulce Nombre de Jesús Nazareno had become the largest, most affluent, and most prominent of the seven confraternities of Holy Week in León. Its procession on the morning of Holy Friday received an audience that numbered in the thousands and was widely recognized as "the important one" in Holy Week, much to the envy of rival confraternities. The initiative taken by the *abad* of El Dulce Nombre de Jesús Nazareno in 1983 to apply to the secretary of state for tourism to seek the designation of "National Touristic Interest" for *Los Pasos* was another way to embellish still further the confraternity's position of prominence in Holy Week. Indeed, leaders of other confraternities reacted angrily to the announcement of the application because their processions in particular and Holy Week in León more generally had not been incorporated into the application.

In light of the preceding historical outline, the unanimous support for the application from all branches of civilian government as well as the diocese and the León Chamber of Commerce can be understood as an important development related to the end of the Franco regime and the transition into the subsequent democratic era. That is, the official promotion of tourism that is contained in the application, as well as its eventual success, represents a new source of political legitimacy for Holy Week that has replaced the imposed religion of National Catholicism from the Franco era. In this connection, it is worth emphasizing the application's recognition of plural forms of participation in present-day Holy Week celebrations. As we have seen, the application contains the reasonably clear implication that the promotion of tourism also involves the promotion of secular participation in the performance of a religious and a civil-religious ritual.

Tourism has not been the only source of new legitimacy for Holy Week since the end of the Franco era. Another source has been the town hall. During the early 1980s, the mayor of León emerged as a well-known patron of the processions of Holy Week. His government initiated a significant financial subsidy that was used by the leadership of the confraternities to pay for the annual advertisement of the processions of Holy Week. His government also sponsored and paid for a new *paso* at the collective request of the leadership of the confraternities. The *paso* cost the considerable sum of more than 2 million pesetas (approximately US$15,000). This new *paso* first appeared in the procession of Holy Monday in 1983, the same year that El Dulce Nombre de Jesús Nazareno submitted its application to the secretary of state for tourism. The particular characteristic of the Holy Monday procession is that all seven confraternities participate together. The new *paso* from the town hall was carried by equal numbers of brothers from the seven confraternities. Opponents of the mayor, including brothers in the confraternities, charged that he was using Holy Week as a way to obtain votes for reelection, even though there was no real opposition to the use of public funds for subsidizing the event. These developments show that, in the wake of the Franco era, the mayor and the leadership of the confraternities have sought to portray Holy Week as a characteristically "Leonés tradition," one that belongs to the city and its province. This image of Holy Week as a Leonés tradition is less concerned with the promotion of outsider tourism than with the promotion of the processions as an image of unity among "the people of the province of León" (*el pueblo de León*). Such an image may also have been beneficial to the well-publicized attempts by the mayor to gain popular support for the establishment of the city and province of León as a semiautonomous political unit (*comunidad autónoma*) in the early 1980s, although no explicit connection of this kind was made at the time.[9] It is also significant that the motivations underlying a politician's promotion of Holy Week "for the people" can now be openly challenged through public criticism and the ballot box "by the people." These democratic activities were, of course, not permitted during the Franco era. This example reveals another facet of the plural participation that has developed since the end of the 1970s in Holy Week, although voices of criticism and challenge "from the people" may not have been part of the vision of the political elites who have been tinkering with the imagery of Leonés identity and tradition.

• • •

Perhaps one of the most interesting assumptions in the application to the secretary of state for tourism is the notion that tourists are "outsiders" because they come from other parts of the country and from abroad. The application suggests that the people of León are participants in Holy Week, either actively, as members of a confraternity such as El Dulce Nombre de Jesús Nazareno, or passively, as members of an urban corporate group (*el pueblo de León*) who come together in the streets and plazas as a community to watch processions such as *Los Pasos*. Generally, the application implies that the participation of the Leoneses is distinct from that of tourists because the former are "insiders" and the latter are "outsiders." It is tempting to take this distinction for granted. However, I suggest that the distinction between "outsider" tourists and "insider" Leoneses is neither as "natural" nor as categorical as it might first appear, since there are indications that the previously mentioned secular aspects of the "outsider" tourists' experience of Holy Week processions can also be detected in the experience of the "insider" Leoneses.[10]

The following four paragraphs are drawn from my observations of Holy Week in 1982:

> In the afternoon of Holy Thursday (after 3:00 P.M.), the eve of the performance of *Los Pasos,* most shops, small industries, and offices close until Monday. The working life of the city abruptly comes to a standstill. Bars, restaurants, hotels, cinemas, and discotheques remain open and are unusually busy.

> Advertisements with the title "Holidays of Holy Week" (*Vacaciones de Semana Santa*) listing package holidays at ski and beach resorts in Spain and abroad are commonplace at the travel agencies of the city. Even those who cannot take a holiday at this time find the idea appealing. As one shopkeeper put it to me, "You know, you always want to leave the place where you are . . . a change of air." Interestingly enough, she did not leave the city because, like other merchants, she did not want to miss the opportunity for business from tourists on Holy Saturday, when some shops reopen.

> One immediate result of the suspension of work is considerable movement. The highways to and from the city are heavy with traffic, and the train station and bus depots bustle with activity. Such movement is characterized by people coming to León, some to be reunited with their families, others to visit León to see the processions, and still others—by far a minority—to participate in them. Hotels will be filled to near capacity by the end of the day.

> People are also leaving the city. Some are traveling to villages of the province or destinations further afield to visit their relatives. The more affluent are packing up ski equipment and heading for the mountains of León or elsewhere to spend these days skiing. Still others are traveling to other parts of Spain to see Holy Week processions or quite simply to have a holiday.

Such movement on the eve of *Los Pasos* was characterized to me in the early 1980s as something new to Holy Week and was also linked with the new conception that Holy Week is a "holiday." Consider the following statement from a brother of El Dulce Nombre de Jesús Nazareno who, along with his actual brother and father, carries one of the twelve *pasos* in the *Los Pasos* procession on the morning of Holy Friday:

> Before, Holy Week was when everybody was in the city. . . . One did the *via crucis* in the afternoon of Holy Thursday. . . . The women went from church to church praying an Our Father or three Ave Marias at each station. The whole city lived it. Now, there is a different, more evolved situation. Now, you see that Holy Week is a mini-holiday in which there is a movement of people who go skiing for these five days, or they go to the country or to another city to see

those processions. So, it is a few days of holiday, to leave the city, to see things . . . which did not happen before.

It is not hard to detect a sense of loss in these remarks that contrast the past, when "the whole city lived" Holy Week, with the present, in which Holy Week is a time "to see things" that do not necessarily include religious processions. It is interesting to note that this contrast between past and present Holy Week also implies that women today no longer fulfill religious obligations. The "more evolved situation" of the present day has meant that Holy Week is an occasion to rest, seek entertainment, and travel. Notice also that the brother's remarks refer to people from León, that is, "insiders." The brother's observations reiterate the theme of plural participation in Holy Week. In one dimension of plural participation, local Leoneses can experience Holy Week from afar through the pursuit of leisure activities, rather than living Holy Week from within by, for example, attending church or donning the tunic of a confraternity brother for a procession. While the tourist remains by definition an "outsider" to León, it is clear that the secular experience of the tourist is also shared by local Leoneses. The locals can and do become tourists, like anyone else, simply by departing from the city on a holiday at Holy Week or by viewing a procession such as *Los Pasos* in the same manner as a tourist, namely, as a spectator.

Nonetheless, the assumption that the tourist is an "outsider" to León allows the leadership of the confraternities to deflect what is perhaps the most vexing criticism that they have been faced with, particularly since the early 1980s, namely, that their processions are folklore, in contradistinction to religion. This assertion is made widely, but it receives an especially potent voice when local journalists raise a "religion or folklore" question about the processions in annual interviews with confraternity leaders. The critical connotations of "folklore" go hand in hand with other critical remarks about processions, such as that they are prone to "exhibitionism" and that their *pasos* are "extravagant." Notice that such pejorative remarks are the opposite of those raised about the poor quality of the *pasos* at the turn of the century. The issue that is activated when the question of folklore is raised is not whether the *pasos* of the processions "excite piety" or "move devotion" but whether there is any religion left in Holy Week at all. "Folklore or religion" represents a discourse of the people in which the issue is debated from differing vantage points. The response by leaders of confraternities is that their processions remain acts of religion. Confraternity leaders are well aware, however, that their point of view is not universally shared among the citizenry of León on whose behalf the processions are claimed to be performed. Introducing tourism into the folklore-or-religion discourse allows leaders of confraternities to say that their processions are "good" for the new and growing audience of tourists and that the tourism of Holy Week benefits the economy of the city, an argument that has widespread acceptance. In other words, another virtue of tourism is that it partially defuses the derogatory accusation that the processions and *pasos* are merely folklore. Confraternity leaders can emphasize the benefits of tourism and the pluralistic form of participation that it implies without necessarily undermining the claim that the content of the processions of Holy Week remains religious and that they are shared religiously by the people of León.

• • •

My discussion of tourism in León takes its point of departure not from actual tourism in the city but rather from the claims and assumptions that have been made in the efforts to promote tourism there for Holy Week. It is evident from the 1983 application to the state tourism office that major public figures in León formally embraced and advocated tourism as a legitimate image and practice in the ritual. I have emphasized that since the early 1980s tourism has represented a new source of political legitimacy for Holy Week in the wake of the National Catholicism of the Franco regime, when the ritual underwent considerable expansion and embellishment. In this sense, tourism in the current era partially fills a political vacuum that was opened when the Franco regime faded into history. The success of the 1983 application made a decisive contribution to situating León's Holy Week within the "new Spain" in which "local traditions" like *Los Pasos* are selected and promoted nationally and internationally by a state agency—the Office of the Secretary of State for Tourism—to further the consumptive practice of tourism. This situation stands in marked contrast to the previous era when Holy Week was as much a demonstration of political allegiance to the Franco regime as the fulfillment of a civil-religious tradition. Tourism has not been the only new source of political legitimacy in the post-Franco era since, as we have seen, there have also been efforts on the part of the mayor and the leadership of the confraternities to promote Holy Week as a characteristically Leonés tradition pertaining to the city and the province.

The kinds of historical developments that I have discussed in this chapter are not peculiar to Holy Week in León. One can turn to Crain's (1992, 1996) discussions of the transformation of El Rocío, the now famous Andalusian pilgrimage in southern Spain, to find comparable themes, such as secularization, tourism, and regional identity. As in the case of León's Holy Week, at El Rocío these kinds of developments are indicative of "how competing sacred and secular discourses intersect as the event conveys divergent meanings to distinct audiences" (Crain 1992, 95–96; see also Eade and Sallnow 1991).[11] Crain also emphasizes forms of opposition and resistance that are employed by pilgrims at El Rocío against the large audience of tourists and mass media people who come to the shrine (1992, 105–8; 1996, 45–50). In this respect, the situation at El Rocío is the reverse of that in the example of León's Holy Week. Tourism in León is widely viewed in positive ways: the audience of tourists enhances the reputation and standing of processions such as *Los Pasos,* tourists financially support the service-based economy of the city, and tourism offers a politically appropriate future direction for the ritual in the aforementioned "new Spain." Indeed, the widespread acceptance of tourism in Holy Week makes a rigid distinction between "insiders" and "outsiders" untenable. As I have shown, "insider" Leoneses can share the same kind of secular experience of processions that is imputed to the "outsider" tourists.

The contentious character of Holy Week is highlighted in differences among "insiders" rather than in differences between "insiders" and "outsiders." A clear example of the differences among "insiders" involves the publicly debated question of whether the processions of Holy Week are folklore or religion. This question is contentious because it underlines markedly different and opposed attitudes about the "true meaning" of the event among ordinary Leoneses.[12] Yet the intensity of this debate is mitigated by the promise of material benefits that can be gained from the promotion of a procession such as *Los Pasos* to a nonlocal audience. It is surely ironic to observe that at the start of the twentieth century the positive value of *pasos* was judged according to their potential for "exciting piety" and "moving devotion," whereas in the latter part of the century *pasos* came to be judged according to how well they would attract tourists for the purpose of consumption and material gain. Nonetheless, the degree to which the processions of Holy Week are marketable for tourism does not preclude both "insiders" and "outsiders" from finding other meanings, including religious ones, for these performances. Rather, the development of a discourse that presents León's Holy Week as a tourist attraction demonstrates a new historical condition that will continue to shape this emergent ritual.

Notes

This chapter is based on research in the city of León between 1981 and 1987, funded by grants from the Wenner-Gren Foundation for Anthropological Research, the Social Sciences and Humanities Research Council of Canada, and the Central Research Fund. I am very grateful to these organizations for their support of my research. Earlier versions of this chapter were presented at the 1996 meetings of both the Canadian Anthropology Society and the European Association of Social Anthropologists. I would like to thank Sharon Roseman and María Cátedra for their invitations to present the papers at these conferences, and I also thank the participants for their comments and suggestions. Lastly, I am grateful to Sharon Roseman and Ellen Badone for the many helpful editorial suggestions they made concerning this chapter. The responsibility for its content is mine.

1. The leader of the confraternity provided me with a copy of the application in 1984 in support of my research on Holy Week in León.

2. Compare Webster's (1999) historical study of Holy Week processions and confraternities in Seville.

3. In the early 1980s, El Dulce Nombre de Jesús Nazareno comprised approximately 3,300 members, all of them male. Approximately 1,300 members donned tunics of "brothers" and participated in the procession on Holy Friday.

4. The escorts come from the Municipal Police, Military Police, National Police, the Civil Guard, and the Red Cross. All escorts wear their dress uniforms for the processions.

5. The mayor cited no source for this estimate.

6. See Lannon (1987) and Payne (1984) for historical overviews of Catholicism and the Franco era; and Behar (1990) for discussion of both the National Catholicism of the Franco period and its aftermath in the province of León.

7. See Driessen (1984) for discussion of the same development in the Holy Week of an Andalusian agro-town.

8. See Moreno Navarro (1982) for discussion of the same development in the Holy Week of Seville.

9. The issue at that time was whether the region of León would form an autonomous political and territorial unit on its own, as had taken place in Catalonia, the Basque Country, Galicia, and other culturally and linguistically distinctive regions in Spain, or whether the León region would be joined with Castile. The latter outcome occurred in 1984 after a great deal of controversy and debate. See Díez Llamas (1993) for a discussion of these events.

10. See Crain (1997) for a related discussion of the shifting employment of insider-outsider distinctions during the El Rocío pilgrimage in Andalusia.

11. A similar point of view is put forward by McKevitt (1991, 94–95) in his analysis of the shrine of Padre Pio in Italy.

12. For another example of contested meanings, see my discussion of parody in Holy Week (Tate 1991).

References Cited

Aparicio Carreño, Luís. 1983. Letter of Support for Correspondence, El Dulce Nombre de Jesús Nazareno. September 29.

Behar, Ruth. 1990. "The Struggle for the Church: Popular Anticlericalism and Religiosity in Post-Franco Spain." In *Religious Orthodoxy and Popular Faith in European Society.* Ed. Ellen Badone. 76–112. Princeton, N.J.: Princeton University Press.

Cayón Waldaliso, M. 1982. *León Semana Santa Cofradía del Dulce Nombre de Jesús Nazareno.* León: Gráficas Cornejo.

Crain, Mary M. 1992. "Pilgrims, 'Yuppies,' and Media Men: The Transformation of an Andalusian Pilgrimage." In *Revitalizing European Rituals*. Ed. Jeremy Boissevain. 95–112. London: Routledge.

———. 1996. "Contested Territories: The Politics of Touristic Development at the Shrine of El Rocío in Southwestern Andalusia." In *Coping with Tourists: European Reactions to Mass Tourism*. Ed. Jeremy Boissevain. 27–55. Oxford: Berghahn Books.

———. 1997. "The Remaking of an Andalusian Pilgrimage Tradition: Debates regarding Visual (Re)presentation and the Meanings of 'Locality' in a Global Era." In *Culture, Power, Place: Explorations in Critical Anthropology*. Ed. Akhil Gupta and James Ferguson. 291–311. Durham, N.C.: Duke University Press.

Díaz Carro, Antonio Miguel. 1983. Letter of Support for Correspondence, El Dulce Nombre de Jesús Nazareno. September 28.

Díez Llamas, D. 1993. *La Identidad Leonesa*. Salamanca: Europa Artes Gráficas, S.A.

Driessen, Henk. 1984. "Religious Brotherhoods: Class and Politics in an Andalusian Town." In *Religion, Power, and Protest in Local Communities: The Northern Shore of the Mediterranean*. Ed. Eric R. Wolf. 73–91. Berlin: Mouton.

Eade, John, and Michael J. Sallnow. 1991. Introduction to *Contesting the Sacred: The Anthropology of Christian Pilgrimage*. Ed. John Eade and Michael Sallnow. 1–29. London: Routledge.

Gutierrez Tejerina, Julián. 1983. Letter of Support for Correspondence, El Dulce Nombre de Jesús Nazareno. September 26.

Lannon, Francis. 1987. *Privilege, Persecution, and Prophecy: The Catholic Church in Spain, 1875–1975*. Oxford: Clarendon Press.

Marne Martínez, Julián. 1983. Correspondence, El Dulce Nombre de Jesús Nazareno. September 28.

Maron, H. 1907. *La Semana Santa en León*. León: C. Gómez.

McKevitt, Christopher. 1991. "San Giovanni Rotondo and the Shrine of Padre Pio." In *Contesting the Sacred: The Anthropology of Christian Pilgrimage*. Ed. John Eade and Michael Sallnow. 77–97. London: Routledge.

Morano, Juan. 1983. Letter of Support for Correspondence, El Dulce Nombre de Jesús Nazareno. September 24.

Moreno Navarro, I. 1982. *La Semana Santa de Sevilla*. Sevilla: Servicio de Publicaciónes del Ayuntamiento de Sevilla.

"Our Processions." 1908. *El Diario de León*. April 15, 1.

Payne, Stanley G. 1984. *Spanish Catholicism: An Historical Overview*. Madison: University of Wisconsin Press.

President of the Provincial Council. 1983. Letter of Support for Correspondence, El Dulce Nombre de Jesús Nazareno. September 29.

Silverman, Sydel. 1979. "On the Uses of History in Anthropology: The Palio of Siena." *American Ethnologist* 6:413–36.

Tate, Mark. 1991. "License, Death and Power: The Making of an Anti-Tradition." In *Religious Regimes and State-Formation: Perspectives from European Ethnology*. Ed. Eric R. Wolf. 261–84. Albany: State University of New York Press.

Webster, Susan Verdi. 1999. *Art and Ritual in Golden-Age Spain: Sevillian Confraternities and the Processional Sculpture of Holy Week*. Princeton, N.J.: Princeton University Press.

7 The Kyoto Tax Strike: Buddhism, Shinto, and Tourism in Japan

NELSON H. H. GRABURN

This chapter focuses on contemporary tourism at the old cultural capital of Japan, Kyoto. The magnificent old temples and shrines are the major attractions for the more than 40 million annual tourists, who supply over 25 percent of the income for today's city. In 1985 the city government asked the major temples and shrines to collect a small head tax to fund repairs and restoration of Kyoto's historical buildings, including religious sites. The Buddhist Association refused to comply, claiming that visitors to shrines and temples were pilgrims, not tourists; some temples stopped charging entrance fees, and others closed their gates. After three years of the "tax strike" and intermittent negotiations, the city revoked the tax. The following discussion analyzes the grounds on which this contest was argued and settled.

For nearly 1,500 years, longer than Japan has been a unified nation, it has been a country with two major religious traditions. The indigenous animistic and shamanistic religion that came to be known as *Shinto* (the way of the gods), is related to East Asian and Siberian animist religions. Buddhism, on the other hand, was brought to Japan from China in the sixth and seventh centuries A.D., partly by way of Korea, along with urbanism, literacy, and many mainland Asian technological advances.

The two religions have had an uneasy coexistence over the millennia; Buddhism has always been the more courtly religion associated with "high" culture, while Shinto has been associated with ordinary people, luck, and the land as well as with the imperial family. Buddhism and tourism are intimately connected, as the common Japanese form of group tourism originated in religious pilgrimages led by priests (Graburn 1983b). Following the Meiji Res-

125

toration of 1868, the nativistic religion of Shinto was elevated to a state religion, with the deified emperor, the descendant of the creator Sun Goddess Amaterasu, at the head. This reaction to European intrusions, after 250 years of self-imposed isolation, led to the chauvinism and militarism that was expressed in the war against Russia in 1904, to colonial expansions in Formosa, Korea, and Manchuria, and eventually to the war against China and to World War II. Since World War II, Shinto has been disestablished, and it has suffered from its reputation of association with militarism and war. The various sects of Buddhism, on the other hand, became dominant in the peace movement and aggressively pursued this identity in Hiroshima and Nagasaki, as well as in peace rallies and rituals in Japan and in their overseas projections.

Shinto and Buddhism in Today's Japan

The simple picture drawn above is historically much more complicated, and the relationship between Buddhism and Shinto has undergone constant adjustment over the centuries. Indeed, at times and in the minds of many ordinary people, the two religions have coalesced, only to be forced apart and even brought into opposition in the early Meiji era. I will start by outlining the basic characteristics of each faith and then describe their mutual interaction institutionally and in the lives of ordinary people. Perhaps one can make the general statement that as both faiths have been practiced by the same people for more than a thousand years, they have come to resemble each other and have mutually "borrowed" many traits.

Shinto

My Japanese mother-in-law used to say, "Shinto is not a religion. To be Shinto is to be Japanese." This statement is true to the extent that all Japanese are Shinto (aside from some Christians), and with few exceptions all the world's adherents of Shrine Shinto are Japanese. It is a religion tied to place, nature, and certain Japanese political institutions. Moreover, it has been less aggressive than Buddhism and various "new religions" (including nonshrine Kyoha Shinto) in accompanying Japanese emigrants who have settled outside of Japan (Graburn, forthcoming).

Shinto is not a religion "of the book," in fact it has no written dogma (Nelson 1996). Shinto was originally a collection of beliefs in the presence of invisible god spirits, or *kami,* inhabiting everything natural (and man-made, as we shall see) in Japan. Shinto probably only emerged as a unitary, named category in its encounter with the fully formed world religion of Buddhism that was brought from overseas and that made the Japanese islanders aware of their own rather disparate set of folk beliefs.

From the dawn of history in the sixth century A.D., we know that each regional ruling clan, or *uji,* had its own protector gods, who were worshipped as ancestors. However, by the late twentieth century, clan membership had been practically forgotten (Nelson 2000). Shinto has always been particularly salient as the religion of the gods of the mountains, fields, and rivers, essential to the annual cycle of rice farmers (Ohnuki-Tierney 1993). But all other places, villages, towns, and fields have their own gods, particularly places of awe, such as caves, waterfalls, or cliffs. Furthermore, with emphases varying throughout history, the Japanese imperial family has claimed to have descended directly from the god creators of the Japanese islands and from the Sun Goddess Amaterasu. Belief in, or at least the continuing relevance of, this 1,400-year-old origin myth is indicated by the fact that even today many Japanese people point out the place where this descent is supposed to have occurred, the sacred mountain Takachiho in the Miyazaki-Kagoshima border area. Life has to be protected against the forces of evil or misfortune by the presence of these local god spirits. Shinto priests and ordinary people pray and chant to bring the local god into the parish's shrine building (*jinja* or *omiya*).

Every parish has at least one *matsuri* festival,[1] during which the local god is asked to enter a portable shrine, the *mikoshi.* This shrine is then carried by the parishioners (usually men), joyously, with chanting and noise, all over the parish and territory, which is thereby purified and protected. At the end of this "tour," the *mikoshi* is brought back to the main shrine building and celebrated with the liquid spirits of the gods, rice wine known as *sake.* One could remark that if pilgrimage is the tour of the faithful to the abode of a god, then the Japanese *matsuri* festival custom is the "tour of the god" to visit the abodes of the faithful. Indeed, Ishimori has pointed out (1994) that the original meaning of the common word for tourism, *kanko,* referred to the "divine light" that the emperor (god) bestowed on his lands and people as *he* toured the country, not to see but to be seen—as the giver of protection and fertility!

This brief account emphasizes that in everyday life Shinto has to do with good luck and protection. People go to shrines at important life-cycle events. Mothers bring their newborn children to visit a shrine forty days after birth. An individual makes a pilgrimage to a shrine at the ages of three, five, and seven, again on becoming an adult (i.e., twenty years of age), and again at marriage. However, Shinto shrines are even more frequently visited to pray for success in one's endeavors; for health, wealth, and travel safety; for admission to good schools; for a good job; for finding a spouse; for getting pregnant (often on the honeymoon); and for overcoming illnesses and problems of all kinds.

Buddhism

Buddhism is a religion of writing, architectural and other art forms, educated priesthoods, the fate of the soul, and cosmological philosophies. Buddhism was originally imported to Japan by a literate elite who spoke and wrote Chinese. This elite convinced the emperor and other ruling families that Buddhism was a religion that would legitimate and consolidate their social power.

Buddhism and Shinto, however, have adapted to each other over the centuries. In Japan, neither religion normally forbids adherence to the other. Thus, if Shinto has to do with fertility, the life cycle, and the ordinary achievements of life, Buddhism has become the religion of death and the ancestors. The Buddhist priesthood, which is *not* celibate in Japan, is trained in the classic texts and is familiar with concepts derived from Indian Buddhism, such as *dharma,* known in Japanese as *daruma,* and the twelve-animal zodiac, based on the animals' race to Buddha's deathbed. The priests officiate at temples (*otera*) in their parishes, but their main contacts with the people involve a series of funeral and postfuneral services attended by the families of the deceased. These services start at death and continue with regularity every few weeks and then at intervals of months and years, for up to thirty-three or fifty years.

The high payments for these obligatory services are the main source of revenue for the wealthy Buddhist sects. Although priests walk the parish with their begging bowls, asking for alms, many live a fairly affluent life. Since World War II, this affluence has been increased by the Buddhist declaration that abortion, Japanese married couples' main method of birth control, is also a human death that must be prayed over for years to come.[2] Thus, sad couples visit small altars in temple precincts where they place teddy bears and toys for their absent children.

Unlike other Buddhist traditions, in Japan it is the good deeds of one's *offspring,* rather than the deeds one performs during one's own lifetime, that push the soul of the deceased into the moral sphere of enlightenment and enable it to "become a Buddha," as the Japanese say. (However, it is publicly stated that the souls of many famous people transform eventually into *kami* and may therefore have Shinto shrines and altars dedicated to them. Privately, it is also said that many ordinary people may also become *kami* after death.) Thus, filial piety is imposed on everyone because one's *parents'* cosmological fate depends on one's own actions in this life.

Buddhism and Shinto as Institutionalized Religions

Japan is a highly technological and apparently secular society. According to numerous surveys conducted by the media and the government, most Japanese say that they do not belong to any particular religion. Perhaps the frequency of this response is the result of the fact that most Japanese do not consciously think of religion as some definable separate entity, for almost everyone partakes of Shinto, and membership in particular Buddhist sects often does not arise until there is a death in the family. These same surveys also show that most Japanese believe in the existence of the human soul, the separation of the soul from the body at death, and a continuing relationship between the living and the dead person as a soul. Nevertheless, the lack of perception of religion as a distinct category may have some bearing on the questions of cultural and religious tourism and pilgrimage discussed below. For instance, in practice most Japanese follow the minor rituals of both Shinto and Buddhism. Shinto concerns luck and fortune, which is bestowed by the omnipresent god spirits, the *kami*. Little shrines are ubiquitous in landscapes and townscapes. According to Reader (1991, 7), more than 60 percent of households have a Shinto shrine (*kami-dana,* or god-shelf), where one claps to attract the god's attention, gives money, and makes various offerings, usually food, to the *kami*. School children, women shoppers, drunken businessmen, happy tourists, and experienced travelers perform this ritual all the time, yet they might deny that they are "religious" (1–4). It might be suggested that the term *shukyo,* for "religion," has in the last one hundred years become identified with an entirely separate religion—Christianity—which entered Japan through missionaries and has made local "religions" appear inseparable from social life itself.

Both Shinto and Buddhism have local parishes, but each shrine and temple (more correctly, the priesthood) belongs to a nationwide network of sects, many of which are headquartered in the old capital of Kyoto. The faithful know that some of the money they contribute at the parish level will make its way to the headquarters and that priests may be trained at seminaries in Kyoto or lesser centers. Furthermore, the faithful like to make pilgrimages to visit the headquarters of their particular sect at least once in their lifetime. For example, devotees of the Zen Buddhist sect may go to the isolated mountain temple complex and seminary of Eiheiji in Fukui Prefecture. Likewise, members of the Inari Shinto sect visit the headquarters of their sect, Inari-jinja, at Fushimi Inari at the southern edge of Kyoto. In the latter case, the spiritual relations between the periphery and the center are maintained through a common belief in the mobile deity spirit of the fox, *kitsune*.

It is said that over 90 million Japanese (four-fifths of the population) are practicing Buddhists and that 115 million, nearly everybody, are Shinto. One does not formally need to "belong" to Shinto. There are, however, certain areas, including parts of Kagoshima on the southern island of Kyushu, where people still believe that Buddhism is a new Chinese religion that has actually harmed Japan. (This belief may have been formed in the mid-Meiji era when the burgeoning official state Shinto was trying to oust the long entrenched power of the Buddhists). Such Shinto practitioners are Shinto when it comes to death, too, and have Shinto rather than Buddhist priests officiate at funerals and burials. Similarly, Japanese Buddhist churches in the United States expect to perform all rites of passage, including weddings, for their congregations because there are no Shinto churches to perform them (Graburn, forthcoming).

Tourism and Religion

Tourism in Japan can be said to have begun hundreds of years ago when the Buddhist temples attempted to gather new adherents (Ishimori 1989, 1995; Vaporis 1995). Priests would visit local communities, asking the people to send a representative from each family to worship at a distant temple to protect the souls of the deceased. The priest, called *oshi* or *sendatsu,* meaning "the one who has gone before," would then lead the villagers out of their community, on a journey that might have been quite frightening in those days, to the temple. The priest knew people in the communities on the route and sometimes arranged for supplies and safe passage. The group of faithful, the *dantai,* took with them the cares and money of the rest of their families, worshipped for them at the temple, and brought back some sacred souvenirs of the visit to show proof of their worship. Shinto shrines instituted the same pattern, though the content of the worship and the souvenirs (*omiyage,* or "shrine gift") were different.

The following patterned sequence is the prototype of all Japanese pilgrimage and most tourism: a representative travels for the group, using its money, with an experienced leader; spends money (and assuages sins) at the site; gets souvenir proofs of worship, religious mementos, and cleansing in exchange for money spent; and travels home to rejoin the group. Modern, secular group tourism to famous sites follows the same pattern, except for the growing popularity of nongroup tourism among some of Japan's younger people today.

The prevalence of this paradigm for sacred and secular journeying provided the title for my book on Japanese tourism, *To Pray, Pay and Play: The Cul-*

tural Structure of Japanese Domestic Tourism (1983b). As I have outlined in that work, Japanese tourism involves the following ten components:

1. Arrangements are made in the home community for some people to go with a guide to some famous or divine place.

2. The group of people going, the *kumi,* actually consists of representatives of other groups, such as their families or work groups. The members of those groups who are not going away may give money, clothes, camera equipment, and other items as parting gifts, or *senbetsu,* which will be used or spent by the tourist/pilgrims on behalf of those left behind.

3. The tourist groups go with their leader, who has made all the arrangements along the way.

4. The tourist attraction or pilgrimage site is framed and set off from the ordinary world by gates, arches, and walls, as well as signs, and most often, by a rise in elevation, providing what MacCannell (1976, 44–45) has called "site sacralization." The visitors usually have to pay an entry fee (except at a shrine) or make a donation, and at a religious place, they must purify themselves by making a short prayer and washing their hands in running water.

5. On entering the precincts, there are various devices to mark the extraordinary character of the place, such as bright banners, music, priests, or others in special clothes, special lamps, and floodlights, or sacred incense smoke.

6. In approaching the central attraction (altar, statue of Buddha, resting place of the god, important historical spot, tourist ride), visitors must pay or make a special donation again, while making another prayer, or calling upon Buddha or God for blessing of whatever is in their mind. Small shrines and altars are often found next to the entrances of secular attractions, so the sequence—to pray, pay, and play—may still hold in the context of so-called secular tourism.

7. In a more relaxed mood, the traveler may visit stalls and buy souvenirs (which can be special foods) characteristic of the place (*omiyage*) to take back to those who gave them *senbetsu* when they started out and to show that the traveler has been to the special place "for them" (Graburn 1987). Conversely, those at home may have laid a place at the table for the absent persons and prayed for them every day.

8. In shrines, people may have their fortunes told, rub themselves on statues of deities, buy *omikuji* (slips of paper foretelling the future, which are tied in sacred trees for the gods to read), and buy *omamori* (amulets and charms) to be taken home for continuing protection.

9. Leaving the special grounds, the travelers can really enjoy themselves. In the old days, brothels were often found outside the gates of shrines and temples. Nowadays, people are likely to have a good meal, go shopping for items known to be famous in the region, or visit and photograph famous regional places. (Significantly, the same term, *meibutsu,* means both the famous "attraction, destination" as well as the "things that are famous to buy." Often the latter are metonymic representations of the former.)

10. On reaching home, the travelers may gather with those left behind, distribute the souvenirs and religious mementos, tell the story of their travels, and show their photos or videos.

My original idea of modern tourism as analogous to, or a replacement for, traditional ritual journeying (Graburn 1977, 1989) was formulated before my research in Japan illustrated the applicability of my hypothesis.[3] Modern Japanese have access to categorical distinctions between tourism and pilgrimage, if they want to dwell upon the difference. While *ryoko* means any kind of journey, *tabi* is a purposeful journey, which can include tourism and *kanko* or *kenbutsu* (seeing things, sightseeing) (Graburn 1983b, 71–82; Ivy 1995, 36–37).

Pilgrimage, which may target the same sites—temples and shrines—as cultural tourism, is known as *henro* (a wide-ranging route) or *junrei* (to make one's rounds to god), words with specifically religious connotations. Pilgrimage, or visiting religious sites, can also be expressed in the form of site-*mairi,* or going to the site out of social obligation, but this common designation does not necessarily imply a religious purpose. Pilgrimages are still outwardly marked in one way or another. For instance, pilgrims may wear special clothing, carry a staff, follow a religious leader (*sendatsu*), be members of a sect, spend extensive time in prayer, follow a traditional pilgrimage route, or travel on foot. Nonetheless, pilgrims still enjoy the other aspects of modern tourism. As Reader points out, "Many Saikoku [a famous thirty-three temple pilgrimage circuit on the island of Shikoku] pilgrims are thus taking part in a cultural tour of their country while having a nice day out with their family, and these interlocking themes, incorporating national pride, family solidarity and enjoyment, are intrinsic to contemporary Japanese pilgrimage and are found in shrine and temple visiting in general" (1991, 159).

Modern nonpilgrimage travel, which very often includes tourism to the same set of sites visited by religious travelers, is rarely completely bereft of "religious" practices. These practices can include purifying oneself by washing one's hands (and mouth) at the entrance to the site, bowing, clapping, and praying at an altar, making offerings, inhaling incense, lighting candles, or purchasing spiritually meaningful souvenirs.

Tourism or Religion: Kyoto as a Definitive Case Study

Kyoto was the imperial capital of Japan almost continuously from 794 A.D. to 1868, when the emperor moved the court to Edo, now called Tokyo. Kyoto now has 1,700 Buddhist temples and 270 Shinto shrines, many of which are architectural wonders and listed as national treasures. Some also serve as headquarters of their national religious sects.

In the early 1980s, the Kyoto city government changed from a Communist plurality to a conservative LDP (Liberal Democratic Party) majority. The new government realized that $11.5 billion, nearly 25 percent of the city's annual income, derived from the nearly 40 million tourists who came each year to see the numerous secular and religious historic wonders of the city. The city authorities also noted that the temples took in well over $100 million a year, perhaps as much as $150 million, in tax-free entrance fees and paid no real estate taxes, even though it was likely that only the fifty most popular could subsist solely on entrance fees. In addition, most of the temples received parishioners' donations and income from urban and rural properties that many of them had owned since medieval times. In spite of the official separation of church and state (discussed below), those temples and shrines that were designated as important national properties or treasures received income for their maintenance directly from the national government in Tokyo.

In order to raise money for historic preservation, necessitated in anticipation of the city's twelve hundredth anniversary celebration in 1994, the city government proposed in 1983 to collect a tax on temple and shrine visitors, to be called the Kyoto Old Capital Preservation Cooperation Tax. The city authorities could not ask the temples and shrines to pay a tax on their income because of the principal of separation of church and state enshrined in the 1946 postwar Japanese Constitution formulated under the American occupation. After two years of legal challenges and negotiations, the city designated the forty most popular tourist attractions, of which thirty-seven were temples (plus one castle and two shrines), as "tax collectors." These attractions were requested to collect approximately $.25 per visitor, which would have raised only about $5 million per year (out of a city budget of $2.15 billion). There was a precedent for an entrance tax, but everyone remembered that when it was abolished in 1964 the mayor had promised that it would never again be reinstituted.

The tax implementation date was July 10, 1985. The Kyoto Buddhist Association, which represented 1,100 of the temples, rebelled by asserting that these were *religious institutions,* not *tourist businesses,* and that their visitors came to *worship,* not to *gaze.* Most people knew that this claim was not entirely true, and the government persisted. The priests said they would not become mere tax collectors for the city, and the debate was hotly argued: some of the temples' authorities thought they should pay, while others were appalled at the city's demands. The government demanded to see the entrance and income accounts of the temples, but the priests refused. They retorted that if they gave in, religious institutions all over Japan would be vulnerable. The government then posted observers near the temple gates to take a head count of visitors, but the priests chased the observers away.

By the end of July 1985, nearly forty of the most famous temples had changed their policies: the priests put up chain-link fences around nineteen of the temples, and another eighteen let in all visitors with free admission. The latter strategy was a boon to tourists and pilgrims, but the closure of the other nineteen temples meant that tens of thousands of Japanese school children and adults on tours and pilgrimages had to change their plans, to say nothing of foreign tourists on a once-in-a-lifetime trip. Hotels, restaurants, souvenir stands, and shops went empty, and some went bankrupt.

Recognizing a crisis situation, the government set up a committee of reconciliation headed by an important businessman, and on August 8 a new compromise was struck. The temples, without admitting acceptance of the government's tax collection scheme, decided to make "donations" to the city, which the city agreed to accept as payment of "taxes." The temples opened their doors again, but this compromise was ruled illegal by the courts. The committee of reconciliation worked to find other solutions, with little success. In November, there was a scandalous rumor about a member of the compromise committee, and some of the leading priests hardened their resolve. On December 8, 1985, the Buddhist leadership split: twenty-five temples decided to pay the tax, but the leaders of twelve other temples refused. These were the most popular temples, whose visitors accounted for more that 50 percent of all temple visits.

These twelve temples remained closed for 115 days. The city was slowly strangling. Since World War II, Kyoto had already lost much of its industry, especially silk weaving, and municipal authorities were afraid of losing even more young people to other areas where employment possibilities were more abundant. In March 1986, the twelve principal temples agreed to open again for three months in the spring but warned that they would close down again at the start of the summer tourist season in June unless the city rescinded its tax law. During these three months, the temples did not charge entrance fees and refused to collect the tax. In fact, the temples would only admit visitors who "donated" their entrance fees in special envelopes printed with the declaration that the donation had been specially invited by the Association to Remove the New Tax, which had been set up by the Buddhists! In June, the popular temples closed again. Business income continued to shrink. Tourism fell off, not only because the most popular "attractions" were closed but because of the frequent news in the media about picketing and protests, fomented in places by the extreme right-wing (fascist) groups that supported the conservative city government. It was even reported that ordinary members of the public—men, women, and children—got into shouting matches and fist fights about the closures. Such public disharmony was anathema to Japanese tourists and pilgrims alike.

Finally, in spring 1988, after months of standoff, the city government gave in. All the gates were reopened, and entrance "donations" were again announced and collected at the gates. In the aftermath, many temples put up signs saying that visitors were to enter for religious purposes, as if to confirm the winning argument that had been waged by the priests. Some temples raised their "entrance fees" to unprecedented heights, up to $17 per person then (but over $30 by the early 1990s), and made the visitors perform *shakyo* (tracing sacred Buddhist texts in ancient characters) or other religious acts before allowing them to tour the gardens or see the sights. The tourists came back in droves, and by contributing over $18.4 billion to the city's coffers by 1992, they became even more crucial to Kyoto's existence.

Thus, the point had been made that ordinary tourists were indeed there for religious purposes when they visited Buddhist temples. The visitors may not have been members of the temple sect or group; indeed, many Japanese have no idea what Buddhist sect they belong to until there is a death in the family (Reader 1991, 3–4). Nonetheless, the priests claimed that visitors benefited from the calm, meditative religious atmosphere and that simply visiting a temple might inspire visitors to adopt some religious practices. Indeed, after the strike, tourists at certain temples told me that they felt that they were being forced to do so!

Conclusion: Religion and Tourism in Japan

There has been much debate in the literature about what, if anything, constitutes the difference between religious tourism and pilgrimage (Morinis 1992; Smith 1992). Indeed, I have made the case elsewhere that modern tourism is a "sacred journey" in a secular world, isomorphic with or taking the place of pilgrimages in more God-fearing societies (Graburn 1977, 1983a). Sometimes, the two kinds of travel seem to merge: how, for instance, can one tell the difference between tourists visiting a remarkable old architectural site and religious devotees who go there regardless of the site's age and heritage value? There have been similar discussions in Europe as well as elsewhere in Asia (Crain 1996, 46–50; Ichaporia 1983, 87–90; Vukonić 1992, 88–90). The case study presented here makes a number of contributions to this debate.

Much as the editors of this volume might like to move beyond the pilgrimage/religion–tourism/secular contrast, we cannot avoid this duality when it exists for actors in any ethnographic case. In Kyoto, not all actors were of one mind: some emphasized the contrast, others wanted to ignore it.

This division between religion and nonreligion is rarely a salient contrast for the majority of Japanese either in daily life or when visiting temples and shrines, although the duality is categorically available for all Japanese. It may be a particularly Christian tendency to separate religion from (the rest of) life. Perhaps it is not irrelevant to point out that many Japanese (as a result of the influence of Shinto, presumably) do not categorically separate human beings from nature (*shizen*) either.

In our analyses, we must therefore clarify *exactly* where and on what grounds the pilgrimage-tourism divide lies in any historical, ethnographic situation. It is not enough to say that "in this culture . . ." or "people at this site . . .," for one must specify which actors insist on maintaining these categories and why. For example, Eade (1992) bases most of his revisionist argument on his status as a long-term "worker"—part of the organizing structure— at a pilgrimage site; even in Turner's most charismatic works (Turner 1969; Turner and Turner 1978), the organizing structure is not claimed to be part of pilgrims' communitas (and it is the omission of this point that weakens the impact of Turner's work). In the Kyoto case, it was the Buddhist priests who protested against the secularization of their functions and of visits to their temples: though the priests claimed that they wished to keep tourism and religion strictly separate, we cannot be sure of the depth of their essentialist arguments. While they could possibly have had sacredness and numinousness in mind, the actual separation was made on legalistic and constitutional grounds (which did not exist before 1946). We could say that the legal separation of church and state has for these Japanese come to stand for and mask the primary essentialist dualism that we anthropologists are now seeking to avoid. Whatever its basis, the duality of pilgrimage as opposed to tourism is certainly an overt and emic division for the officials and priests in Kyoto.

One of the problems with Turner's work on pilgrimage and with the work of those who both follow and oppose it is that these approaches are far too explicitly based on Christian cases. This problem raises the issue of ethnocentrism for anthropologists who come from a Euro-American background. For instance, the three types of pilgrimages proposed by Eade and Sallnow (1991) would be quite unsuited for Japanese cases if, for instance, one were to look for saints and miracles, bodies or relics, or even sacred texts as key categorical markers. Shinto, for instance, possesses no sacred texts. Among the most interesting and challenging ethnographic studies on our topic are those that have focused on Asian or non-Christian settings; for instance, Pfaffenberger (1983) on Sri Lanka; Ichaporia (1983) on Kajuraho; Cohen (1992) on Thailand; and Morinis (1984) and Gold (1988) on Hindu pilgrimages.

The most important research direction involves attempting to gain insight into the meaning of any touristic act within the broader context of the lives of the actors. We have seen that different actors occupying different status positions in the Kyoto scene have different interpretations of the events during the tax strike, based on their own interests and preoccupations. We have also seen that mere questioning of actors, in this case ordinary Japanese, cannot fully reveal the meaning of their practices. Intensive research, including many of those works mentioned in the previous paragraph, has shown that even actors occupying similar status positions may differ in their interpretations. Ongoing research, such as that of Frey (in this volume; 1998) and Gold (1988) is breaking ground in innovative ways by interviewing travelers not only at the target site but also at later stages in their lives, back in their home environment. Only in this way may we learn when and how the essentialist dualism between sacred and secular, like other categorical and fluid sets of meanings, constitutes a part of actors' experiences.

Notes

This work is dedicated to Kimura Mikio-sama, whom I knew for twenty years as a connoisseur, retired art consultant, and dedicated Communist. He was an enthusiastic, poverty-stricken, but ever-humorous guide to all things in Kyoto, especially shrines, temples, artists, local politics, cheap lunches, and naked festivals. He introduced me and my family as well as many friends to people and places that he felt were interesting and important, first in 1978 and on many later occasions, until 1994. He wrote to us regularly when we were not in Kyoto. Born in Shikoku as World War II was beginning, he died in 1995 and is survived by his mother.

An earlier version of this paper titled "Religion, Tourism, Peace and War: Shinto and Buddhism in Japan" was presented at the session "Religion, Tourism and Peace" at the Conference "I pellegrini della modernita: I giovani, i viaggi e la pace," organized by Dr. Nicolo Costa, University of Milan, and the Italian Association of Catholic Bishops, May 31–June 2, 1996.

1. *Matsuri* literally refers to prayer or worship, but for ordinary Japanese the term always refers to parish festivals of the type described here.

2. The "pill" was banned in Japan, except for experimental uses, which started in 1996, until a few months after Viagra was approved in 1999 (IMS-Global 2003).

3. The reader should note that my earlier work (1977, 1989) on the structuring of tourism as ritual made no mention of Turner's work or ideas; it was based almost entirely on the work of my mentor at Cambridge, the anthropologist Edmund Leach (1961), something that critics such as Eade (1992) and Nash (1984) failed to recognize.

References Cited

Cohen, Erik. 1992. "Pilgrimage Centers: Concentric and Excentric." *Annals of Tourism Research* 19:33–50.

Crain, Mary M. 1996. "Contested Territories: The Politics of Touristic Development at the Shrine of El Rocío in Southwestern Andalusia." In *Coping with Tourists: European Reactions to Mass Tourism.* Ed. Jeremy Boissevain. 27–55. Oxford: Berghahn Books.

Eade, John. 1992. "Pilgrimage and Tourism at Lourdes, France." *Annals of Tourism Research* 19:18–32.

Eade, John, and Michael J. Sallnow. 1991. Introduction to *Contesting the Sacred: The Anthropology of Christian Pilgrimage.* Ed. John Eade and Michael Sallnow. 1–29. London: Routledge.

Frey, Nancy L. 1998. *Pilgrim Stories: On and Off the Road to Santiago.* Berkeley: University of California Press.

Gold, Ann G. 1988. *Fruitful Journeys. The Ways of Rajasthani Pilgrims.* Berkeley: University of California Press.

Graburn, Nelson H. H. 1977. "Tourism: The Sacred Journey." In *Hosts and Guests: The Anthropology of Tourism.* Ed. Valene L. Smith. 17–31. Philadelphia: University of Pennsylvania Press.

———. 1983a. "The Anthropology of Tourism." In "The Anthropology of Tourism," ed. Nelson H. H. Graburn. Special issue, *Annals of Tourism Research* 10:9–33.

———. 1983b. *To Pray, Pay and Play: The Cultural Structure of Japanese Domestic Tourism.* Aix-en-Provence: Centre des Hautes Etudes Touristiques.

———. 1987. "Material Symbols in Japanese Domestic Tourism." In *Mirror and Metaphor: Material and Social Constructions of Reality.* Ed. Dan Ingersoll and Gordon Bronistky. 15–27. Lanham, Md.: University Press of America.

———. 1989. "Tourism: The Sacred Journey." In *Hosts and Guests: The Anthropology of Tourism.* Ed. Valene L. Smith. 2nd ed. 21–36. Philadelphia: University of Pennsylvania Press.

———. Forthcoming. "When *Uchi* Goes *Soto:* The Travels of the Gods in the Shinto Diaspora." In *The Diaspora of Japanese Religions.* Ed. Ronan A. Pereira and H. Matsuoka. Berkeley, Calif.: Center for Japanese Studies.

Ichaporia, Niloufer. 1983. "Tourism at Khajuraho: An Indian Enigma." *Annals of Tourism Research* 10:75–92.

IMS-Global. 2003. "Viagra and the Pill Approved in Japan." <http://www.ims-global.com/insight/news_story/news_story_990426.htm>.

Ishimori, Shuzo. 1989. "Popularization and Commercialization of Tourism in Early Modern Japan." In *Japanese Civilization in the Modern World.* Vol. 4, *Economic Institutions.* Ed. Tadao Umesao et al. 161–78. Senri Ethnological Studies no. 26. Osaka: National Museum of Ethnology.

———. 1994. "Introduction: Kanko." Paper delivered at the Conference on New Directions in Tourism Research, organized by Shuzo Ishimori and Nelson Graburn, National Museum of Ethnology, Osaka.

———. 1995. "Tourism and Religion: From the Perspective of Comparative Civilization." In *Japanese Civilization and the Modern World.* Vol. 10, *Tourism.* Ed. Tadao Umesao et al. 11–24. Senri Ethnological Studies no. 38. Osaka: National Museum of Ethnology.

Ivy, Marilyn. 1995. *Discourses of the Vanishing: Modernity, Phantasm, Japan.* Chicago: University of Chicago Press.

Leach, Edmund R. 1961. "Time and False Noses." In *Rethinking Anthropology.* 132–36. London: Athlone.

MacCannell, Dean. 1976. *The Tourist: A New Theory of the Leisure Class.* New York: Schoken Books.

Morinis, E. Alan. 1984. *Pilgrimage in the Hindu Tradition: A Case Study of West Bengal.* New York: Oxford University Press.

———, ed. 1992. *Sacred Journeys: The Anthropology of Pilgrimage.* Westport, Conn.: Greenwood.

Nash, Dennison. 1984. "The Ritualization of Tourism: Comment on Graburn's 'The Anthropology of Tourism.'" *Annals of Tourism Research* 11:503–22.

Nelson, John K. 1996. *A Year in the Life of a Shinto Shrine.* Seattle: University of Washington Press.

———. 2000. *Enduring Entities: The Guise of Shinto in Contemporary Japan.* Honolulu: University of Hawaii Press.

Ohnuki-Tierney, Emiko. 1993. *Rice as Self: Japanese Identities through Time.* Princeton, N.J.: Princeton University Press.

Pfaffenberger, Bryan. 1983. "Serious Pilgrims and Frivolous Tourists: The Chimera of Tourism in the Pilgrimages of Sri Lanka." *Annals of Tourism Research* 10:57–74.

Reader, Ian. 1991. *Religion in Contemporary Japan.* Honolulu: University of Hawaii Press.

Smith, Valene L., ed. 1992. "Pilgrimage in Tourism: The Quest in Guest." Special issue, *Annals of Tourism Research* 19.

Turner, Victor. 1969. *The Ritual Process.* Chicago: Aldine.

Turner, Victor, and Edith Turner. 1978. *Image and Pilgrimage in Christian Culture: Anthropological Perspectives,* New York: Columbia University Press.

Vaporis, Constantine N. 1995. "The Early Modern Origins of Japanese Tourism." In *Japanese Civilization and the Modern World.* Vol. 10, *Tourism.* Ed. Tadao Umesao et al. 25–38. Senri Ethnological Studies no. 38. Osaka: National Museum of Ethnology.

Vukonić, Boris. 1992. "Medjugorje's Religion and Tourism Connection." *Annals of Tourism Research* 19:79–91.

8   Extending the Metaphor: British Missionaries as Pilgrims in New Guinea

WAYNE FIFE

In 1871, two London Missionary Society evangelists, the Reverend A. W. Murray and the Reverend Samuel MacFarlane, set out by boat to scout the Torres Strait Islands between Australia and New Guinea in order to find suitable locations for the establishment of mission stations. Their purpose was to create a series of "stepping stones" on the Torres Strait Islands, with the eventual goal of establishing a mission within New Guinea itself. The mission to New Guinea was conceived to be part of a sacred quest. As Murray proclaimed in 1872, when the first chapel was built on Darnley Island, "How many Christian temples will follow in its train as the light spreads throughout the many isles around, and the great land [New Guinea] with all the lesser lands that skirt its shores" (31). To bring light to New Guinea, that "dark and heathen land," was characterized as a task worthy of all missionaries and of almost any sacrifice.

In this chapter, I am interested in extending "pilgrimage" as a metaphor in order to gain a greater understanding of the early years of the pioneering mission in New Guinea and at the same time to develop a more flexible definition of pilgrimage itself. To fulfill this task, I seek to convince the reader that many of the essential elements by which anthropologists have defined pilgrimage were present in the New Guinea mission as it was carried out by a handful of British evangelists between the years 1871 and 1914.

In making my argument, I stretch the boundaries of what has normally been considered pilgrimage. The "sites" that I refer to here are not the standard sacred shrines to holy persons, places, or texts (compare Eade and Sallnow 1991, 9). Instead, these sites are shrines to an activity—the activity of evangelism itself. The act of evangelical improvement, centrally located in the mission compounds of Papua New Guinea, turned mission work there into a sacred movement toward a new religious location and the compound itself into a type of "shrine" that gave meaning to evangelization. This type of spiritual movement, I contend, constitutes a form of pilgrimage and as such needs to be taken into account when we formulate our definitions of that religious activity. This theme will be taken up again at the end of the chapter, when I ask the reader to consider an expanded definition of pilgrimage.

If we rethink some of the previous interpretations of pilgrimage, it becomes apparent that the one offered here is not radically different from those of previous researchers. For example, if we deemphasize the rhetoric opposing structure to liminality in Victor Turner's work, we see that he views pilgrimage primarily as sacred movement through time and space that helps to develop temporary as well as more durable connections among people of disparate social stations and even of different cultures (e.g., Turner and Turner 1978). I suggest that there is much in the context of the New Guinea missions that is encompassed by this perspective on pilgrimage.

In comparing tourism with pilgrimage, Nelson Graburn (1977) makes the salient point that both offer socially valued statuses "back home" after the "trip" has been successfully completed. He further notes that, during the journey, an important contrast emerges between the "ordinary time" of life at home and the experience of an extraordinary and in some sense "sacred time" away from home. These insights also apply to my material, despite the fact that for many missionaries "time away from home" was measured in years or even decades, rather than in weeks or months. One of the points to which I return at the conclusion of this chapter concerns the necessity of extending the time dimension implicit in our definitions of the pilgrimage process. With few exceptions (Morinis 1992; Dubisch 1995), researchers have thought of pilgrimages as relatively restricted both in time and space. I argue that we now need to redefine the category of pilgrimage as a process independent of temporal and spatial boundaries. Accomplishing this task will expand our insight into the various forms of travel that constitute pilgrimage journeys.

John Eade and Michael Sallnow (1991, 5), writing in response to the work of "modernist" anthropologists such as Turner, claim that today "the analytical emphasis shifts from positivistic, generic accounts of the features and functions of pilgrimage, and of the extrinsic characteristics of its focal signs, towards an investigation of how the practice of pilgrimage and the sacred powers of a shrine are constructed as varied and possibly conflicting representations by the different sectors of the cultic constituency, and indeed those outside it as well." Despite their continued reliance on older models of what constitutes a shrine and the concomitant limiting of the sacred space involved in pilgrimage, I share with these authors a focus on the central importance of practice. Pilgrimage is something that people do. In the case that I offer below, I suggest that the British missionaries who went to New Guinea in the early years were, in some fundamental ways, "doing pilgrimage."

Of those anthropologists working on pilgrimage, Alan Morinis (1992) adopts a perspective that comes closest to my own. As he states, pilgrimages may be allegorical—inner, spiritual journeys instead of geographical ones (4). Extending this insight, I argue that a spiritual journey can be created through, rather than in place of, a geographical journey. According to Morinis, "a journey is undertaken because in some way movement from here to Other is called for to realize the quest of the pilgrim. . . . We know that here is incomplete and unsatisfactory, and so we set out, hoping to find the Other through the act of going forth itself" (13). In the case presented in this chapter, English missionaries could certainly have been said to be going forth in order to encounter the Other (something that can also be said of many people engaging in journeys that are labeled as tourism). That statement, however, would not by itself completely describe what the missionaries were doing in New Guinea. The missionaries were there to convert a pagan Other into a new sort of Christian self. Along the way, missionaries hoped to transform their own former selves into new ones—evangelists who were closer to an imitation of the sacred actions of Jesus himself. Turning an old self into a new self and setting out to transform the Other is, I would contend, a much more intricate form of pilgrimage than Morinis may have had in mind, but it is nevertheless a form of pilgrimage. This position is reinforced by Morinis's own definition, in which the *transforming* encounter between the self (the familiar) and the Other is at the very heart of the pilgrimage experience (26).

For Morinis, the pilgrimage "is always a quest, and the quarry is usually an extraordinary place" (17). He elaborates this notion by suggesting that such an "extraordinary place" is usually a location with a privileged relationship to the divine, as well as a place of condensed cultural ideals (4, 17). In the New Guinea example, I suggest that in addition to the notion of journeying toward a "sacred space" we need to add the concept of journeying toward a place that can be *made sacred* through the actions of its pilgrims. In this sense, British missionaries went to New Guinea not to visit a sacred shrine but rather to create a sacred space—a "somewhere" that existed only as a projection in the future, during the real time of the mission journey.

This consideration brings us to the important dimension of time. Morinis, like most anthropologists working on pilgrimage, views it as an activity that normally occurs over a relatively short period: "Pilgrims tend to be people for whom the sacred journey is a limited break from the routines and familiar context of an ordinary, settled, social life" (19). In contrast, however, New Guinea missionaries usually measured their time away from home in years or even decades. In the sections that follow, I build upon Morinis's work by suggesting that we expand our ideas about sacred space and erase the limitations we often place upon time within our definitions of pilgrimage.

In keeping with the other chapters in this volume, I would also like to suggest that the situation that I am discussing in this chapter has parallels to certain aspects of nineteenth-century tourism and travel in both Great Britain and North America. Wendy Joy Darby (2000), for example, has written about how the Lake District in England gradually became a sacred destination inextricably entwined with national sentiments about "being English." Speaking of this and other British landscapes that became nationally important in the 1800s, Darby states, "what was at stake was an aesthetic nationalism located in landscape, what was to become perhaps a secular religion of the countryside embodied in the aptly named National Trust" (107). In a similar manner, places such as Niagara Falls, Mammoth Cave, the White Mountains, and Yosemite became "sacred places" in the nineteenth century in the United States (Brown 1995; Sears 1998). In the first half of the 1800s, for example, Niagara Falls was both difficult to reach and difficult to experience once there. As Sears (1998, 13) suggests, "Visitors to the Falls sometimes referred to themselves as 'Pilgrims.' . . . They descended staircases to the bottom of the Falls, crossed the rapids, and walked on trembling walkways to Terrapin Tower on the edge of Horseshoe Fall. They struggled over slippery rocks, were wetted with spray and buffeted by winds. Such tourist rituals recapitulate, if only faintly, the trials experienced by pilgrims on their journey toward Canterbury, Rome, or Jerusalem and their initiation into the mysteries of the sacred place." The amount of effort required to visit a place like the falls played an instrumental role in making it "sacred" (see, e.g., Seibel 1985; and Sears 1998). When such efforts were removed, the quasi-religious character of the tourism destination also faltered. "As the falls became more accessible, through the Erie Canal, finished in 1825, and later thanks to the railways, and as hotels and sightseeing platforms were erected, the falls lost some of their sublimity" (Löfgren 1999, 30).

As I am arguing here for pilgrimage and missionaries in New Guinea, British and American tourism in the nineteenth century seemed to involve the possibility of rendering a site sacred because of the effortful movement that was required to both physically visit and metaphorically "understand" the site. In other words, that effort of movement is a defining feature of turning a physical space into a sacred place—whether the situation involves tourism or missionary activities (and hence pilgrimage).

Evangelism: The Sacred Mission

We need to begin with a brief consideration of the sacred aspects of evangelism. If early missionaries in Papua New Guinea were on a sacred journey, what were the main elements that made this journey sacred?

In the early 1870s, the London Missionary Society (LMS), was composed primarily of Congregationalists and a small number of evangelical Anglicans. Here, I will address only of a few of the most important taken-for-granted assumptions that missionaries from such backgrounds would carry with them into the new mission fields.

Jean and John Comaroff have noted that British evangelists in the first half of the nineteenth century wanted to mold the "heathens" who inhabited the colonies not into an image of real British society but rather into a projected ideal of what Great Britain could be:

> And what they wished to see was a neat fusion of three idealized worlds: the scientific, capitalist age in its most ideologically roseate form, wherein individuals were free to better themselves and to aspire to ever greater heights; an idyllic countryside in which, alongside agrarian estates, hardworking peasants, equipped with suitable tools, might produce gainfully for the market; and a sovereign Empire of God, whose temporal affairs would remain secure under the eye, if not the daily management, of divine authority. (1991, 59)

What brought these elements together was the common assumption that each person had a duty to strive for both spiritual and material self-improvement throughout his or her life. Such improvement could only occur within the context of the acceptance of evangelical Christianity as the best of all possible religions and British colonialism as the best of all possible social organizations; nothing else would encourage the "proper" development of native peoples.[1] In the report of the first visitation from the home office to New Guinea, the Reverend R. W. Thompson remarked that "The value of the Mission as an elevating and civilizing agency among tribes notorious for their barbarism and degradation is frankly admitted by those who, looking at it from this point of view, have been best able to judge its work" (1897, 57). Within this cultural context, the role of the missionary was not only to improve himself or herself through evangelical work but also to serve as a role model and inspiration for any "pagans" who might be persuaded to "improve themselves" as well.

When the New Guinea mission began in the 1870s and for several decades thereafter, the goal of self-improvement through sacrifice, hard work, and correct spiritual attitudes remained the dominant model for evangelists to emulate. This message had a special poignancy for the LMS missionaries to New Guinea, who shared a common background as members of the lower middle or upper working classes. These class origins were not true of the LMS as a whole, as most members of the Congregationalist churches from which the organization drew its supporters in Great Britain actually came from a solidly middle-class background during that time period (Bebbington 1989, 110). Diane Langmore (1989, 17) further points out that "During the forty years between 1874 and 1914, LMS recruitment in general was moving away from the artisans and skilled workers toward those of middle-class occupations. But this trend was not reflected in the Papuan mission." Langmore also suggests that class improvement was by no means a small motivation for the missionaries who went to New Guinea during its earlier period of missionization (44).

Along with self-improvement came the desire to help others move toward the "higher" path of Christian life. David W. Bebbington (1989, 141) notes that in this period we can see a common message in many novels and other popular works of literature: "The belief was spreading that the greatest need of humanity was not rescue from its futile ways through salvation, but effort that would apply knowledge for the betterment of the world. The resulting stance has been labelled 'meliorism,' the belief that, if only skills were exerted, the human race would make rapid progress." While rejecting the secular component of these messages, the British evangelical missionaries of the late nineteenth century were nevertheless strongly influenced by the belief in the possibility of human progress. This belief was fostered by a long-standing preoccupation with the idea that life itself could be thought of as a pilgrimage, presented most prominently in the various editions of John Bunyan's *The Pilgrim's Progress* published from the late seventeenth century onwards. As John Gillis (1996, 31) suggests, from the 1600s Protestants increasingly rejected the idea that one needed to go on a pilgrimage to a sacred shrine in order to properly experience "the journey of life" that would eventually lead to a sacred union with God (see also Reader and Walter 1993, 4). It is a short step from this notion to the one I am suggesting—that one could go forth on a missionary journey and through the expression of correct internal spiritual states create sacred sites where none had existed before. In the case of New Guinea missionaries, this process was to be achieved through the application of Christ's message of salvation. The twin goals of improvement for "self" and "other" became inseparable in the New Guinea mission and formed a constant subtext for the evangelical work carried out there.

New Guinea missionaries were of course heavily influenced in the direction of their work by the time and place from which they came. And as Richard Altick (1973, 170) states, "Of all the maxims in the sententious Victorian vocabulary, 'Heaven helps those who help themselves' was amongst the most ubiquitous." The metaphor that was constantly in use in New Guinea among the missionaries themselves was that of a journey from the darkness of savagery to the light of the gospel. The Reverend A. W. Murray, for example, wrote the following in a journal in 1872 regarding his trip to an outstation run by the very charismatic Polynesian teacher Mataika:

> To us it was a wonderful and delightful sight to see such a congregation assembled for the worship of God on this land so lately covered with the grossest darkness and filled with the habitations of cruelty. Of course, it is dark still, and the people are virtual heathens still, but it is no small thing that they are now mild, harmless and docile, and that they come together week after week to join in the worship of the true God and hear of him who is able to raise the lowest, and pardon the guiltiest, and cleanse the vilest of the children of Adam. (34)

The sacred journey to New Guinea was conceived of in the contexts of both self-improvement and other-improvement, with no strong differentiation made between the spiritual and the material benefits that were to come from these personal and social transformations. The sign of God's grace was to be seen though the transformation itself. The easiest way to trace the enactment of God's grace was through the changing conditions found within the Christian compounds that were built by the LMS from the opening of the mission in the 1870s until the outbreak of World War I. These compounds served as markers that allowed the missionaries to measure their own progress as pilgrims toward the new kingdom of light and life within New Guinea.

Mission Compounds as Sacred Sites

The missionaries who came to New Guinea in the late nineteenth century and early twentieth century faced a long and uncomfortable journey, either from England or from other Pacific Islands to the east of New Guinea. In the latter case, they had previously traveled from Great Britain at an earlier stage in their mission career. Despite the length and difficulty of these journeys, their missionary diaries, reports, and other documents do not linger on the hardships, mentioning virtually nothing except for simple variations on the theme of "We are here at last." We know that early local trips in small vessels between Australia and the Torres Strait Islands, or a little later around the shores of New Guinea itself, were often unpredictably difficult. Reverend Murray, for example, almost refused to make further local trips until London headquarters saw fit to supply the mission with a permanent and more "suitable ship." In his 1873 report, he states that "The late short voyage has tried me more than a six months voyage would have done in a suitable vessel. Such being the case I feel that only very urgent circumstances will justify my undertaking another such voyage . . . I do trust, should I be spared to make another visitation of the stations, that I shall be able to obtain a larger and more commodious vessel" (27–28).

The lack of attention paid to the voyage from England in the writings of missionaries suggests that, despite the parallel this long trip has with classic definitions of pilgrimage, in the eyes of the missionaries the trip itself was not the defining feature of their experience. The real pilgrimage, in the sense of both an internal and an external movement or transformation of self, took place within New Guinea. However, we can assume that the long, initial voyage must have shaped the perceptions of the men and the women who undertook it regarding the importance of their undertaking as a whole. Clearly, missionary work in New Guinea was not like the local charity services provided by LMS workers in Britain, which involved, for example, commuting to poor neighborhoods of London to assist in soup kitchens. The New Guinea endeavor was something quite different. In this regard, it can be compared to the journeys that took place in the nineteenth century to see famous tourism sites, such as Niagara Falls or the Lake District, which were sacred in a nationalistic sense. In each case, the journey to the site *and* the journey around the site were key components to instilling a sense of the sublime (i.e., the sacred) in the participants. Moving around the mountains of the Lake District or negotiating a difficult path to try to get a better view of the falls were just as important (and often more important) in evoking a feeling of awe and delight than the trip initially required to reach these landscapes. This was also the case, I would argue, for the British missionaries in New Guinea.

The sense of difference and heightened importance associated with the New Guinea mission can be seen quite clearly from the missionaries' own words. From the beginning, the missionaries expected New Guinea to be an especially difficult mission.[2] As stated at the beginning of this chapter, Murray and MacFarlane left the York Peninsula in Australia in 1871 to scout for coastal sites where Polynesian teachers could be left to begin a series of stations from which missionaries could eventually move into the mainland itself. After setting up the very first station on Darnley Island, Murray remarks in his notes that this action "will undoubtedly prove the first of a series which will issue in the overthrow of the reign of darkness throughout New Guinea and the almost numberless islands that skirt its shores, and the establishment in its room of the kingdom of light and life. No wonder therefore that it should have had to encounter opposition; the wonder would have been if it had been otherwise" (1871, 32). Many years later, the Reverend H. P. Schlencker offers reasons why, by 1915, the mission work had not been as successful in terms of conversions as the LMS directors in London might have wished, while at the same time illustrating his faith that the situation would ultimately improve. Having been in New Guinea for twenty years at this point, he offers the theory that mission work must go through three stages:

> The first we may call the Novelty Stage, when the Missionary is new and strange, + the people crowd to the service out [of] respect for him, or curiosity. . . . The second stage we may call the Indifferent Stage, when the novelty has worn off; because there is no spiritual root the seeming enthusiasm withers away. The people find that there is nothing of a very material nature to be gained, + because they have not grasped the meaning of Christianity they are disappointed, + the interest dwindles to a very low ebb. The third stage we may call the Genuine Stage when the good seed of the Kingdom is taking root + striking down into the good soil, when a few followers come round, not from novelty, but a genuine hunger for the unadulterated Bread. Between the first and the last stage there may be a period of many years; but if faithfulness mark the life + work of the Sower, the third stage is as sure and certain as the very Promise of God. (1915, 3)

In the above quotation, we can see that, even though forty-four years separate the writing of their reports, Schlencker and Murray, like other missionaries, habitually expected movement or transformation to occur despite the difficulties of working in New Guinea. This movement constituted a "progress" that was to bring about the Kingdom of God within this particular corner of the universe. The main task of the missionary was to serve as the center for such movement—a faithful, living beacon of light that might draw the Others from darkness so that they, too, might experience "genuine" faith.

The main location and the main means for attempting to bring about the desired changes and for exercising one's faith in the inevitability of a new Kingdom of God was the compound or settlement style of mission station (see Langmore 1989). In this pattern, separate Christian settlements were built near but not within areas of village concentration. From the very beginning, these compounds, which were often quite extensive, were fenced—an important symbolic gesture that suggested that something special was going on inside these new Christian settlements. A good example of the separateness expected as a normal result of the erection of these compounds is the description provided in 1897 by a visiting deputation led by the Reverend R. W. Thompson: "The mission buildings at Vatorata consist of a very commodious and comfortable house with outhouses and store, a large well-built lecture-room, a native teacher's house and twenty houses for students. The property originally consisted of 150 acres of land. This has been added to by a gift of about nineteen acres by James Burns, Esq. The whole is being enclosed by wire fence, and will provide ample ground for plantations for the students" (19).

European visitors were often extremely impressed by what they saw as the "civilized and civilizing" designs of the mission enclosures. Witness the description of the Reverend Joseph King, who visited New Guinea in 1905:

> At Orokolo I found Mr. and Mrs. Holmes living in a well-fenced and spacious enclosure; the paths were long and broad, and bordered with ornamental shrubs, the grounds were planted with useful trees, there were many well-built houses in the compound, a neat building serving at present for schoolhouse and church, the Rarotongan teachers' house, a row of cottages for the young men of the settlement, the missionaries' commodious residence, and near the entrance of the compound was a large store. All this represents much labour, and it is native labour. The houses are a greatly improved adaptation of aboriginal workmanship. . . . The store bore its testimony to a new industrial enterprise, for it was filled with prepared sago packed in bags for sending away to help the food supply of distant mission stations, and outside the store were stacks of building material to be conveyed in the "John Williams" for the erection of the churches or schools in other districts. (1905, 29–30)

That these areas were considered to be special, even sacred spaces is readily apparent in King's words when he gives us a different sort of description of the situation at Orokolo earlier in the same 1905 report:

> I had not been so far west in the Gulf before, and the long line of large [local village] houses visible as we approached the breakers showed that there were many people here needing help. Landing at this spot, we were within the spheres of missionary influence, but in the confines of barbarians of the worst kind. In the regions only a few miles beyond there is a thick population of timid, suspicious, and cruel savages, amongst whom cannibalism is no crime, but a mistaken "virtue." With the black shadow of this darkness resting upon us, we landed, and we were met by a most welcome sight, a missionary compound cut out of the tangled, tropical bush, with its straight paths, its useful and ornamental shrubs, its spacious house (European in design, but made out of native material), its row of student houses occupied by the sons of savages, and its combined school-house and church. Our way to the place of worship that Sunday morning had been unique. (7)

As the above quotation shows quite clearly, some British missionaries felt as though they were surrounded by darkness—a darkness that threatened to close in upon them and extinguish the coming light of Christianity. Anyone who had the privilege of living within the fenced compound was expected to act as a model Christian or at least work steadily toward becoming the "best Christian" possible under the circumstances. Areas outside of the compound were in some sense tainted. Missionary records are full of their authors' disparagement of the "wild heathens" whom they had come to tame in the name of Jesus. Notice that in a curious parallel, as Nelson Graburn (1977) suggests for both pilgrims and tourists, these missionaries considered themselves to be living not only in a different place from their native land but also in a different time than the local villagers. In the same 1905 report, for example, Reverend King outlines what he considers to be the difficulties of providing education in such "backward" places: "In providing schools for children whose parents are only just emerging from their stone age, much and careful thought must, of necessity, be given to method. What is a model education for advanced races is not necessarily suitable to the child races of the world" (20). Everyday terms used to describe non-Christianized Papuans include "people of the stone age," "heathens," "primitive children," "a barbarous and uncivilized race," and "a degraded savage race." Common to such epithets is what Johannes Fabian (1983, 31) has termed the "denial of coevalness"; that is, the idea that Papuans did not live within the same temporal era as the "civilized" British missionaries who had come to work among them.[3]

Most missionaries felt that Papuan adults were a lost cause and that the only hope for Christianity lay in convincing as many people as possible to give up their children to the missionaries' care. These children were separated from their parents and raised within the confined haven of the compound itself. A concern for the social and moral purity of the compound reached its height after the turn of the century (Fife 2001). In 1908, members of a deputation that had just visited New Guinea noted that the Reverend Charles Abel "is intending to place a village which will contain no foreign element, and will, no doubt, prove of great service in raising native life to a higher level" (Johnson 1908, 47–48). In a report of 1915–16, the years when the LMS decided to abandon the compound style of missionary work as a system that promoted too much separation between those few who lived and were educated on the station and the majority of Papuans, the Reverends A. J. Viner, G. J. Williams, and Frank Lenwood eulogized the compounds in the following manner:

> Yet it is true that each of our Mission stations is a haven of peace and beauty. . . . Where the system is followed, the Mission station forms an oasis in the middle of what seems to be a very thirsty land. There is a sense of activity about a station, the long training helps to promote a higher measure of ability, and the life of such a community with its games, its discipline, and its comparatively keen intellectual interest must be like paradise for those who have the opportunity of dwelling within it. (1915–16, 214–15)

Internal Movement as Pilgrimage

Despite the desire to create as heavenly a place as possible, in the midst of what were perceived to be a savage people living in a wild land, it was never intended that missionaries or their helpers should remain segregated within the compounds. In fact, it was part of the evangelical duty of missionaries to venture forth and undertake numerous journeys in search of new people to missionize, as well as to visit the small satellite outstations that were maintained by the numerous South Sea teachers who had entered the New Guinea mission field with the British missionaries. These outstations were not considered to be as purely Christian as the "headstations" and were therefore thought to be in need of constant visiting (Fife 2002). In a sense, spiritual guidance emanated from the headstations outward into their regions of influence, like ripples moving outward from a pebble thrown into a pond; the farther a person was from the "center" of a headstation, the less likely he or she was to receive "proper" spiritual instruction.

Individual missionaries differed in the energy they expended upon visiting outstations and on scouting for new and as yet untouched village clusters for possible evangelism. A restless man like the Reverend James Chalmers spent much of his time on such journeys, while the Reverend William Lawes and his wife seemed content to invest most of their time at the headstation in Port Moresby. Most British missionaries, however, spent a considerable amount of their time journeying throughout their regions of responsibility, and the written records that they left behind indicate that many were profoundly affected by these travels. In 1905, the Reverend W. J. V. Saville recalled the difference between his first contact with a particular village and the situation two years later, after a South Sea teacher and his wife had been living there:

> Two years ago I was frequently climbing 1,500 feet to their mountain-top village, where they appeared to be living like conies in the rocks, and in the depths of squalor. On those occasions the children used to be huddled by their parents into their dirty houses out of my sight, lest they should be hurt by the spirit of the foreigner. Last time I made a state visit to their new coast village the teacher had got the children to collect a great quantity of food, which they carried from the village and laid down in front of me at the teacher's house. I was quite overcome by these different state of things, and warmly thanked those dirty, little, naked youngsters for their gift, and also their Heavenly Father for His goodness in letting me see His hand at work. (156)

Despite the arrogance of Saville and many of the other missionaries in these situations, one also gets the impression that few had their faith left unchanged by the experiences gained on their journeys within New Guinea.

Most British missionaries assumed that their Polynesian teacher "helpers" were either incapable of or unwilling to exercise the correct, modern form of Christian discipline among their congregations. The generally sympathetic Reverend Samuel MacFarlane, who helped the Polynesian teachers gain a better financial reward for their labors from the LMS directors in London, was nevertheless fond of pointing out examples of what he regarded as the failures of Polynesian teachers at the outstations and the concomitant reasons why the European missionary must constantly travel from the headstation to the outstations in order to keep a watchful eye on them. In an 1875 report, for example, MacFarlane notes his disgust with the Polynesian teachers' "unsatisfactory progress" at several closely connected outstations, where they had as yet failed to build a single church. "Yet when a Sheller [trader] established a station at Tauan [Dauan Island], the teachers could find time to build him a house, disagreeing afterwards about the division of the payment! They are not likely to repeat this [because of the dressing down that MacFarlane had given them]. And I merely mention these things to show you how desirable it is that the teachers should be frequently visited and stimulated in their work" (13). Doctrine, too, was a concern, and in the same report, MacFarlane notes that he has constantly warned the Polynesian teachers against what he terms the "negative Christianity" of the Old Testament: "They generally begin at the wrong end by forbidding the natives to continue their games and superstitions, instead of dwelling upon the example and precept of Christ. When they begin to love the Saviour they will begin to abandon those things which are displeasing to him" (16). Such words suggest that it is not simply discipline that emanates from the headstation but also spiritual truth. MacFarlane, as one of the most important leaders of the early mission, was constantly worried about the kind of Christianity that the Polynesian evangelists were teaching the Papuan villagers. In his 1876 report to the directors in London, he includes a lengthy example about a major theological error made by two teachers at Katau station—an error that he attributes to their lack of language skills:

> They asked for the name of their god, the great spirit of whom they spoke, and were informed that it was Malaki. So in their preaching and public prayers they spoke of Jehovah as the True Malaki, but were rather astonished to find that the natives believed in two great spirits, a good and an evil one, and that Malaki was the name of the latter, to whom they traced all their misfortunes, + whom they greatly feared. Consequently the teachers had been representing the true God as the great, and true, and only Devil! (6)

Polynesian teachers were often thought to be willing but simply not capable of providing the correct forms of disciplined spirituality for their students and their congregations. In 1915, for example, the Reverend William N. Lawrence wrote that "The schools in the outstations of the district are very much what they always have been . . . but all could be greatly improved. The teachers, or at any rate the majority of them do their best but as I said in my last year's report, their best leaves much to be desired" (4). Two years later, Lawrence was still complaining about the teachers: "At best they are indifferent. . . . More could be accomplished with the teachers that we have if one had more time to give to visitation and superintendance [sic] throughout the district" (1917, 5).

Until World War I, the British missionaries who lived on the headstations constituted the sole judges of who would be allowed into the Christian life of the mission compounds (on both headstations and outstations) and who would have to leave this charmed spiritual life. Reports are full of references to the dismissals of Polynesian teachers, the Papuan teachers who came along later, and even common lay members of their congregations for moral turpitude. In a rare report from a female missionary,[4] Edith Turner notes a typical situation in the compounds: "During the year we had with much sorrow to expel one couple, as the man was found guilty of wrongdoing with the wife of another student. The second couple have been suspended temporarily." She goes on to note that the woman involved in the second adulterous affair had been especially promising. "It may be that for her husband's sake [he, too, was expelled, though he had nothing to do with the affair] she will be allowed to return to Vatorata, and we hope that the discipline of disgrace has brought home to her a sense of sin, and that her future life may be but another proof of the saving power of Christ" (1916, 2). Such expulsions were particularly common at the head compounds, as if there were a special need to keep such places as "holy" as possible. There is not a single record of Polynesian teachers, for example, expelling members from the church at outstations for "moral laxity"; and such issues only seem to have arisen on the outstations during visitations from British missionaries. It seems clear that Polynesian teachers were quite aware of the British preoccupation with sexual misconduct and sometimes used this preoccupation to their advantage. An example can be drawn from the 1876 report of Samuel MacFarlane, who writes that "Our chief business at the meeting was to investigate and decide upon the charges of immoral conduct brought by the widow of one of the teachers against the teachers Matika + Isaun which I mentioned in a former letter" (6). The two male teachers were removed from their duties and replaced with others. In this example, the widow, who would ordinarily have been subordinate to the male teachers, effects their dismissal and reverses normal power relationships by manipulating the concern of the British missionaries to maintain sexual purity.

Just as the English missionaries felt compelled to check on discipline at the outstations and on the Polynesian teachers who maintained them, so, too, did the missionaries feel pressure to maintain a constant watch over their own behavior and that of their converts within the head compound (see Fife 2001). Disciplined behavior was an important yardstick for measuring the growth of Christian endeavors within New Guinea while also measuring the improvement of both self and other in following the path of Jesus. Discipline also seems to have been part of an attempt to keep these compounds "pure" or, as the 1915–16 report of Viner, Williams, and Lenwood puts it, as much "like paradise" as possible. There is no doubt that virtually all British missionaries of the LMS working in New Guinea in the years 1871–1918 thought of the large head compounds as special places. In 1917, as rumors circulated that the directors in London were thinking of closing down the separate compound system and moving to a more integrated boarding system, the well-respected Reverend J. H. Holmes spoke for most missionaries when he stated in his report to the directors, "Eliminate mission settlements in Papua and we [will have] put back the hands of the clock 25 yrs" (5). In less than fifty years, the mission compound had become so much the center of Christian spirituality in the LMS mission in New Guinea that it had become unthinkable for the working evangelists to conceive of continuing the mission without it. Compounds had become a kind of shrine—a shrine to the act of evangelism and what it could accomplish in what most still thought of as a dark and savage land.

Some missionaries, perhaps, were also unwilling to give up the almost godlike status that they had achieved within these compounds. This status is clearly apparent in the following story by the Reverend A. Porritt in an undated newspaper report (1908?) about his friend Charles Abel, who was an influential missionary in New Guinea at the turn of the century. After explaining to his readers that a missionary who was visiting from Samoa had very much wanted to speak with the Reverend Mr. Walker (who lived some distance away) but was on a tight schedule and had to leave from Kwato station within two days, Porritt continues:

> Mr. Abel called one of his most trusty "boys," told him to pick a crew of six reliable comrades, and go by whale boat for Mr. Walker. In half an hour's time the "boys" had left Kwato, knowing that they had to paddle a hundred miles, find Mr. Walker, and paddle a hundred miles back with him in forty-eight hours.
>
> Mr. Abel at Kwato scarcely expected them to succeed; but forty-four hours afterwards the "boys" arrived back with Mr. Walker in their boat. . . . This incidence [sic] . . . gives us a glimpse of the devotion of his "boys" to Mr. Abel;

and again it enables us to take the true measure of a man who can inspire such devotion in natives just emerging from savagery. (202)

Conclusion: Toward a More Inclusive Definition of Pilgrimage

Eade and Sallnow (1991) have suggested that we adopt a practice approach to pilgrimage, focusing not upon positivistic sets of attributes but rather on the often conflictual forms of behavior exhibited around sacred sites. Together with these researchers, I argue that we should turn more of our attention to what it is exactly that pilgrims are doing when they "do pilgrimage." Put in the context of this chapter, in what way can the early missionaries to Papua New Guinea be said to have been doing pilgrimage in the New Guinea mission?

British missionaries to New Guinea traveled to their mission sites in much the same way as pilgrims travel to sacred shrines or tourists travel to nationally sacred sites. Missionaries, like pilgrims, held the expectation that they would experience significant spiritual transformation through their encounters with the "Other," to use the language of Morinis (1992). That the missionaries often stayed for ten or twenty years before returning to their point of departure, and that their travels in and around New Guinea seemed to be more important to their spiritual journey than the initial voyage outward, should not blind us to the very real similarities between missionary expeditions and pilgrimage. Both experiences are fundamentally concerned with the transformative encounter between Self and Other and its potential for spiritual growth and renewal, an encounter that Morinis quite rightly identifies as lying at the heart of the pilgrimage experience.

This insight can be expanded through rereading the work of Victor Turner (e.g., Turner 1974; and Turner and Turner 1978). Leaving aside some of his more essentialist notions, Turner was among the first to understand the potential of pilgrimage for breaking down the everyday barriers of culture, class, and caste. Following Eade and Sallnow's (1991) focus on the often conflicting practices of pilgrims does not necessarily preclude the possibility of gaining insights from the Turnerian perspective. In the right times and places, many social and cultural barriers can be at least temporarily erased in a mutual quest for spiritual growth. Neither conflict nor communitas can be assumed to dominate the pilgrimage process, and we should always be open to the possibility of discovering both forms of social interaction when conducting pilgrimage research. The British missionaries of the LMS in New Guinea were actively conspiring to break down old social and cultural barriers while at the same time busily constructing new ones; creating the communitas of Christian fellowship while simultaneously forming racial barriers in a newly colonized frontier. Spiritual movement, rather than social barriers, lay at the heart of the emic experience of the missionary pilgrimage within New Guinea.

Paralleling both pilgrims and tourists (Graburn 1977), these British missionaries suggest through their words and deeds that their New Guinea sojourn was part of a sacred time away from home in Great Britain—a time to be used in building the new sacred spaces of the mission compounds: places of "light" that were surrounded by the dark night of "savagery." This metaphorical reading of missionary work implies that pilgrimage phenomena need not be limited to events that occur within a specifically circumscribed and relatively short period of time or around particular, well-defined locations. As both Morinis (1992) and Coleman and Elsner (1995) point out, one defining feature of pilgrimage is movement itself.

Pilgrimage is an internal and external journey toward an ideal destination. The individuals involved in this form of physical and spiritual movement, which normally involves hardships and difficulties, expect the experience to change their relationship with the sacred. As a definition, this seems to bear a strong relationship to the experiences that many nineteenth-century tourists in Great Britain and the United States expected to have when visiting sacred national sites, such as Yosemite or the Lake District. In both forms of phenomena, the key sign seems to involve an effort of movement (both literal and metaphorical)—one powerful enough to change an indistinguishable space into a sacred place through desires expressed in movement itself.

Following the above definition, it seems reasonable to conclude that the British missionaries who went to New Guinea before World War I as members of the LMS were in some sense engaged in a form of pilgrimage. The ideal destination was an as yet nonexistent Christian New Guinea. Physical movement occurred both before reaching the new mission and continued as part of their duties within it, while spiritual movement revolved around striving for self-improvement through serving others. Both conversion as an act of evangelism and one's self-improvement through living a Christian life were thought to bring one closer to God and therefore to alter one's relationship with the sacred—a primary goal of pilgrimage.

If early LMS activities in New Guinea are not a kind of pilgrimage, then why do the two forms of religious activity variously labeled pilgrimage and missionization (and, we might also ask, at least some forms of tourism) share so many common elements? One answer might be that all of these practices are subsets of an as yet undefined and much larger spiritual phenomenon. In the absence of such a definable category, however, it may be concluded that early British missionizing efforts in New Guinea have a metaphorical likeness to classical pilgrimage experiences and that the men and the women who undertook these outer and inner journeys may therefore be seen as unconventional, though recognizable, pilgrims.

Notes

I would like to thank the Social Sciences and Humanities Research Council of Canada for funding that helped to make the research work for this essay possible. I would also like to thank Sharon Roseman and Ellen Badone for all the work they have put into this project and for bringing the participants together initially for a Canadian Anthropology Society conference session to discuss our common (and divided) issues. Sharon in particular, who is both my partner and my closest colleague, has been extremely helpful in my quest to rethink parts of this chapter—it was in fact her suggestion that I consider missionaries in the light of pilgrimage in the first place. She was correct—it has been a fruitful rumination.

1. On the "romance" of imperialism and its appeal to the missionaries who went to New Guinea, see Langmore (1989, 46).
2. For a brief discussion of the image of the "savage Melanesian" in the European imagination, see Fife (1995, 62).
3. For a similar division between modern people and "the Folk," see McKay (1994); and for one between tourists and hosts, see Löfgren (1999).
4. Wives of male missionaries were considered to be evangelists in their own right, but they were not paid salaries.

References Cited

Altick, Richard D. 1973. *Victorian People and Ideas*. New York: Norton.
Bebbington, David W. 1989. *Evangelism in Modern Britain*. London: Unwin Hyman.
Brown, Dona. 1995. *Inventing New England: Regional Tourism in the Nineteenth Century*. Washington: Smithsonian Institution.
Bunyan, John. 1965. *The Pilgrim's Progress*. New York: Holt, Rinehart and Winston. (Originally published in 1678.)
Coleman, Simon, and John Elsner. 1995. *Pilgrimage Past and Present in the World Religions*. Cambridge, Mass.: Harvard University Press.
Comaroff, Jean, and John Comaroff. 1991. *Of Revelation and Revolution*. Chicago: University of Chicago Press.
Darby, Wendy Joy. 2000. *Landscape and Identity: Geographies of Nation and Class in England*. Oxford: Berg.
Dubisch, Jill. 1995. *In a Different Place: Pilgrimage, Gender, and Politics at a Greek Island Shrine*. Princeton, N.J.: Princeton University Press.
Eade, John, and Michael J. Sallnow. 1991. Introduction to *Contesting the Sacred: The Anthropology of Christian Pilgrimage*. Ed. John Eade and Michael Sallnow. 1–29. London: Routledge.
Fabian, Johannes. 1983. *Time and the Other*. New York: Columbia University Press.
Fife, Wayne. 1995. "Education and Society in Papua New Guinea: Toward Social Inequality, 1870–1945." *Man and Culture in Oceania* 11:61–79.

———. 2001. "Creating the Moral Body: Missionaries and the Technology of Power in Early Papua New Guinea." *Ethnology* 40:251–69.

———. 2002. "Heroes and Helpers, Missionaries and Teachers: Between Mimesis and Appropriation in Pre-Colonial New Guinea." *People and Culture in Oceania* 18:1–22.

Gillis, John R. 1996. *A World of Their Own Making: Myth, Ritual, and the Quest for Family Values.* Cambridge, Mass.: Harvard University Press.

Graburn, Nelson H. H. 1977. "Tourism: The Sacred Journey." In *Hosts and Guests: The Anthropology of Tourism.* Ed. Valene L. Smith. 17–31. Philadelphia: University of Pennsylvania Press.

Holmes, Rev. J. H. 1917. "Namau Report." CWM Papuan Reports. Box 3, folder 1. School of Oriental and African Studies, University of London.

Johnson, Rev. A. N. 1908. "Report: Deputation to New Guinea." CWM Collection. School of Oriental and African Studies, University of London.

King, Rev. J. 1905. "New Guinea Mission Report." CWM Collection. School of Oriental and African Studies, University of London.

Langmore, Diane. 1989. *Missionary Lives: Papua, 1874–1914.* Honolulu: University of Hawaii Press.

Lawrence, Rev. William N. 1915. "Dec. 31 Report: Mission House, Papua New Guinea." CWM Papuan Reports. Box 1, folder 1. School of Oriental and African Studies, University of London.

———. 1917. "Dec. 31 Port Moresby Report." CWM Papuan Reports. Box 3, folder 1. School of Oriental and African Studies, University of London.

Löfgren, Orvar. 1999. *On Holiday: A History of Vacationing.* Berkeley: University of California Press.

MacFarlane, Rev. Samuel. 1875. "Annual Report." CWM Journals. Box 1. School of Oriental and African Studies, University of London.

———. 1876. "Annual Report." CWM Journals. Box 1. School of Oriental and African Studies, University of London.

McKay, Ian. 1994. *The Quest of the Folk: Antimodernism and Cultural Selection in Twentieth-Century Nova Scotia.* Montreal: McGill-Queens University Press.

Morinis, E. Alan. 1992. "Introduction: The Territory of the Anthropology of Pilgrimage." In *Sacred Journeys: The Anthropology of Pilgrimage.* Ed. E. Alan Morinis. 1–27. Westport, Conn.: Greenwood.

Murray, Rev. A. W. 1871. "Report of a Missionary Voyage to New Guinea." CWM Journals. Box 1. School of Oriental and African Studies, University of London.

———. 1872. "Annual Report." CWM Journals. Box 1. School of Oriental and African Studies, University of London.

———. 1873. "Annual Report." CWM Journals. Box 1. School of Oriental and African Studies, University of London.

Porritt, A. [1908?]. "Civilizing Cannibals: A Missionary Hero at Work." Offprint, *Sunday Strand* (London), vol. 21, no. 26, n.d. CWM Papuan Personals. Box 2, folder 2, Misc. Letters. School of Oriental and African Studies, University of London.

Reader, Ian, and Tony Walter, eds. 1993. *Pilgrimage in Popular Culture.* London: Macmillan.

Saville, Rev. W. J. V. 1905. "Old and Young in New Guinea." *The Chronicle* (London), n.s., 14:156. CWM Collection. School of Oriental and African Studies, University of London.

Schlencker, Rev. H. P. 1915. "Report for 1915 (Orokolo)." CWM Journals. Box 3, folder 1. School of Oriental and African Studies, University of London.

Sears, John F. 1998. *Sacred Places: American Tourist Attractions in the Nineteenth Century.* Amherst, Mass.: University of Amherst Press.

Seibel, George A. 1985. *Ontario's Niagara Parks: A History.* Niagara Falls: Niagara Parks Commission.

Thompson, Rev. R.W. 1897. "Report of the Deputation to New Guinea and South Seas." CWM Collection. School of Oriental and African Studies, University of London.

Turner, Edith. 1916. "Women's Work at Vatorata." CWM Papua Reports. Box 3, folder 1. School of Oriental and African Studies, University of London.

Turner, Victor. 1974. "Pilgrimages as Social Processes." In *Dramas, Fields and Metaphors: Symbolic Action in Human Society.* 166–230. Ithaca, N.Y.: Cornell University Press.

Turner, Victor, and Edith L. B. Turner. 1978. *Image and Pilgrimage in Christian Culture: Anthropological Perspectives.* New York: Columbia University Press.

Viner, Rev. A. J., Rev. G. J. Williams, and Rev. Frank Lenwood. 1915–16. "Report: Deputation to the South Seas and Papua." CWM Collection. School of Oriental and African Studies, University of London.

JENNIFER E. PORTER

Victor Turner (1974a, 263) once urged students of religion to take note of the genre of science fiction, for in science fiction could be seen futuristic frameworks expressing mythic and liminal states and concerns. More recently, anthropologist Michael Jindra (1994, 28) has argued that the popularity of the science fiction television series *Star Trek* "is one location in which to find religion in our society."[1] These observations, linked to the suggestion of Turner and Turner (1978, 20) that "a tourist is half a pilgrim, if a pilgrim is half a tourist" and to the argument that secular journeys are the "inheritors" of pilgrimage (Coleman and Elsner 1995, 200; Graburn 1989), form the impetus for the current work. Drawing upon fieldwork with *Star Trek* fans at conventions in Pasadena, California, and Toronto, Ontario, from 1995 to 1997, this chapter examines the possibility that *Star Trek* convention attendance represents, for some participants, contemporary pilgrimage. Viewing convention attendance through the lens of anthropological understandings of pilgrimage can allow us to explore aspects of pilgrimage processes, theoretical models of pilgrimage, and the meanings invested in secular journeys in new ways. By contextualizing *Star Trek* convention attendance within the anthropology of pilgrimage, new insights into both pilgrimage and popular culture emerge.

As the introductory chapter to this volume demonstrates, the picture of pilgrimage that has emerged in the anthropological literature is one of a theoretically ambivalent concept that is "betwixt and between" a universalist, essentialist, and paradigmatic model on the one hand and a contested, multivocal, and constructivist framework on the other hand. What this ongoing debate into the nature of pilgrimage processes has accomplished, if not consensus, is a broadening of the boundaries of pilgrimage. If one can no longer take for granted previous notions about the nature of pilgrimage, and yet pilgrimage remains in some respects an identifiable process, the boundaries of pilgrimage can perhaps be made to encompass journeys previously relegated to other domains.

"Secular" Pilgrimage

What, then, is "pilgrimage" for the purposes of this chapter? Although Turner's views of liminality and communitas retain some theoretical utility in the study of contemporary pilgrimage, *Star Trek* convention attendance fits within the broader definitions of pilgrimage as a negotiated, constructed, and heterogeneous process, rather than within more restricted notions of pilgrimages as journeys in pursuit of perceived theophanies.[2] According to anthropologist E. Alan Morinis (1992, 4–5), secular journeys can fall within the boundaries of pilgrimage if made in pursuit of embodied ideals. Pilgrimage, he writes, can be defined as any "journey undertaken by a person in quest of a place or a state that he or she believes to embody a valued ideal." The destinations of such journeys, he suggests, "share being an intensified version of some ideal that the pilgrim values but cannot achieve at home." Pilgrimage centers are the embodiment of these intensified ideals, which represent "the collective ideals of the culture" (4). These collective ideals, in turn, can be understood as "sacred" in that they "are the image of perfection that a human being sets out to encounter or become on a pilgrimage . . . it is the pursuit of the ideal (whether deified or not) that defines the sacred journey" (2).

Morinis's definition of pilgrimage allows us to encompass secular journeys within the boundaries of pilgrimage, provided such journeys are undertaken in pursuit of "sacred" ideals. The concept of sacred, as Morinis (1992, 2) points out, is somewhat problematic, however, given the universalist connotations imparted to the term by sociologist Emile Durkheim (1995) and other scholars, such as Mircea Eliade (1987) and Victor Turner.[3] Morinis nonetheless advocates the continued use of the term, provided that Durkheim's emphasis on the social dimension of the sacred is expanded to include a cultural dimension.[4] In the case of complex, industrialized societies, however, Durkheim himself acknowledges, in a little-known essay titled "Individualism and the Intellectuals," that it is within the cultural dimension of commonly held ideals, rather than within the social dimension of common rites, structures, and practices, that religion will be located.[5] In particular, he suggests, it is within the culturally differentiated concept of "humanity" that the future of the sacred lies:

To what, after all, should collective sentiments be directed in future? As societies become more voluminous . . . each mind finds itself directed towards a different point of the horizon, reflects a different aspect of the world and, as a result, the contents of men's minds differ from one subject to another. One is thus gradually proceeding towards a state of affairs, now almost attained, in which members of a single social group will no longer have anything in common other than their humanity. . . . This idea of the human person, given different emphases in accordance with the diversity of national temperaments, is therefore the sole idea that survives, immutable and impersonal, above the changing tides of particular opinions; and the sentiments which it awakens are the only ones to be found in almost all hearts. (Durkheim 1969, 25–26)

Durkheim consequently suggests that within the confines of complex, industrialized societies, the sacred will be increasingly manifest within a "religion of humanity" or a "cult of man" (27–28). In this religion, the value and nature of human beings become central religious concerns, and the pursuit of individual liberty, justice, and equality for all human beings become central religious goals. Sacred ideals, within this context, become the ardent support and communal defense of the rights of the individual, for "whoever makes an attempt on a man's life, on a man's liberty, on a man's honour inspires us with a feeling of horror. . . . Nowhere are the rights of man affirmed more energetically, since the individual is here placed on the level of sacrosanct objects" (21–22). Within the "cult of man," diversity, individuality, freedom, justice, equality, and concern for the common weal become the sacred ideals that govern human life.

Although it is beyond the scope of this chapter to discuss the applicability of Durkheim's "cult of man" model to religion and secularization generally, his suggestions regarding the future expression of sacred ideals within a secularized context are remarkably applicable to the *Star Trek* convention context. *Star Trek* conventions clearly fall within what Turner (1977, 41) calls the "leisure domain" of human activity, and traveling to attend such conventions is therefore an overtly secular act. As Morinis (1992, 5) argues, however, even secular contexts can provide a forum for the pursuit of sacred ideals, provided those ideals are understood to be embodied in the place or state that acts as the center of the pilgrimage process.[6] Although *Star Trek* conventions are admittedly secular forums, they are forums that are understood by many fans to embody cultural ideals. It is the pursuit of these "cult of man" ideals in the convention context that transforms convention attendance for many fans from a purely leisure pursuit to that of a sacred journey.

The Convention Context

The fans are the single most noticeable and significant element of the *Star Trek* convention experience. Predominantly young, white, and middle class, although there are significant minorities of Asian, African American, and Hispanic fans, they line up while patiently waiting to buy admittance tickets, and their lines sometimes circle the entire convention site. Fans hold midnight vigils for the chance to purchase next year's tickets in advance. They fill surrounding hotels and motels, coffee shops, restaurants, and bars during lunch breaks and after hours, talking animatedly to other fans whose names they don't know, others who are likewise drawn to the celebration of *Star Trek*. They wear costumes, T-shirts, ball caps, jackets, and jewelry with *Star Trek*–inspired designs. Fans paint pictures and portraits; write scripts, short stories, novels, and poems; design costumes, build models, and buy merchandise inspired by their favorite television show. And they talk, and listen to others talk, about the "true" meaning of *Star Trek*.

The very first *Star Trek* convention, held in 1973, was organized by fans. Following the cancellation of the original *Star Trek* series after its third season in 1968, many fans felt the need to share their continuing love of the show with others. As one fan expressed it, she wanted to "put back into *Star Trek*, for others, the joy it has given me . . . [and] to communicate with fellow Trek followers" (quoted in Irwin and Love 1984, 136). Motivated by similar sentiments, the organizers of the first *Star Trek* convention prepared to greet what they had initially expected would be a crowd of several hundred like-minded fans. More than three thousand fans arrived for this convention. They were drawn from across the continent and from around the world.[7] One young woman dying of leukemia flew in from Hawaii to attend (Winston 1979, 43). Other fans came from Europe, from South America, and from across Canada and the United States. The international appeal and high attendance rate of this first convention continues to be matched or surpassed yearly at conventions throughout the world.[8]

The Fieldwork Context

Fieldwork for this study was conducted at the Trek 30 and Grandslam IV conventions held in Pasadena, California, in 1995 and 1996, and at the TorontoTrek 10 and TorontoTrek 11 conventions held in Toronto, Ontario, in 1996 and 1997. Like the original 1973 convention, the TorontoTrek conventions are fan-organized. Running from Friday to Sunday, the conventions highlight discussion panels dedicated to various themes within *Star Trek* and science fiction, such as the "Anthropology of *Star Trek*" or "Women in Science Fiction" panels at TorontoTrek 11. Conventions also typically include a costume competition or "Masquerade," in which *Star Trek*–inspired and other types of costumes are modeled; "filk" singing sessions in which popular folk songs rewritten with *Star Trek*–inspired lyrics (such as "The Yellow Bird of Prey/Yellow Submarine") are sung with enthusiasm by fans; a writing competition for amateur science fiction authors; and a costume ball. Reruns of favorite *Star Trek* episodes are shown, guest speakers (usually including at least one actor and one screenwriter or director from one of the *Star Trek* television series) are invited, and *Star Trek*–related merchandise is sold. Additionally, fans who come for the full two-and-a-half-day convention and stay in the hotel where the convention is located hold room parties and private get-togethers with other fans, whom they may meet only in the context of the annual *Star Trek* conventions. Approximately six thousand people attended the TorontoTrek 10 convention in August 1996, and another six thousand attended the July 1997 TorontoTrek 11 convention.

In contrast to the TorontoTrek conventions, Trek 30 and Grandslam IV are professionally organized conventions sponsored by Creation Conventions, an American company that also organizes conventions for other popular television shows. The Creation Conventions–sponsored events included a masquerade, one or more costume balls, merchandise rooms, many more guest speakers than at fan-organized conventions, and music montage videos with popular rock music set to *Star Trek* episode and movie scenes. Approximately twelve thousand people attended the Trek 30 convention in November 1995. More than sixteen thousand people attended the Grandslam IV convention in April 1996. As in the case of the fan-organized conventions, the fans themselves often organized room parties and private functions in conjunction with the professionally organized convention.

Star Trek *Convention Attendance as Pilgrimage*

The primary motivation for convention attendance, according to fans themselves, is "fun." *Star Trek* conventions are fun for a variety of reasons, including the enjoyment garnered from seeing favorite television stars, collecting autographs, watching reruns of favorite shows, and browsing or buying the voluminous merchandise associated with *Star Trek*. Fun, however, is not exclusive of pilgrimage.[9] Moreover, upon reflection, many fans identify as their reason for participation precisely the goal identified by Morinis (1992) as a key criterion of pilgrimage journeys: that is, the pursuit of embodied ideals.[10] The ideals identified by fans as central to the *Star Trek* context are precisely those identified by Durkheim as constitutive of the "cult of man": that is, individualism, liberalism, freedom, justice, equality, and tolerance for diversity.

Star Trek, for these fans, is still just a television show.[11] But it is a show in which these deeply meaningful ideals are embedded, and it is out of respect for and in pursuit of these ideals that many fans are drawn to the convention context.[12] According to media studies scholar Henry Jenkins (1992, 116), almost every fan identifies *Star Trek*'s optimistic vision of the future and the embodiment of these ideals in the context of fandom as central to their understanding of the true meaning of *Star Trek*—ideals characterized by humankind's attainment of peaceful coexistence among all nations and with non-human species; the acceptance of equality for all regardless of ethnic, racial, gender, species or other difference; and the mastery of technology in the peaceful pursuit of space exploration.[13] This vision of the future, as fans acknowledge, is a deeply personal, rather than abstract fictional, ideal.[14] Many fans attempt to live up to this ideal in their everyday lives, and for a few short days in the context of *Star Trek* conventions, they feel that they have participated in and achieved it.

The true meaning of *Star Trek,* for these fans, is encapsulated within the *Star Trek* doctrine of IDIC—an acronym for Infinite Diversity in Infinite Combination—which has been adopted and elaborated by fans since it was introduced in the third and final season of the original television show. The words of one teenage fan reveal the depth to which this "IDIC ethic" can be internalized. "All beings have a right to exist," he told me, "regardless of their beliefs or actions. It is IDIC which gives the universe its meaning. *Star Trek* is not about special effects, or even space exploration, but a vision of humanity greater and better than today's humanity. IDIC is [*Star Trek* creator] Gene [Roddenberry]'s philosophy, and Gene's philosophy is my philosophy."

The private adoption and internalization of the IDIC ethic is so prevalent among individual fans that it has become what Turner and Turner (1978, 10) might characterize as the "root paradigm" of *Star Trek* fandom. A root paradigm involves structures of thought and feeling that underlie all of the sensorially perceptible symbols at a pilgrimage site. Such paradigms derive "from the seminal words and works of the . . . founder" and allow pilgrims to enter into the symbolically constructed world that is the founder's legacy (10–11). The "founder" of *Star Trek* is its creator, Gene Roddenberry, and fans frequently refer to the philosophy of IDIC as Roddenberry's "vision."

Star Trek fans find fun in their pursuit of the ideals encapsulated within Roddenberry's vision and in their entrance into the symbolic world of *Star Trek* in the convention context. The fun of *Star Trek* fandom has an edge of serious social consciousness, for many of the fans are very active in charitable works, which they consider to be an integral part of their dedication to the series. In the following conversational exchange, two women at the Toron-toTrek II convention reveal the idealistic basis for their participation in fandom and their perception that their affiliation with the ideals of *Star Trek* are somehow grounded in the convention context:

> Marjorie: Most of us just like the whole idealism that is portrayed by *Star Trek*. Which is like, you know, Infinite Diversity in Infinite Combination should be accepted. It's there in the world today. We just don't have aliens running around. We do have all kinds of different races. We should be able to get along. We should . . .
>
> Karen: Yeah, yeah. I think [the convention participants] wouldn't be here if they didn't believe that. There's a lot of people that come out for the first time, and they're curious to see what's going on. But it doesn't take too long before you're sort of infected with it, and you really want to be a part of it . . .
>
> Marjorie: We go to Red Cross banks. We raise money, I personally campaigned all over Ottawa for Easter Seals one cold, cold day . . . Dressed up as a Klingon.
>
> Karen: You go to the malls, and then you're doing blood drives, and the people see the Klingons, and you say, 'Come on in . . .'
>
> Marjorie: So there's a whole aspect of the fandom that a lot of people don't know about.
>
> Karen: Why would people care to [come here], why would people bother if they didn't believe in Gene Roddenberry's vision that eventually everybody's going to come together and love each other? You know? And there's not going to be all of this racism and criticism and poverty and hunger and . . . You get these people who are fans . . . And they're raising money, and this is Gene Roddenberry's vision that they embraced. Well, if we're going to call ourselves the U.S.S. whatever [fan club/ship name], then we're going to get ourselves together and organize ourselves. We're going to do the blood drives, we're going to go do the Ronald McDonald House, whatever the need is, they're going to try and do something. United Way, you know, Cancer Society in April, and the Easter Seals. And they do all this in the name of their ship. They dress up in uniform to make it fun for everybody. See what I mean? And then you get all back down in here [to the convention], and then they get more people in and say, well this is what we do. You go up and ask any of those people at those [fan club information] tables, they'll say, "What we do is help people." That's what we want to do, and this all comes back to Gene Roddenberry's vision—of having an Asian man at the helm, a black woman at navigation, a Vulcan at science—you know what I mean?

According to Durkheim (1969, 21–22), the ideals inherent in the "cult of man" are centered on the rights of the individual. This individualistic emphasis, however, has as its center not the glorification of the self but of humankind in general. As a result, "its motive force is not egoism but sympathy for all that is human, a wider pity for all sufferings, for all human miseries, a more

ardent desire to combat and alleviate them, a greater thirst for justice."
Durkheim (24) then asks, "Is this not the way to achieve a community of all
men of good will?" For *Star Trek* fans, this motivation to alleviate the sufferings of others in pursuit of a "community of all [people] of good will" is precisely the basis of their affiliation with the vision of *Star Trek*.

Fans enter into the symbolically constructed world of Roddenberry's *Star
Trek* through fan club-sponsored charity events. They also enter into that
world through the private, individual adoption and internalization of IDIC
as a guiding philosophy of life. Pilgrimage, however, is characterized, according to anthropologist Morinis (1992, 4), by the pursuit of a place or state in
which intensified ideals not attainable at home are embodied, and this is true
of the convention context. While individual fans can internalize the values
promulgated within the television show, and fan clubs can act on those ideals through their dedication to charity, it is only in the convention context,
in the company of other fans, that the embodiment of the IDIC ethic truly
emerges. Cultural ideals can be embodied in many places—Graceland (Davidson, Hecht, and Whitney, 1990; King 1993), Walt Disney World (Moore 1980;
Ritzer and Liska 1997), and war memorials (Walter 1993), to name only a few.
Cultural ideals are also embodied, however, in the people who hold and as-
pire to them, and it is within the people, not the places, of *Star Trek* conventions, I would suggest, that these intensified ideals can be found.

Decentered Space

The centrality of "place," or "space," has rarely been questioned in the context of pilgrimage. Although scholars of pilgrimage pay frequent lip service
to the idea of nongeographically centered pilgrimage, very little detailed research into such journeys has been undertaken. Critics of Turner have questioned his assumption of paradigmatic meaning inherent in sacred space and
his Eliadian view of sacred space as "theophany," but the importance of space
itself within anthropological conceptions of pilgrimage remains. One exception to this ongoing emphasis on the centrality of space is the argument by
anthropologists John Eade and Michael Sallnow (1991, 6–7) that pilgrimage
can sometimes be person centered, in the bodies of saintly mortals or incarnate deities. In the *Star Trek* convention context, however, we find an even
more radical decentering of space than that proposed by Eade and Sallnow.
Although it may be ironic to stress the "decentering" of space in connection
to the popularity of a television show that begins with the preamble "Space,
the final frontier," such decentering can point to the value of applying the
insights of the anthropology of pilgrimage to journeys that have no geograph-

ical center, as such. A convention, after all, can be held anywhere—any town, any country—and fans will attend.[15] This irrelevancy of space or place is epitomized in the November 1995 response of one fan to the question of whether the Pasadena location of the convention had influenced his decision to attend: "Who wouldn't go, no matter where it is?" In the *Star Trek* convention context, it is not space or place but rather fandom that represents the true center of the convention pilgrimage process.

The Dialogic Center

Many *Star Trek* fans identify as one of their primary motivations for convention attendance the opportunity to meet with, and more important, to speak with, other fans. The center for the *Star Trek* convention pilgrimage process is a dialogic, rather than a spatial, one. Fans discuss, negotiate, and impose meaning on both the convention experience and the experience of fandom through an interactive process involving a "core" of meaning found within the television shows themselves and within interpretations and elaborations of that meaning developed through thirty years of ardent fan interest. The doctrine of IDIC is one example of negotiated meaning and elaboration of a core concept taken from the television shows. Although Turner's model of pilgrimage implies that the meaning of pilgrimage centers is given to participants in pure, paradigmatic form (Turner 1974b, 189), critics of Turner have suggested that the meaning of pilgrimage shrines is the product of social and historical construction and negotiation among participants (Eade and Sallnow 1991; Morinis 1992). This is the case with the IDIC ethic in the convention context.

The concept of IDIC itself is mentioned in only a single *Star Trek* episode titled "Is There in Truth No Beauty?" but it has become the central ethic of *Star Trek* fandom. It is within the context of conventions that the concept of IDIC is elaborated, negotiated, and expressed. Fans of the *Star Trek* series often learn of this concept for the first time while attending a convention. One fan at the Trek 30 convention, when asked if he could explain the concept of IDIC, replied, "No! I know it's important, but I don't know what it is! This is my first convention. And I've heard it mentioned several times, but I don't know what it is!" For this fan and many others, the context of the convention provides their first introduction to the concept of IDIC. Through negotiation with other fans, they learn to see IDIC as central to the philosophy of *Star Trek*. More important, they learn to see IDIC as central to the convention experience.

During *Star Trek* conventions, fans come to perceive, articulate, and embody IDIC. "Just look around you," one man at the Trek 30 convention told

me, "everyone here is different. Infinitely so. This is it. This is IDIC." A woman later told me much the same thing. "*Star Trek,*" she said, "gives a positive,
hopeful outlook for the future. People are treated equally, not judged by race
or color. It's evident at conventions—no one cares who or what you are—
you're just another Trek fan!"

This perceived embodiment of the IDIC ideal in the convention context,
readily apparent in the discourse of fans, is perceived by fans to be absent in
the broader social context. The majority of fans see contemporary society as
filled with social inequities and prejudicial attitudes that are only temporarily overcome in the convention context. According to Morinis (1992, 1), pilgrimages are motivated by the desire "for solution to problems of all kinds that
arise within the human situation [and] the belief . . . that somewhere beyond
the known world there exists a power that can make right the difficulties that
appear so insoluble and intractable here and now." This desire for a solution
to seemingly insoluble problems and the belief that a solution and temporary
alleviation of those problems can be found within the convention context
and the IDIC ethic was articulated by another fan at the Trek 30 convention:
"[We live in an] extremely turbulent world, with . . . terrible problems that
seem unsolvable. *Star Trek* gives people hope that the future can be a much
better place for humanity. Being here tells me that perhaps we can overcome
all our petty grievances." Although individual fans can and do adopt and internalize the ideals of *Star Trek* on a personal basis, and fan clubs seek to actualize the vision of Roddenberry through charity work, it is only in convention
contexts that the IDIC ethic, or the ethic of tolerance for diversity, is truly
perceived to be lived or embodied.[16] For many fans, participation in and experience of this embodiment is reason enough to journey to as many conventions as possible.[17]

The centrality of the convention community and its role in embodying
the ideals of *Star Trek* for fans can be seen in the words of a woman who has
actively been attending conventions since the late 1970s. "I am so grateful to
Star Trek," she told a roomful of fans during a panel discussion on the enduring popularity of *Star Trek* at the TorontoTrek 10 convention in 1996. "Finding *Star Trek* let me find the conventions. We're together [here]. We're family." For this woman and many others, the television series is incidental to the
true meaning of *Star Trek* as embodied in the community of fandom in the
convention context. She is grateful to the show not for its entertainment value, or even for the philosophy that it promulgates, but for its role in introducing her to the convention community of fans. That it is fandom, rather than
the television show, the guest speakers, or some other facet, that lies at the
center of the convention pilgrimage process becomes even more evident in

the following statement by another fan at TorontoTrek 11: "Even without *Deep Space Nine* and *Voyager* and whatever other *Star Trek* show that's going to come along, years from now, down the pipe—*that* doesn't matter. It's nice to come here and see a guy from *Voyager*. But, I mean, he could be a guy from *Dr. Who*—it doesn't matter who the [guest] star is. People are going to come here, and they're going to get together, and they're going to share ideas and philosophies and talk." Meeting and talking with other fans therefore forms the impetus for the majority of fan attendance at conventions. Guest speakers, and by implication all the other facets of a *Star Trek* convention, such as merchandise rooms and costume competitions, are incidental to the true center of the convention. It is the meeting and talking together of fans that forms the dialogic center of the convention pilgrimage process.

Negotiating the Center

Although meeting and talking with other fans lies at the center of the *Star Trek* convention pilgrimage process, the convention community is not without discord. The spontaneous and normative communitas of Turner's model, implying as it does some kind of emergent, implicit consensus of experience among participants, is tempered here by divergent perceptions of fans. The convention context therefore reflects to some extent the theoretical insight of Eade and Sallnow (1991, 5), who argue that pilgrimage is characterized by the diverse and discrepant perceptions of participants. Fans come to the convention with a wide variety of opinions, expectations, and goals. The divergent and discrepant expectations and perceptions of fans, however, are tempered by a mutual adherence to the "cult of man" ideals of tolerance, diversity, and freedom encompassed within the philosophy of IDIC. According to *Star Trek* fans Marjorie and Karen, the ethos of the convention comes down to this tolerance for diversity that unites rather than divides:

Marjorie: You don't judge, you don't judge people.
Karen: No you don't, you don't.
Marjorie: You have your *opinion,* they have *their* opinion. You can sit there and debate it all night if you want to, but you're not going to walk away mad because "Hey, well I think [the character of] Q's best and you think [the character of] Worf's best" and like.
Karen: Well, no, hey. We can do this and get into really heated discussions with people about what they think was the best episode. I mean, there are people who will just really get on you about what was the best episode. But they're not going to break your face over it [laughs]. You know what I mean? Whereas if you met at a bar, and a few people had a few drinks, and you started discussing politics or something—that gets, that can get violent. That can

get downright nasty. And it just doesn't, it just doesn't get nasty [here] . . . because, the underlying theme of it all . . .
Marjorie: Infinite Diversity in Infinite Combination.

The embodiment of IDIC in the convention community as perceived by fans is the consequence of the careful construction, negotiation, and sometimes coercive imposition of this view between and among participants.[18] The center of the convention pilgrimage process is dialogic, for it is in the negotiation of the meaning of the convention experience that the IDIC ideal is realized and expressed. The dialogic, interactive nature of the convention pilgrimage center can be seen very briefly in the following conversational exchange. Following upon an ardent and sometimes heated debate about the relative merits of the five *Star Trek* television series and the major characters portrayed in each during a workshop session at the TorontoTrek 10 convention in 1996, the following exchange between Robert and Angela, two panelists at the session, and Mark, a member of the audience, took place:

Mark: Don't you find, though, that some people have the totally opposite opinion, I mean, I personally think *Voyager* sucks, but I've heard people say how they can't stand *DS9,* and how they love *Voyager,* so . . . ?
Robert: Yes, but that's just my point. We're arguing among ourselves. Of course, everyone is entitled to their own opinion. But I think what we really need is another dry period to bring people together. I mean, back in the beginning, in the 1970s, people said, "Let's get together," they didn't have *Star Trek* anymore, and so they started meeting and talking about this show that they all loved. And they said, "Hey, I guess I'm not the only *Star Trek* geek out there!" But now . . .
Angela: Yes, now you can watch *Star Trek,* I think it's something like twelve hours a week, in some areas, with *Next Gen* reruns and classic *Trek,* plus *Deep Space Nine* and *Voyager* . . .
Robert: Yes! And all we seem to do is argue about whether *Deep Space Nine* is too dark and political, or if the story lines from *Voyager* are too weak . . .
Mark: But they are! I mean, how many other shows are given two whole seasons to work things out, most only get thirteen weeks [interjected from the floor: "Or less!"].
Angela: Well, that might be so, but that's not what *Star Trek* is about.
Robert: No, what it's about is this, where we all love *Star Trek,* and we all get together to celebrate *Star Trek.* I really think we need another dry spell, when there is no new *Star Trek,* so we can remember that . . .
Angela: We always seem to come back to this. It's the fans that make a difference.

This conversational exchange is a clear illustration of the dialogic nature of the convention pilgrimage center, for here the three speakers are negotiating the "true meaning of *Star Trek,*" and this meaning is being constituted through the very act of negotiation in which the fans are engaged. Although outsiders might think that the central core of *Star Trek* fandom is the five television series, this perception is inaccurate. Instead, the true meaning of *Star Trek,* we are told in the above narrative exchange, is understood to be the community of fandom itself.

Discord and diversity of opinion about the television shows among fans is a common facet of fan interaction. Everyone has a favorite character, actor, series, or episode. Everyone has criticisms of plots, actors, writers, or producers. With five *Star Trek* television series and ten major motion pictures to date to discuss, differences of opinion among fans are rampant. These disagreements have reached the point, according to Robert in the above dialogue, where they are threatening the very core of the true meaning of *Star Trek.* Every individual, Robert insists, is entitled to his or her own opinion, and this reverence for individual rights is part of the philosophy of *Star Trek.* But the various series themselves are undermining the very philosophy that unites fans, for fans can watch so many hours of *Star Trek* per week that the subsequent differences of opinion that arise are undermining fan unity. Mark, in the above dialogue, is attempting to engage in just such a divisive debate. Robert and Angela, however, shift the focus of the discussion away from the divisive topic of television shows and onto the topic of fandom itself. According to Angela, it does not matter how warranted criticisms of the television series might be, for the shows are peripheral to the true meaning of *Star Trek.* This true meaning, Robert insists, is embodied in the fans who come together in the convention context to celebrate their love of *Star Trek.* Diversity and discord, acknowledged and even anticipated within an ethic that idealizes tolerance for diversity, nonetheless contravene the spirit of the IDIC ethic. The "true meaning of *Star Trek,*" it consequently emerges through this discussion, is a tolerance for diversity of opinion that unites, rather than divides, the community of fandom. The true meaning of *Star Trek* lies in the IDIC ideal, as embodied in the fandom/convention context.

Conclusion

Morinis (1992, 4) suggests that pilgrimage is a journey in pursuit of an embodied ideal, and that a pilgrimage center is a place in which intensified ideals not attainable at home are thought to be found. If we accept this as a working definition of pilgrimage, then *Star Trek* convention attendance truly does constitute pilgrimage in a secular context, and the center of that pilgrimage is not the place or space in which the conventions are held but is instead to be found in the community of fans who journey to attend them. What follows from this brief examination of *Star Trek* convention attendance as pilgrimage, therefore, are the conclusions that the boundaries of pilgrimage can readily encompass such secular journeys and that such journeys need not have a spatial center in order to represent for participants the meaningful pursuit and active embodiment of cultural ideals.

Within the convention context, the concept of space proves largely inconsequential in terms of the goals, motivations, and meanings that fans bring to the convention process. Although in the late 1990s, the organizers of these conventions began to restrict events to a few, recurring locales, fans have not (at least to date) conceptualized the space or place of the convention as integral to the experience. In place of sacred space, I suggest that the center of the convention process can be found in the community of fans who collectively interpret, negotiate, and embody the ideals that *Star Trek* is understood to symbolize. If "decentered space" has structural parallels in other pilgrimage contexts, this concept can suggest new avenues of inquiry within the field of pilgrimage studies.

Connected to the idea of a spaceless center is the related issue of "travel" in the convention context. As with "space," the concept of "journey" is largely irrelevant to the experience of fans in the analysis of convention attendance as pilgrimage. While many fans told me that the journey added to their excitement at attending the convention, many others insisted that the journey detracted from the overall experience or was largely irrelevant. With the ready availability of modern means of transportation, the convention is simply a plane ticket away for many fans. The impact of modern means of travel on the experience of convention attendance is similarly reflected in religious pilgrimage contexts. If one relocates the object of scholarly attention from the space and the journey as integral frames to pilgrimage processes, however, and focuses instead on the participants as the "sacred center," the scope of pilgrimage studies suddenly becomes much more broadly defined. Since the anthropology of pilgrimage—like ethnography more generally—is moving away from a study of bounded structures to an appreciation for unbounded processes (compare Clifford 1997), emphasizing the interactive core of pilgrimage, rather than the geographic boundaries, can lead to new insights in the field.

What also follows from this brief examination is the observation that conflicting or discrepant perceptions of a pilgrimage experience among participants does not inhibit the common pursuit of cultural ideals. The concept of a dialogic center and the negotiation of cultural ideals raises questions both about Turner's assumption of paradigmatically given meaning of pilgrimage shrines and also about the more radical assertion by Eade and Sallnow (1991, 15) that pilgrimage centers are religious and ritual voids lacking any consensus of meaning. In the *Star Trek* convention context, we have a center—the fans themselves—who negotiate the meaning of the pilgrimage/convention experience internally, but that meaning is constrained by the ideals embedded and perceived by fans within the television shows themselves. Meaning is therefore negotiated and embodied, but not just any meaning will do. This is a circumstance that may well be found in other pilgrimage contexts.

It further follows from the above analysis that it is the community of fandom, rather than the show, or the actors, or some other factor, that is central to the meaning of *Star Trek* and to the entire convention experience for fans. Also evident in the dialogues cited above is the implicit assumption that the convention context can and should embody the ideals that *Star Trek* fosters. It is this embodiment of ideals that constitute what *Star Trek* is "really" about. If we accept Morinis's assertion that pilgrimage represents a journey in pursuit of embodied ideals and Durkheim's argument that sacred ideals can nonetheless be found in secular contexts, then the above analysis suggests new ways for understanding sacred journeys in secular contexts. Durkheim suggests (1969, 24) that the sacred ideals of the "cult of man" are based on individual human rights but that this individualism does not prevent the construction of consensus among a community of individuals. An analysis of *Star Trek* convention attendance in light of Durkheim's ideas regarding the "cult of man" can suggest a middle ground between the Durkheimian/Turnerian emphasis on communal experience in pilgrimage processes, therefore, and the more radical individualist emphasis within the works of more contemporary pilgrimage scholars. This would allow the field of pilgrimage studies to benefit from the insights found within Turner's work, while simultaneously maintaining an emphasis on the complex, heterogeneous nature of pilgrimage processes.

Star Trek conventions are clearly not typical pilgrimage sites. They are, however, places to which people journey in pursuit of collective ideals. As such, they can be seen to constitute pilgrimage in a secular context. Broadening the boundaries of pilgrimage to encompass such secular journeys can shed new light on pilgrimage processes, theoretical models of pilgrimage, and the meanings invested in secular journeys. By broadening the boundaries of pilgrimage to encompass such secular journeys, pilgrimage scholars can perhaps boldly go where they've never gone before.

Notes

1. Other scholars suggest that the popular *Star Trek* television franchise reveals evidence of the enduring power of religious and cultural themes, as expressed in overtly

secular, fictional frameworks. For discussion of *Star Trek* as revealing of cultural themes, see Goulding (1985); Jewett and Lawrence (1988); Kreuziger (1986); and Selley (1990).

2. For an analysis of *Star Trek* convention attendance as pilgrimage within the framework of Turner's model, see Porter (1999).

3. For an example of a universalist understanding of the sacred in the context of pilgrimage, see Turner and Turner (1978).

4. Durkheim (1995, 206) is, of course, best known for his assertion that religion equals the sacralizing or deification of society itself.

5. This cultural ideal is nonetheless a product of social forces, according to Durkheim (1969, 28): "The religion of the individual is a social institution like all known religions. It is society which assigns us this ideal as the sole common end which today is capable of providing a focus for men's wills. To remove this ideal, without putting any other in its place, is therefore to plunge us into that very moral anarchy which it is sought to avoid."

6. However, as Turner (1982, 29–30) also notes, "modern" pilgrimages also fall squarely within the leisure domain, and such "sacred" journeys are not devoid of the playful, "leisure" components that characterize touristic journeys. As the introductory chapter in this volume argues, the boundaries between sacred and secular journeys, between touristic travels and pilgrimage, are not clear.

7. The organizers of the first *Star Trek* convention were founding members of an organization named the Welcommittee, established to facilitate contacts between *Star Trek* fans. The Welcommittee ultimately organized and ran four conventions—from 1973 to 1977—at which point the committee retired from the convention business (although not from fandom). Other fan organizations and professional convention organization companies have continued to offer conventions. See Winston (1979).

8. Fans from Australia, Brazil, England, and Germany in particular often travel to attend North American conventions. Fans from each of these countries were present in large numbers at each of the conventions during the fieldwork period.

9. Anthropologist Valene L. Smith suggests (1989, 1) that conventions and conventiongoers are somewhat anomalous within the framework of anthropological definitions of tourism. In the *Star Trek* convention context, the majority of fans identify fun as their primary motivation for participation, and as one woman told me, conventions represented "holiday time" in clear distinction to the "work time" she experienced at home. According to anthropologist Nelson Graburn (1989, 24–25), vacation time or holiday time is understood and experienced in juxtaposition to "work" or "ordinary" time, for fundamental to vacation or holiday time is "the contrast between the ordinary/compulsory work state spent 'at home' and the non-ordinary/voluntary 'away from home' sacred state." Although Turner's characterization of pilgrimage is framed within the context of the historical, creedal, universalist religious system of Christianity, he does suggest (1974a, 260) that "leisure" or holiday time can manifest the same "liminoid" characteristics as religious pilgrimages in secular contexts. As Turner notes (1977, 43), within complex, industrialized societies, "many of the symbolic and ludic capacities of tribal religion have . . . migrated into nonreligious genres."

10. Not all fans seek or experience anything beyond the fun of conventions. As Morinis (1992, 6) notes, however, this situation is true of all pilgrimage processes: "the message of ideals is an inner voice, or implicit paradigm, of the shrine. Not all pilgrims come to hear this voice, although some do." In the convention context, some fans come sim-

ply out of curiosity, others to complete memorabilia collections, to get autographs, or simply to take a break from everyday work worlds. Others, however, particularly those who return time and again to conventions, are seeking and experiencing something more: the pursuit of the ideals that Morinis identifies.

11. *Star Trek* fandom is clearly a stigmatized category (Jenkins 1992), as epitomized in an infamous *Saturday Night Live* television sketch that characterized fans as brainless consumers of worthless products and accumulators of worthless knowledge; as social misfits and sexual nerds whose infantile behavior reveals their inability to distinguish fantasy from reality; as those who desperately need, to quote actor William Shatner (*Saturday Night Live* 1986), to "Get a Life!" Fans are careful, therefore, to stress that they "have a life" and are aware that *Star Trek* is "just a television show," particularly to researchers who might be inclined to portray them as "hard-core trekkies." Henry Jenkins (1992, 19–21) and Cassandra Amesley (1989, 338) note that the category of hard-core trekker may be entirely fictional. As cultural studies scholar Amesley (38) notes, "I have yet to find a self-identified 'hardcore Trekkie'. . . . The idea of a 'hardcore Trekkie' influences [fan] beliefs concerning their own behaviour, but does not, except in theory, exist."

12. Within the context of *Star Trek* fandom, fans identify in *Star Trek* what sociologist Jay Goulding (1985, 4) calls the ideals of "a healthy liberal democracy: equality, peace, expansion, freedom." Goulding (12) is critical of this embodiment of ideals within *Star Trek,* for he argues that *Star Trek* simultaneously violates these ideals within the framework of story lines and characterization, while positing a society within which the goals have putatively been reached. The contradiction teaches fans, Goulding suggests (21–22), to condone inequality while hypocritically claiming to abhor it.

13. These ideals are seen by fans to be embedded within the story lines and characterizations of the episodes themselves. One fan recalled her first exposure to *Star Trek* during a period of cynicism and pessimism following Vietnam war protests and the assassination of Martin Luther King:

> For a diversion one evening I absently turned on a syndicated show called *Star Trek.* It depicted man two hundred years in the future. I saw blacks, Asians, and whites all working as a team. It looked good, but I was still a skeptic. It revealed how man had gone beyond his own confines and reached out to other beings with peace and friendship. Aliens from distant worlds labored side by side with our own future generations. My cynicism was slipping. I saw hope amid the present despair, and a new vision for mankind. People in the future had learned from our mistakes and our lofty ideals were not so unrealistic after all. Our years of turmoil must serve as a lesson, a dark period to overcome and prosper as rational, sensitive beings. *Star Trek* gave me confidence and foresight. It expressed a positive standard worthy of incorporating into my life, as well as the philosophy that we can prevail through the direst of adversities. (quoted in Irwin and Love 1986, 129)

14. Well-known fan author Joyce Tulloch, for example, writes, "The feelings evoked in and by *Star Trek* are deep, mysterious. No wonder some think of it as cultist, for there is no good bread-and-butter, black and white way to describe to an outsider what *Star Trek* means to those who number themselves among its fans. It has a lot to do with the mysterious, surrealistic magic of science fiction, of course. And with the powerful literary presence of such ideas as isolation, alienness, of hope for the future, of the imperativeness of human brotherhood" (1986, 33).

15. Attendance at conventions is, of course, influenced by individuals' work and financial constraints.

16. This embodiment may not in fact reflect real sociological factors. Although there is a significant representation of "visible minorities" among fans, the majority of fans are drawn from primarily white, middle-class, educated groups. When fans speak of diversity, they often refer to "Klingons," "Romulans," and "the Federation," rather than Asians, African Americans, or Latin Americans. Fans are aware of sociopolitical tensions involving racial, ethnic, and gender groups, but few seem to recognize that fandom itself is largely exclusive in membership. Further research will need to be conducted to explore this point further.

17. Fans will often attend multiple conventions. One woman at the Trek 30 convention in November 1995 had attended ten conventions during that year alone. Fans also often ask for the same stories to be told by actors time after time and ask questions to elicit information that is already familiar to long-term fans. This sense of security and of a ritual reenactment of belonging is characteristic of *Star Trek* conventions. Further research needs to be conducted on this point.

18. An illustration of preemptive coercion can be seen in the story told by one fan about the TorontoTrek 9 convention in 1995. A fan stood up just as actor Walter Koenig was about to speak, informed him that the fans had come to enjoy *Star Trek* and the convention experience, and asked Koenig to "keep this in mind" when speaking. Koenig responded, "Oh, you mean no Shatner-bashing, then!" The fan, embarrassed but determined, agreed. And so Koenig, who is known to dislike fellow actor William Shatner, refrained from making any negative remarks about him. Fans were treated to stories that stressed the good times and enjoyable experiences of making *Star Trek,* not the negative ones that they knew all about but were not interested in hearing.

References Cited

Amesley, Cassandra. 1989. "How to Watch *Star Trek.*" *Cultural Studies* 3 (3): 323–39.

Clifford, James. 1997. *Routes: Travel and Translation in the Late Twentieth Century.* Cambridge, Mass.: Harvard University Press.

Coleman, Simon, and John Elsner. 1995. *Pilgrimage Past and Present in the World Religions.* Cambridge, Mass.: Harvard University Press.

Davidson, J. W., Alfred Hecht, and Herbert A. Whitney. 1990. "The Pilgrimage to Graceland." In *Pilgrimage in the United States.* Ed. Gisbert Rinschede and Surinder M. Bhardwaj. 229–52. Berlin: Dietrich Reimer Verlag.

Durkheim, Emile. 1969. "Individualism and the Intellectuals." Trans. S. Lukes. *Political Studies* 17:14–30. (Originally published in 1898.)

———. 1995. *The Elementary Forms of the Religious Life.* Trans. Karen E. Fields. New York: Free Press. (Originally published in 1915.)

Eade, John, and Michael J. Sallnow. 1991. Introduction to *Contesting the Sacred: The Anthropology of Christian Pilgrimage.* Ed. John Eade and Michael Sallnow. 1–29. London: Routledge.

Eliade, Mircea. 1987. *The Sacred and the Profane: The Nature of Religion.* New York: Harcourt Brace.

Goulding, Jay. 1985. *Empire, Aliens and Conquest: Critique of American Ideology in "Star Trek" and Other Science Fiction Adventures.* Toronto: Sisyphus Press.

Graburn, Nelson H. H. 1989. "Tourism: The Sacred Journey." In *Hosts and Guests: The Anthropology of Tourism*. Ed. Valene L. Smith. 2nd ed. 21–36. Philadelphia: University of Pennsylvania Press.

Irwin, Walter, and G. B. Love. 1984. *The Best of Trek*. Vol. 7. New York: Signet Books.

———. 1986. *The Best of Trek*. Vol. 10. New York: Signet Books.

Jenkins, Henry. 1992. *Textual Poachers: Television Fans and Participatory Culture*. London: Routledge.

Jewett, Robert, and John S. Lawrence. 1988. *The American Monomyth*. Lanham, Md.: University Press of America.

Jindra, Michael. 1994. "*Star Trek* Fandom as a Religious Phenomenon." *Sociology of Religion* 55:27–51.

King, Christine. 1993. "His Truth Goes Marching On: Elvis Presley and the Pilgrimage to Graceland." In *Pilgrimage in Popular Culture*. Ed. Ian Reader and Tony Walter. 92–112. London: Macmillan.

Kreuziger, Frederick A. 1986. *The Religion of Science Fiction*. Bowling Green, Ohio: Popular.

Moore, Alexander. 1980. "Walt Disney World: Bounded Ritual Space and the Playful Pilgrimage Center." *Anthropological Quarterly* 53:207–17.

Morinis, E. Alan. 1992. "Introduction: The Territory of the Anthropology of Pilgrimage." In *Sacred Journeys: The Anthropology of Pilgrimage*. Ed. E. Alan Morinis. 1–27. Westport, Conn.: Greenwood Press.

Porter, Jennifer E. 1999. "'To Boldly Go': *Star Trek* Convention Attendance as Pilgrimage." In *"Star Trek" and Sacred Ground: Explorations of "Star Trek," Religion, and American Culture*. Ed. Jennifer E. Porter and Darcee L. McLaren. 245–70. Albany: State University of New York Press.

Ritzer, George, and Allan Liska. 1997. "'McDisneyization' and 'Post-Tourism': Complementary Perspectives on Contemporary Tourism." In *Touring Cultures: Transformations of Travel and Theory*. Ed. Chris Rojek and John Urry. 96–109. London: Routledge.

Saturday Night Live. 1986. NBC, December 20.

Selley, A. 1990. "Transcendentalism in *Star Trek: The Next Generation*." *Journal of American Culture* 13:31–34.

Smith, Valene L. 1989. Introduction to *Hosts and Guests: The Anthropology of Tourism*. Ed. Valene L. Smith. 2nd ed. 1–17. Philadelphia: University of Pennsylvania Press.

Tulloch, Joyce. 1986. "The Brilliant Door." In Irwin and Love 1986, 27–34.

Turner, Victor. 1974a. "Passages, Margins, and Poverty: Religious Symbols of Communitas." In *Dramas, Fields and Metaphors: Symbolic Action in Human Society*. 231–71. Ithaca, N.Y.: Cornell University Press.

———. 1974b. "Pilgrimages as Social Processes." In *Dramas, Fields and Metaphors: Symbolic Action in Human Society*. 166–230. Ithaca, N.Y.: Cornell University Press.

———. 1977. "Variations on a Theme of Liminality." In *Secular Ritual*. Ed. Sally Falk Moore and Barbara Myerhoff. 36–52. Amsterdam: Van Gorcum.

———. 1982. "Liminal to Liminoid, in Play, Flow, Ritual: An Essay in Comparative Symbology." In *From Ritual to Theatre: The Human Seriousness of Play*. 20–60. New York: Performing Arts Journal Publications.

Turner, Victor, and Edith L. B. Turner. 1978. *Image and Pilgrimage in Christian Culture: Anthropological Perspectives.* New York: Columbia University Press.

Walter, Tony. 1993. "War Grave Pilgrimage." In *Pilgrimage in Popular Culture.* Ed. Ian Reader and Tony Walter. London: Macmillan Press.

Winston, Joan. 1979. *The Making of the Trek Conventions.* Chicago: Playboy.

10 Crossing Boundaries: Exploring the Borderlands of Ethnography, Tourism, and Pilgrimage

ELLEN BADONE

"Religion is the quest, within the bounds of the human, historical condition, for the power to manipulate and negotiate one's 'situation' so as to have 'space' in which meaningfully to dwell" (Smith 1978, 291). This definition, formulated by Jonathan Z. Smith, one of the foremost contemporary scholars of comparative religion, is particularly apposite to an examination of the symbolic significance of travel. For Smith, religious thought and action constitute a process of mapping the social and natural cosmos. Maps are key to all journeying, spiritual and intellectual as well as physical. In this short concluding chapter, I seek to sketch, however incompletely, the outlines of a map of the territory bordering ethnography, pilgrimage, and tourism. Like all travelers, I am indebted to those who have passed this way before, especially Nelson Graburn (1983a, 1983b, 1989, 1995) but also Bruner (1989, 1991, 1996), Crick (1985, 1989, 1995), Dubisch (1995), Frey (1998), Galani-Moutafi (2000), Gewertz and Errington (1989), Harkin (1995), Harrison (2003), MacCannell (1976), Nash (1995, 1996, 2001), and Edith and Victor Turner (1978).

At the outset, it is important to caution against reification and homogenization of the categories "ethnographer," "tourist," and "pilgrim." As Cohen (1972, 1974, 1979), V. Smith (1989), and others (see, e.g., Harrison 2003; and Wickens 2002) have shown, touristic travel takes multiple forms, and tourists have varying motivations. Tourists do not speak with a single voice, any more than ethnographers or pilgrims. Likewise, we need to be attentive to Nash's (2001, 495) reminder that more empirical data are needed before making conclusions "with confidence about the differences and similarities of the inner worlds of different kinds of travelers" (see also Nash 1984). Nonetheless, it is worthwhile to set forth some tentative propositions about the relationships among tourists, ethnographers, and pilgrims, if only to provide the basis for further fieldwork-based enquiries.

In this chapter, I argue for a theoretical perspective that situates all three forms of travelers in an interstitial border zone, a metaphorical space "betwixt and between" cultures where social actors have the potential to reformulate meanings and negotiate identities. Here, I am following the work of Bruner (1996), with specific reference to tourism, and Rosaldo (1989), on border crossings more generally (see also Gupta and Ferguson 1992). Rosaldo suggests that the concept of the borderland has both literal and metaphorical connotations. Similarly, Berdahl (1999, 7), argues that "As intersecting, overlapping, and often, mutually constitutive cultural fields, border zones need not be spatially grounded, although they may also have real spatial dimensions and implications." Berdahl's formulation articulates neatly with Bruner's (1996, 158) metaphor of the touristic border zone as an empty stage, waiting for performers—the "natives"—and for the audience—the "tourists." For Bruner, this stage is "a creative space, a site for the invention of culture on a massive scale, a festive liberated zone, one that anthropology should investigate, not denigrate" (159). For too long, tourism has been one of the "blindspots" of classic anthropology to which Rosaldo (1989, 208) refers, partly because it is largely a phenomenon of the presumed "postcultural" world of the ethnographer. This chapter seeks to illuminate this blindspot by highlighting its parallels with both pilgrimage and ethnography.

The work of Johannes Fabian has been instrumental in recognizing the cosmological character of ethnography. As Fabian (1983, 111–12) observes, "When modern anthropology began to construct its Other in terms of topoi implying distance, difference and opposition, its intent was above all . . . to construct ordered Space and Time—a cosmos—for Western society to inhabit." Other ethnographers have also commented on the connections between ethnography and cosmology. Quoting Geertz (1973, 10), Danforth concludes, "An anthropological perspective or world view, no less than a religious one, is a 'mode of seeing, . . . a particular manner of construing the world'" (1989, 296; see also Dubisch 1995; and Badone 1991).

Clearly, ethnography—like all cultural products—is multivocal and multifaceted. Its cosmological modality is only one of its many dimensions that are not hierarchically ranked or mutually exclusive but rather become more or less salient under specific historical and social circumstances. To highlight the significance of ethnography as cosmology does not undermine its significance as political discourse or as a means of enabling us to hear the voices of individuals and groups of people who would otherwise be ignored. Moreover, if as Fabian (1983) and others have demonstrated, the cosmological schemata constructed through ethnography have in the past been largely evolutionary models that legitimated Western imperialism and colonialism, currently ethnographic "mappings" are undergoing transformation in the direction of more dialogical relationships "in a world of culturally, socially, and economically interconnected and interdependent spaces" (Gupta and Ferguson 1992, 14; see also Tedlock 1979).

At its most basic level, ethnography—like pilgrimage and tourism—involves travel. Even when ethnographers work "at home," some physical displacement is involved between those places or "centers" framed as fieldwork sites and those unmarked places that the ethnographer inhabits when he or she is occupying roles other than that of field-worker. A pattern of movement to and from unmarked and marked spaces imbued with significance—sacred centers for pilgrimage, destinations for tourism, and fieldwork locations for ethnography—is shared by all three forms of travel. All three processes construct a "there" where "goods" not available "here" are perceived to be accessible: knowledge, self-transformation, or leisure and recreation. While at the abstract level, the quest for one of these goods may predominate in a particular type of journeying—knowledge in ethnography, self-transformation in pilgrimage, leisure and recreation in tourism—in practice, all three goods contribute in varying degrees to the experience of each type of travel. Recreation implies the re-creation of the self, just as knowledge leads to self-transformation, and both pilgrims and ethnographers, like tourists, engage in leisure activities. As a result, the boundaries separating pilgrimage, touristic travel, and ethnography are indeed blurred.

The perception that valued goods are localized in other places or historical periods is closely connected to the notion of authenticity and its identification with the Other. Since the publication of MacCannell's *The Tourist* (1976), the concept of authenticity has evoked considerable debate in the social-scientific literature on tourism. For present purposes, I see authenticity not as an absolute value but rather as a culturally and historically situated ideal that is *believed* to exist by individuals or groups of individuals in specific social settings (compare Graburn 1995). Although authenticity may dissolve into a chimera of simulacra from some analytical vantage points in anthropology, sociology, and cultural studies, the quest for authenticity can remain a powerful motivating force for on-the-ground behavior, including travel.[1]

Building on a framework inspired by a number of previous researchers (Graburn 1983a, 1983b, 1989, 1995; MacCannell 1976; Bruner 1991; Taylor 2001), I would like to suggest that, at least since the late eighteenth century in the West, certain forms of touristic travel have been indelibly impregnated with Romantic values reflecting the ongoing influence of the Christian worldview in an increasingly secular society (see Fife, in this volume, on the connections with nineteenth-century missionary travel). It is not without significance, as Graburn (1995, 163) points out, that one of the founders of modern mass tourism, Thomas Cook, was a Methodist minister who sought to combat the spiritual impoverishment of the British industrial working classes by organizing affordable day tours for the urban poor to the country-side. For Cook, therefore, the encounter with alterity, in the form of Nature, was fundamentally re-creative and redemptive. This paradigm remains influential to the present, as urban alienation leads to the "search for more 'authentic' experiences for people seeking connectedness and community, imagining it is found in 'simpler, gentler' lifestyles . . . in rural cultures" (Graburn 1995, 167).

As Taylor (2001, 10) points out, contemporary touristic travel to non-Western cultural destinations is embedded in a discourse in which the "spiritually pure primitive" becomes "a means of reconstituting the Christian eschatological narratives of sin, sacrifice and redemption. 'They' become the lost sacredness of Western culture, they become its Other, and they are ascribed a spiritual and physical authenticity which the 'materialist' West has somehow lost." Likewise, Bruner (1993, 324) observes that "built into our Western metaphysics is the notion of a privileged original, a pure tradition, which exists in some prior time, from which everything now is a contemporary degradation. . . . Tourists are searching for 'experience' and for their 'origin' through the rural, the primitive, the childlike, the unpolluted, the pure, and the original. They are returning to the Garden."

The mythic paradigm of the Fall, combined with notions of sacrifice and redemption, provides continuing legitimation for the structuring of time and labor in industrial and postindustrial Western society. For the majority of individuals, temporal organization alternates between long periods of work—characterized as spiritually unrewarding, based on instrumental relationships, and lacking in creativity—and relatively short periods of vacation, associated with the cultivation of affective relationships, leisure, and self-renewal. These latter values are perceived as being attainable, at least in part, through travel. In line with the vestigial Protestant work ethic, long periods of monotonous work are understood to be morally uplifting, and vacation time involving travel is viewed as labor's legitimate reward. Here, my indebtedness to Turnerian notions of liminality and communitas, as well as to Graburn (1989), is apparent.

Turner and Turner's (1978) application of the rite-of-passage model to pilgrimage is well known, and Graburn and others have suggested that touristic travel likewise serves as a rite of passage resulting in a temporary elevation of status for the traveler that persists in the form of accumulated social capital after the return home (see also Crick 1985; and Harkin 1995). Likewise, it is almost an anthropological truism that long-term fieldwork constitutes a rite of passage initiating the ethnographer both into the complexities of another culture and into the "inner sanctum" of disciplinary discourse (see, e.g., Peacock 1986, 55–57; and Crick 1985, 82).

The significance of touristic travel, as with pilgrimage, lies largely in its liminality. The *perceived* potential for self-renewal increases when one is physically removed from the structures of everyday social interaction. Note my emphasis on perception. While Bruner (1991) may well be correct in his assertion that touristic encounters with non-Western Others result in very little self-transformation for the tourists, what counts for the tourist—as for the pilgrim—is the perception that one may be changed. Liminality is also construed as being critical to the acquisition of ethnographic understanding. As most first-year anthropology students learn, defamiliarization heightens cultural awareness. In one's own society, culture—like the air we breathe—is taken for granted. Only through a radical separation from familiar practices and immersion in those of Others do we come to recognize that both are socially constructed, rather than part of the natural world.

The trope of the Fall remains implicitly central to the worldview of the post-Christian West. Since Christianity no longer provides a compelling means of redemption, alternative avenues are sought.[2] These include the encounter with alterity in the form of Nature or other cultures. For at least some ethnographers and tourists, part of the motivation for travel lies in the quest for connection with an enduring entity—social or natural—that is larger than the self (compare Frey 1998, 258; and Harrison 2003, 90). In this respect, tourism and ethnography are clearly similar to pilgrimage, even though the latter form of travel has traditionally been conceptualized as linked to institutionalized religious structures. Benedict Anderson's (1991) observations on the similarities between nationalism and religion are relevant to my argument here: both posit "imagined communities" that outlast the lifetimes of their individual members. For some tourists and ethnographers, as for members of some diaspora groups, travel is motivated by the desire to establish a link with such an imagined community, through return to one's own or adopted ethnic roots (see Ebron 1999; Danforth 1989; Delaney 1990; and Storper-Perez and Goldberg 1994). These travelers seek a form of immortality or self-transcendence through identification with a timeless heritage—cultural, architectural, and material, or natural—that persists beyond the individual lifetime. Coleman's "heritage pilgrims" at Walsingham (in this volume) fall into this category, as do some of Frey's late twentieth-century pilgrims on the Camino de Santiago (1998, and in this volume).

Paradoxically, however, as Graburn (1995), Bruner (1991, 246), and others point out, drawing upon Rosaldo's (1989) concept of "imperialist nostalgia," tourism inevitably desacralizes its object and generates a continuing search for people and places that are more authentic than those already visited. "The moment that culture is defined as an object of tourism, or segmented and detached from its indigenous sphere, its aura of authenticity is reduced . . . modernity 'touches' and tarnishes the prelapsarean, mythological ideal" (Taylor 2001, 15).

Reviewing the anthropological literature on tourism, Crick (1985, 77) observes a degree of "'emotional avoidance'" and "repugnance" toward the topic. He suggests that "one of the reasons tourism has not become a matter for greater attention in anthropology is precisely because tourists are relatives of a kind; they act like a cracked mirror in which we can see something of the social system which produces anthropologists as well as tourists. More than that, tourists remind us of some of the contexts, motives, experiential ambiguities and rhetoric involved in being an anthropologist" (78). For many ethnographers, therefore, the comparison between themselves and tourists is "a painful experience" (76). Likewise, the analogy between touristic travel and pilgrimage is also problematic for some religious practitioners (see, e.g., O'Grady 1982, 59). This tendency to reinforce categorical distinctions among the three types of travel stems in part from the prevalent Western characterization of tourism as frivolous and hedonistic. I suggest that this characterization is derived from a set of implicit oppositions in Western thinking that are themselves the product of the Judeo-Christian and classical heritage. These oppositions can be outlined as follows:

money	asceticism
consumption	poverty
evil	good
low	high
material	spiritual
tourism	pilgrimage

In a tongue-in-cheek parody of Lévi-Straussian structuralism, it could perhaps be suggested that ethnography serves as a mediator for these oppositions, since the ethnographer (like the tourist) comes from an affluent, morally decadent, materialist consumer society but (like the pilgrim) voluntarily assumes a reduced standard of living and a degree of scholarly asceticism through fieldwork in an alien but more spiritually enlightened society!

Bauman's (1996) distinction between the pilgrim and the tourist as meta-phors for the modern and postmodern life strategies, respectively, is struc-tured by the kind of oppositional hierarchy I have just outlined. For the pil-grim, according to Bauman, the concept of a destination gives form and coherence to life's wanderings, and the successful life strategy involves build-ing a solid personal identity, delaying gratification, maintaining an orderly record of the past, and ensuring a predictable future. In contrast, in the world of the tourist, time has no directionality, and success involves avoiding com-mitments, escaping from rootedness in place, and the fragmentation of ex-perience into "an arbitrary sequence of present moments" (24). Clearly, in Bauman's schema, as in much of the social science literature, the persona of the tourist is denigrated (see, e.g., Boorstin 1964; and Fussell 1980). Frey (1998, 26) points out that this tendency is not restricted to the academic literature: modern-day travelers on the Camiño de Santiago draw distinctions among themselves, labeling those who make the journey by foot "true pilgrims," while those who travel by car or bus are "tourists."

Ethnographers, too, seek to define the boundaries between themselves and tourists, despite the logic of arguments to the effect that both types of travelers use the same infrastructure and are products of the same historical conjuncture in the political economy of the world system (Bruner 1996; Crick 1985, 77; 1995; Graburn 1983a). While recognizing that ethnographers and tourists may be in competition with one another, since both travel "to foreign lands and return with representations of their experience," Bruner contends that postmodern ethnography has moved beyond the touristic "quest for the exotic, authentic original" (1993, 324–25).[3] Harkin (1995, 668) seems less sym-pathetic to postmodern ethnography, concluding that "Postmodernism in both tourism and anthropology promises (or threatens) to bring the two prac-tices much closer together." Similarly, Gewertz and Errington (1989) distance themselves from what they see as postmodern anthropological relativism. They differentiate ethnographers from tourists on the basis of the greater depth of knowledge about alien cultures acquired by the former and their obligation to be politically engaged and attentive to global issues of power and domination. Nash's later work is characterized by a more positive view of tour-ists. Noting the many varieties of touristic travel, he suggests that "the notion of tourism as a form of imperialism may be at times inapplicable" (1995, 192–93). Moreover, he poses the question, "Is it possible that the tourist may have a point of view that is as authoritative as that of the ethnographer?" (194).

In my own estimation, the response to Nash's question must be an affir-mative one. Rather than devaluing ethnographic discourse, my position strives to overcome simplistic binary stereotypes about frivolous, materialistic tourists and serious, ascetic ethnographers and pilgrims, which, as I have shown, have their unexamined roots in the religious and philosophical structuring of Western thought. As social scientists, we need to take seriously the ways in which individuals in our own society ascribe meaning to experience. Rather than precluding political engagement or advocacy, the recognition that ethnography—like pilgrimage and tourism—is in part a meaning-making enterprise should serve to sharpen its analytical focus.

Notes

1. See Bendix (1997) for a historical deconstruction of the concept of authenticity. Although Bendix focuses specifically on the discipline of folkloristics, the implications of her argument extend to other fields of scholarship and to nonacademic practices in Western society such as tourism.

2. It would be incorrect to state that Christianity is irrelevant to contemporary Western society, and that is not my argument here; evangelical and fundamentalist groups in the United States, for example, have experienced membership growth and gained political and social influence since the 1980s (Harding 2000; Miller 1997). Nonetheless, meaning is also sought in a variety of ways that fall outside the Christian paradigm, which include an interest in such "exotic" religions as Buddhism and through travel.

3. Significantly, Bruner (1996, 163, 176–77) also observes that authenticity was not a key concern for the tourists he interviewed in Indonesia. For Bruner, it is the porosity of the boundaries between tourism, art, and ethnography that should be of key interest to anthropologists. Documenting historical developments in Bali, he concludes, "Cultural innovation that arises in the borderzone as a creative production for tourists, what anthropologists formerly called 'inauthentic' culture, eventually becomes part of Balinese ritual and may subsequently be studied by ethnographers as 'authentic' culture" (167; see also Harrison 2003, 208).

References Cited

Anderson, Benedict. 1991. *Imagined Communities: Reflections on the Origin and Spread of Nationalism.* London: Verso. (Originally published in 1983.)

Badone, Ellen. 1991. "Ethnography, Fiction, and the Meanings of the Past in Brittany." *American Ethnologist* 18:518–45.

Bauman, Zygmunt. 1996. "From Pilgrim to Tourist—or a Short History of Identity." In *Questions of Cultural Identity.* Ed. Stuart Hall and Paul Du Gay. 18–36. London: Sage.

Bendix, Regina. 1997. *In Search of Authenticity: The Formation of Folklore Studies.* Madison: University of Wisconsin Press.

Berdahl, Daphne 1999. *Where the World Ended: Re-unification and Identity in the German Borderland.* Berkeley: University of California Press.

Boorstin, Daniel J. 1964. *The Image: A Guide to Pseudo-Events in America.* New York: Harper and Row.

Bruner, Edward M. 1989. "Of Cannibals, Tourists, and Ethnographers." *Cultural Anthropology* 4:439–49.

———. 1991. "Transformation of Self in Tourism." *Annals of Tourism Research* 18:238–50.

———. 1993. "Epilogue: Creative Persona and the Problem of Authenticity." In *Creativity/Anthropology*. Ed. Smadar Lavie, Kirin Narayan, and Renato Rosaldo. 321–34. Ithaca, N.Y.: Cornell University Press.

———. 1996. "Tourism in the Balinese Borderzone." In *Displacement, Diaspora, and Geographies of Identity*. Ed. Smadar Lavie and Ted Swedenburg. 157–79. Durham, N.C.: Duke University Press.

Cohen, Erik. 1972. "Towards a Sociology of International Tourism." *Social Research* 39:164–82.

———. 1974. "Who Is a Tourist? A Conceptual Clarification." *Sociological Review* 22:527–55.

———. 1979. "A Phenomenology of Tourist Experiences." *Sociology* 13:179–201.

Crick, Malcolm. 1985. "'Tracing' the Anthropological Self: Quizzical Reflections on Fieldwork, Tourism and the Ludic." *Social Analysis* 17:71–92.

———. 1989. "Representations of International Tourism in the Social Sciences: Sun, Sex, Savings, and Servility." *Annual Review of Anthropology* 18:307–44.

———. 1995. "The Anthropologist as Tourist: An Identity in Question." In *International Tourism, Identity and Change*. Ed. Marie-Françoise Lanfant, John B. Allcock, and Edward M. Bruner. 205–23. London: Sage.

Danforth, Loring. 1989. *Firewalking and Religious Healing: The Anastenaria of Greece and the American Firewalking Movement*. Princeton, N.J.: Princeton University Press.

Delaney, Carol. 1990. "The *Hajj*: Sacred and Secular." *American Ethnologist* 17:513–30.

Dubisch, Jill. 1995. *In a Different Place: Pilgrimage, Gender, and Politics at a Greek Island Shrine*. Princeton, N.J.: Princeton University Press.

Ebron, Paulla A. 1999. "Tourists as Pilgrims: Commercial Fashioning of Transatlantic Politics." *American Ethnologist* 26:910–32.

Fabian, Johannes. 1983. *Time and the Other*. New York: Columbia University Press.

Frey, Nancy L. 1998. *Pilgrim Stories: On and Off the Road to Santiago*. Berkeley: University of California Press.

Fussell, Paul. 1980. *Abroad: British Literary Travelling between the Wars*. New York: Oxford University Press.

Galani-Moutafi, Vasiliki. 2000. "The Self and the Other: Traveler, Ethnographer, Tourist." *Annals of Tourism Research* 27:203–24.

Geertz, Clifford. 1973. "Thick Description: Toward an Interpretive Theory of Culture." In *The Interpretation of Cultures*. 3–30. New York: Basic Books.

Gewertz, Deborah, and Frederick Errington. 1989. "Tourism and Anthropology in a Post-Modern World." *Oceania* 60:37–54.

Graburn, Nelson H. H. 1983a. "The Anthropology of Tourism." In "The Anthropology of Tourism," ed. Nelson H. H. Graburn. Special issue, *Annals of Tourism Research* 10:9–33.

———. 1983b. *To Pray, Pay and Play: The Cultural Structure of Japanese Domestic Tourism*. Aix-en-Provence: Centre des Hautes Etudes Touristiques.

———. 1989. "Tourism: The Sacred Journey." In *Hosts and Guests: The Anthropology of Tourism*. Ed. Valene L. Smith. 2nd ed. 21–36. Philadelphia: University of Pennsylvania Press. (Originally published in 1977.)

———. 1995. "Tourism, Modernity, Nostalgia." In *The Future of Anthropology: Its Relevance to the Contemporary World*. Ed. Akbar S. Ahmed and Cris N. Shore. 158–78. London: Athlone.

Gupta, Akhil, and James Ferguson. 1992. "Beyond 'Culture': Space, Identity, and the Politics of Difference." *Cultural Anthropology* 7:6–23.

Harding, Susan Friend. 2000. *The Book of Jerry Falwell: Fundamentalist Language and Politics.* Princeton, N.J.: Princeton University Press.

Harkin, Michael. 1995. "Modernist Anthropology and Tourism of the Authentic." *Annals of Tourism Research* 22:650–70.

Harrison, Julia. 2003. *Being a Tourist: Finding Meaning in Pleasure Travel.* Vancouver: University of British Columbia Press.

MacCannell, Dean. 1976. *The Tourist: A New Theory of the Leisure Class.* New York: Schoken Books.

Miller, Donald E. 1997. *Reinventing American Protestantism: Christianity in the New Millennium.* Berkeley: University of California Press.

Nash, Dennison. 1984. "The Ritualization of Tourism: Comment on Graburn's 'The Anthropology of Tourism.'" *Annals of Tourism Research* 11:503–22.

———. 1995. "Prospects for Tourism Study in Anthropology." In *The Future of Anthropology: Its Relevance to the Contemporary World.* Ed. Akbar S. Ahmed and Cris N. Shore. 179–202. London: Athlone.

———. 1996. "On Anthropologists and Tourists." *Annals of Tourism Research* 23:691–94.

———. 2001. "On Travelers, Ethnographers and Tourists." *Annals of Tourism Research* 28:493–96.

O'Grady, E. 1982. *Tourism in the Third World: Christian Reflections.* New York: Orbis.

Peacock, James L. 1986. *The Anthropological Lens: Harsh Light, Soft Focus.* Cambridge: Cambridge University Press.

Rosaldo, Renato. 1989. *Culture and Truth: The Remaking of Social Analysis.* Boston: Beacon.

Smith, Jonathan Z. 1978. *Map Is Not Territory: Studies in the History of Religions.* Leiden: E. J. Brill.

Smith, Valene L. 1989. Introduction to *Hosts and Guests: The Anthropology of Tourism.* Ed. Valene L. Smith. 2nd ed. 1–17. Philadelphia: University of Pennsylvania Press.

Storper-Perez, Danielle, and Harvey E. Goldberg. 1994. "The Kotel: Toward an Ethnographic Portrait." *Religion* 24:309–32.

Tate, Mark. 1991. "License, Death and Power: The Making of an Anti-Tradition." In *Religious Regimes and State-Formation: Perspectives from European Ethnology.* Ed. Eric R. Wolf. 261–84. Albany: State University of New York Press.

Taylor, John P. 2001. "Authenticity and Sincerity in Tourism." *Annals of Tourism Research* 28:7–26.

Tedlock, Dennis. 1979. "The Analogical Tradition and the Emergence of a Dialogical Anthropology." *Journal of Anthropological Research* 35:387–400.

Turner, Victor, and Edith L. B. Turner. 1978. *Image and Pilgrimage in Christian Culture: Anthropological Perspectives.* New York: Columbia University Press.

Wickens, Eugenia. 2002. "Sacred and the Profane: A Tourist Typology." *Annals of Tourism Research* 29:834–51.

CONTRIBUTORS

ELLEN BADONE is an associate professor of anthropology and religious stud-ies at McMaster University. She is the author of *The Appointed Hour: Death, Worldview, and Social Change in Brittany* (1989) and the editor of *Religious Or-thodoxy and Popular Faith in European Society* (1990). Her current research fo-cuses on a Marian apparition site in Brittany, France, and on *pardons*, or pil-grimages, to local Breton shrines.

SIMON COLEMAN is a reader in anthropology at the University of Durham. His research focuses on conservative Protestantism, pilgrimage, and, current-ly, the aesthetics of hospital space. His recent books include *The Globalisation of Charismatic Christianity: Spreading the Gospel of Prosperity* (2000) and the co-edited volumes *Pilgrim Voices: Narrative and Authorship in Christian Pilgrimage* (2002) and *Reframing Pilgrimage: Cultures in Motion* (2004).

WAYNE FIFE is department head and associate professor of anthropology at Memorial University of Newfoundland. His articles on contemporary school-ing and the historical ethnography of missionization in Papua New Guinea have been published in such journals as the *Journal of the Polynesian Society* and *Ethnology*. He recently completed a book, tentatively entitled "Doing Ethnog-raphy: Educational Research among Disadvantaged Groups." He has received a grant from the Social Sciences and Humanities Research Council of Canada to conduct research on the Northern Peninsula of Newfoundland in relation to the conflicts that occur between different social groups over the use of tour-ism sites such as national parks and heritage sites.

NANCY L. FREY obtained her doctorate in anthropology from the University of California, Berkeley, based on her research of the contemporary Camino de Santiago pilgrimage. She is the author of *Pilgrim Stories: On and Off the Road to Santiago* (1998). She currently resides in Galicia, Spain.

NELSON H. H. GRABURN is a professor of anthropology at the University of California, Berkeley. He is the editor of *Ethnic and Tourist Arts: Cultural Expressions from the Fourth World* (1976) and a contributor to *Hosts and Guests: The Anthropology of Tourism* (1977, 1989), *The Future of Anthropology: Its Relevance to the Contemporary World* (1995), and *Consuming Tradition, Manufacturing Heritage* (2000).

PAULA ELIZABETH HOLMES-RODMAN is a research associate in the Department of Anthropology at McMaster University and adjunct faculty in the Department of Religion and Culture at Wilfrid Laurier University. She is the author of *A Rumor of Miracles: Tales of Tekakwitha and the Creation of a Native American Saint* (forthcoming). She has worked among the Pueblo, Navajo, and Apache peoples in the American Southwest, and her interests include Native American religions, folk Catholicism, saints and miracles, women's devotional narratives, and postcolonial religious history.

JENNIFER E. PORTER is an assistant professor of religious studies at Memorial University of Newfoundland. She is the coeditor of *Star Trek and Sacred Ground: Explorations of Star Trek, Religion, and American Culture* (1999). Her current research deals with the impact of the Star Wars Saga on the spiritual lives and convictions of Star Wars fans, and she plans a book based on this research, tentatively titled "Religion: Jedi."

SHARON R. ROSEMAN is an associate professor of anthropology at Memorial University of Newfoundland. She is editor of *Identities, Power, and Place on the Atlantic Borders of Two Continents* (2002) and a contributor to *Feminist Fields: Ethnographic Insights* (1999) and *Las Expresiones Locales de la Globalización: México y España* (2003). Over the past decade, she has been writing about politics and culture in twentieth- and twenty-first-century Galicia in relation to waged and unwaged labor, developmentalism discourses, rural rights claims, nationalism, and, more recently, the period of the Franco dictatorship.

MARK TATE is an assistant professor of anthropology at Memorial University of Newfoundland. He is a contributor to *Religious Regimes and State-Formation: Perspectives from European Ethnology* (1991). His chapter in this volume is part of a larger study on the fiesta of Holy Week in twentieth-century Spain.

INDEX

Abel, Reverend Charles, 150
abortion, 128
Abu-Lughod, Lila, 28, 72, 73, 74
addiction to pilgrimage, 104
Adler, Judith, 89, 107n4
aftermath of pilgrimage, 89–109; Christian,
    96; experience of, 97, 99, 100–101, 102, 103;
    Hindu, 95; Islamic, 95; lack of attention to,
    95–96; lasting effects of, 98–100; memories
    of, 100–102; readjustment of, 99–100; and
    reunions, 105; and transition period, 97–98;
    and trends, 101
Alfonso II, King, 76
Alonso, Ana María, 72
Alonso Romero, Fernando, 96
Altick, Richard, 145
Amaterasu, 126, 127
Amesley, Cassandra, 176n11
Andalusian El Rocío *romería,* 19n9
Anderson, Benedict, 184
Angelus, 34, 48n6
Anglican pilgrimage, 56–58
anthropological travel, 7–8
antitourist, 9, 18n6
Aparicio Carreño, Luis, 111, 114
Appadurai, Arjun, 9
appropriation, 58, 59, 61, 62, 63
Archdiocese of Santa Fe, 24–25
architectural replication, 58, 62
Ashworth, Gregory J., 83
Asian pilgrimage, 136
authenticity, 14, 182, 187n1, 187n3
Aviva, Elyn, 102

Badone, Ellen, 8, 17, 123n, 157n, 181
Barcelona, 84n5
Bauman, Zygmunt, 18n6, 186
Bebbington, David W., 145

Behar, Ruth, 43, 50n12, 75, 110, 123n6
Belgian juvenile penal system, 107n5
Bendix, Regina, 187n1
Berdahl, Daphne, 181
birth control, 128, 137n2
Blair, Reverend Oswald H., 56
blessings, 31–32, 49n10
Boissevain, Jeremy, 71, 72
Boniface, Priscilla, 72
Boorstin, Daniel J., 6, 7, 18n3, 186
borderland, 181
Borneman, John, 81
boundaries, of ethnography, tourism, pil-
    grimage, 180–89
Bowman, Glenn, 53
Boyd, Charlotte, 55, 56
British missions, 16, 140–59
Brown, Dona, 143
Bruner, Edward: authenticity and, 187n3;
    tourism and, 181, 182, 183, 185; tourism and
    ethnography, 7–8, 186, 187n3; tourism and
    pilgrimage, 180, 184
Buber, Martin, 14
Buddhism: contemporary, 128; history of,
    125; as institutionalized religion, 129–30;
    Shinto and, 128; Zen sect, 129
Buddhist pilgrimage, 15, 130–32
Bunyan, John, 145

Camiño (also Camino) de Santiago: after-
    math of, 13–14, 89–109; authenticity of par-
    ticipation, 107n3; definition of, 90; experi-
    ence of, 92, 94, 97, 99, 100, 104; Friends of
    the Camino, 105; influence in history, 79;
    motivations for, 91; nature of, 90–92, 94;
    reanimation of, 90, 107n8; social implica-
    tions of, 105–106; spelling of, 19n8; trans-
    portation methods, 92, 107n3

The University of Illinois Press
is a founding member of the
Association of American University Presses.

Composed in 9/13 ITC Stone Serif
with ITC Stone Sans display
by Jim Proefrock
at the University of Illinois Press
Manufactured by Maple-Vail
Book Manufacturing Group

University of Illinois Press
1325 South Oak Street
Champaign, IL 61820-6903
www.press.uillinois.edu